ANTI-FEDERALISTS
VERSUS
FEDERALISTS

Chandler Publications in
POLITICAL SCIENCE
VICTOR JONES, *Editor*

ANTI-FEDERALISTS

VERSUS

FEDERALISTS

Selected Documents

EDITED BY

John D. Lewis

OBERLIN COLLEGE

CHANDLER PUBLISHING COMPANY
124 SPEAR STREET, SAN FRANCISCO, CALIFORNIA 94105

Selections from *The Federalist* are reprinted by permission of the publishers from Benjamin Wright, editor, *The Federalist*, Cambridge, Mass.: The Belknap Press of Harvard University Press, Copyright, 1961, by the President and Fellows of Harvard College.

************ CONTENTS ************

v

************ PREFACE ************

Since the appearance of the letters of *The Federalist* in 1787–
1788, there have been numerous editions of the series, not only in
English but also in the principal languages of the world. Why
then, one may properly ask, should there be another? The answer
is that this is not a new edition of the most famous American
treatise on government. It is, rather, an attempt to show what the
authors of *The Federalist* thought they were talking about and
why they thought it necessary to talk about such matters. A
tract for the time which has become a timeless handbook of political wisdom tends to live in a rarefied intellectual atmosphere.
Scholars analyze arguments in terms of the timeless reasons given in their support; they criticize the structure of argument in terms of its cogency and consistency. All this is
perfectly proper and useful. But clearly it is not quite enough,
either for the historian or for the political scientist. It is important
to keep clearly in mind the widespread fears and misgivings of
those who opposed the new Constitution.

In the extensive literature on *The Federalist,* a good deal of
common ground of interpretation has been established, in spite
of the fact that no two analysts are likely to give quite the same
interpretation. The statement in the Introduction will take for
granted some knowledge of common interpretations and will
stress particularly those aspects of *The Federalist* that have been
less generally observed.

There have not been numerous editions of the writings of the

ix

anti-Federalists, nor have non-Americans found it useful to translate them. The relative neglect of anti-Federalist writings is not due merely to the fact that the Federalists won the debate over the immediate issue, ratification of the Constitution; in the end, the moderate anti-Federalists also won an historically important victory, the approval of the first ten amendments. Nor is it due merely to the fact that the Federalists were in general looking to the future rather than to the past. Nor, although one must acknowledge the intellectual superiority of the case presented by *The Federalist*, has that been the only explanation. There is the further important explanation that, with all the writing and all the talking on the anti-Federalist side, there was no single Anti-Federalist. There was no comprehensive, systematic statement of the case against the Constitution that combined general principles with specific arguments and with close textual analysis. This is not to say that there were no good arguments on the anti-Federalist side. But good arguments were too often mixed with poor arguments; there were varying degrees of criticism and diverse motives for opposition; and, although a common pattern of basic objections emerged early, different writers often reached the same conclusions by different routes.

It is not my purpose to help to rescue from obscurity the arguments of the lesser party, but to present the arguments of both sides in a form that makes cross-reference and comparison possible and that suggests the general significance of the debate.

In dealing with the arguments of the anti-Federalists, it has been necessary to approach their common assumptions and generalizations by way of their numerous specific objections. To have done otherwise would have been to risk imposing upon an unsystematic body of scattered literature a convenient pattern of generalizations drawn from what later readers would expect to find. This technique has unfortunately been much used in hasty interpretations, and the results have impeded rather than advanced genuine understanding. In Parts I and III, I have given a number of representative samples of anti-Federalist arguments, both long and short, making some necessary deletions, but attempting in general to preserve the manner in which they were originally set forth. This method of presentation entails some repetition, but it seemed preferable to sorting out and reorganizing arguments according to subject. Allowing the debaters to speak for themselves on their understanding of the relationships between the separable points will enable the reader to interpret their attitudes as well as their arguments. My own interpretation appears in the Introduction.

Of the many recent editions of *The Federalist*, most follow the text of 1788, as edited by Henry Cabot Lodge in 1888. Benjamin F. Wright's edition of the text of 1788 corrects many minor errors found in the Lodge edition. The letters reprinted here and their titles are from Wright's edition, and all references to *The Federalist* are to that edition. The anti-Federalist documents are from various sources, as indicated. Many of the titles are my own abridgments of the original titles. Throughout the book, footnotes have been renumbered to run in series throughout a selection.

I am glad to acknowledge the courtesy of Harvard University Press in granting permission to reprint letters of *The Federalist* from the Wright edition. For instigating this project and gently insisting that it be completed, I am grateful to Professor Victor Jones of the University of California, Berkeley; for criticism and indispensable assistance, to Ewart Lewis; and for typing, to Miss June Wright, Mrs. Lois Wasem, Mrs. Claudia Braxton, and Miss Ellen Lewis.

J.D.L.

Oberlin, Ohio
1966

ANTI-FEDERALISTS
VERSUS
FEDERALISTS

☆☆

Brief Documentation Used
in Footnotes and Source Notes

☆☆

Elliot. Elliot, Jonathan, ed. *The Debates in the Several State Conventions on the Adoption of the Federal Constitution.* 4 vols., 2nd ed.; Washington, D.C., 1854.

Farrand. Farrand, Max, ed. *The Records of the Federal Convention of 1787.* 3 vols.; New Haven, Conn.: Yale University Press, 1911.

Ford, *Essays.* Ford, Paul Leicester, ed. *Essays on the Constitution of the United States, Published During Its Discussion by the People, 1787–1788.* Brooklyn, N.Y., 1892.

Ford, *Pamphlets.* Ford, Paul Leicester, ed. *Pamphlets on the Constitution of the United States, Published During Its Discussion by the People, 1787–1788.* Brooklyn, N.Y., 1888.

McMaster and Stone. McMaster, John B., and F. D. Stone, eds. *Pennsylvania and the Federal Constitution, 1787–1788.* Lancaster, Pa., 1888.

Introduction

THE ANTI-FEDERALIST CASE

When the Philadelphia Convention met for the first time in May 1787, some who had been designated to represent their states declined to attend. The state of Rhode Island, having refused to name delegates, was unrepresented. When the Convention concluded its work on September 17, a number of delegates who had at some time attended were absent, and three of those present refused to sign the completed document. Thus the campaign against ratification of the Constitution was already brewing while the Convention met, and debates that had gone on behind discreetly closed doors at Philadelphia were soon being aired loudly and publicly. That favorite subject of constitutional historians and jurists, "the intentions of the fathers," promptly became a subject of heated debate.

On September 15, Edmund Randolph and George Mason of Virginia and Elbridge Gerry of Massachusetts explained to the Convention why they could not sign the Constitution; their explanations anticipated the lines of argument that much of the later debate would take. To the views of these nonsigners were added later the opinions of Robert Yates and John Lansing of New York, who had left the Convention in protest on July 10, and of Luther Martin of Maryland, who had left on September 4. Martin's "Genuine Information" about the Convention and its work purported to reveal to the legislature of Maryland the full details of the Philadelphia plot to destroy the sovereign inde-

1

pendence and equality of the states and to establish an oppressive centralized monarchy over freedom-loving Americans. This extravagant early statement [1] provided material for the demagogic argument that an antirepublican plot was afoot.[2]

The composite anti-Federalist case varied a great deal in cogency, relevance, rhetoric, moderation, and emphasis from writer to writer. Furthermore, the anti-Federalist campaign was, in effect, waged by a loose negative coalition. Common arguments reappeared, however—some with boring regularity and often in identical language. Hence a general pattern of anti-Federalist argument can be sketched. In this pattern, one finds some elements that were similar to those of *The Federalist* and some that were different. To some extent the differences represented divergence of basic principle; to some extent they were related to different views of factual situations and different expectations of future American developments; to some extent they were convenient debater's points.

The most common anti-Federalist argument was the claim that the new Constitution must inevitably lead to a new "consolidated system" of government. To this contention was usually added the claim that the leaders of the majority at Philadelphia intended such a system and that the "consolidated system" would in the end destroy republican government and individual liberty as well as the independence of the states. Yates and Lansing, explaining the reasons for their dissent, declared that they would have opposed any system "which had in object the consolidation of the United States into one government." [3] "The

---

[1] It was presented to the Maryland legislature in November 1787 and printed in revised form December 1787–February 1788. See Max Farrand, ed., *The Records of the Federal Convention of 1787* (New Haven, Conn.: Yale University Press, 1911), III, 172.

[2] See, e.g., "Observations on the New Constitution, and on the Federal and State Conventions. By a Columbian Patriot. Sic transit gloria Americana," Paul Leicester Ford, ed., *Pamphlets on the Constitution of the United States, Published During Its Discussion by the People, 1787–1788* (Brooklyn, N.Y., 1888), pp. 3–23. (Portions of this pamphlet appear in this book at p. 181, "Observations by a Columbian Patriot.")

[3] Jonathan Elliot, ed., *The Debates in the Several State Conventions on*

Constitution proposed has few, if any, federal features," declared Gerry, "but is rather a system of national government." [4] Martin explained that the party at Philadelphia that wished to "abolish and annihilate all state governments, and to bring forward one general government over this extensive continent, of a monarchical nature," had been able to combine with the less extreme party that sought "undue power and influence" for particular states, thus paving the way for "the *destruction of the state governments*, and the introduction of *monarchy*." [5] The minority of the Pennsylvania Ratifying Convention vigorously protested the "annihilation of state governments." The powers to be given Congress, they maintained,

> must necessarily annihilate and absorb the legislative, executive, and judicial powers of the several States, and produce from their ruins one consolidated government, which from the nature of things will be *an iron handed despotism* . . . .

Nothing short of despotism, they implied, could bring the states under one government.[6] The anti-Federalists could acknowledge no middle ground between the continuation of a loose confederate structure and one completely national, thoroughly centralized, and thoroughly dangerous. Thus, in a famous comment, Samuel Adams declared:

> I confess, as I enter the Building I stumble at the Threshold. I meet with a National Government, instead of a Federal Union of

---

the Adoption of the Federal Constitution (2nd ed.; Washington, D.C., 1854), I, 480.

[4] "Letter Containing the Reasons of the Hon. Elbridge Gerry, Esq., for Not Signing the Federal Constitution," Elliot, I, 493. (Portions of this letter appear in this book at p. 80, "Letter to the Legislature of Massachusetts.")

[5] "Luther Martin's Letter on the Federal Convention of 1787," Elliot, I, 350 f. (Portions of this letter appear in this book at p. 83, "Genuine Information, to the Legislature of Maryland.")

[6] "The Address and Reasons of Dissent of the Minority of the Convention of the State of Pennsylvania to Their Constituents," John B. McMaster and F. D. Stone, eds., *Pennsylvania and the Federal Constitution, 1787–1788* (Lancaster, Pa., 1888), p. 465. (Portions of this address appear in this book at p. 127, "Reasons of Dissent.")

Sovereign States. [The Convention has proposed a system of] Imperia in Imperio justly deemd a Solecism in Politicks, [and] highly dangerous, and destructive of the Peace Union and Safety of the Nation.[7]

The recipient of Adams's letter found the whole Constitution vitiated by its first seven words.

With all the complexity of the new system, "consolidation pervades the whole constitution."[8] The anti-Federalists supported and illustrated this theme in a multitude of ways, giving their own interpretation of the features of the proposed government. They explored endlessly and often with imaginative ingenuity the powers of Congress, of the President, and of the courts. They speculated on the inevitable abuse of such powers. The Federalists exercised a good deal of imagination in spelling out the future interstate rivalries and conflicts, which would eventually dissolve the confederate union, if the Constitution were not approved. But the eager imagination of Luther Martin and of some other anti-Federalists far surpassed that of the Federalists in dire warnings of the cupidity, the brutality, and the tyranny of the future unrestrained officers of the proposed government, and in confident prediction of the coming enslavement of the people. Without attributing antilibertarian motives to the framers or supporters of the Constitution, even moderate anti-Federalists argued that, because of the extensive territory and dispersed population of America, the Constitution would necessarily lead to tyranny.

Exclusive of our objections originating from the want of power, we entertained an opinion that a general government, however guarded by declarations of rights, or cautionary provisions, must unavoidably, in a short time, be productive of the destruction of the civil liberty of such citizens who could be effectually coerced by it, by reason of

---

[7] Letter to Richard Henry Lee (3 Dec. 1787), H. A. Cushing, ed., *The Writings of Samuel Adams* (New York, 1908), IV, 324.

[8] Pennsylvania Minority, McMaster and Stone, p. 470.

the extensive territory of the United States, the dispersed situation of its inhabitants, and the insuperable difficulty of controlling or counteracting the views of a set of men (however unconstitutional and oppressive their acts might be) possessed of all the powers of government, and who, from their remoteness from their constituents, and necessary permanency of office, could not be supposed to be uniformly actuated by an attention to their welfare and happiness . . . .[9]

When they came to particulars, the anti-Federalists found especially ominous the power of Congress to raise revenue by levying and collecting its own taxes ("a power very odious in its nature"[10]) and the power of Congress to regulate interstate and foreign commerce. Federal taxation would require a huge national bureaucracy. It would require also "a great number of Congressional ordinances, immediately operating upon the body of the people"; these would "continually interfere with state laws," until one or the other system of laws would be destroyed.[11] The constitutional definition of restrictions upon Congress would not prevent abuse, for Congress would itself determine what was "necessary and proper" to the exercise of its delegated powers; and, by virtue of the supremacy clause, national laws would prevail over state constitutions and laws.[12]

If then . . . they have unlimited power to drain the wealth of the people in every channel of taxation, . . . this system must be too

---

[9] "Letter from the Hon. Robert Yates and the Hon. John Lansing, Jun., Esquires, to the Governor of New York, Containing Their Reasons for Not Subscribing to the Federal Constitution," Elliot, I, 481. (Portions of this letter appear in this book at p. 59, "Letter to Governor George Clinton on Their Reasons for Leaving the Convention.")

[10] Luther Martin, "Genuine Information," Elliot, I, 368.

[11] Richard Henry Lee, "The Federal Farmer, Letter III" (10 Oct. 1787), Ford, *Pamphlets*, p. 302.

[12] Curiously enough, Luther Martin had proposed the substance of the important supremacy clause. His proposal was made, however, as an alternative to a clause which would have given Congress the power specifically to nullify laws passed by the states contrary to the Constitution or to treaties made under constitutional authority. See Farrand, II, 26–29.

formidable for any single State, or even for a combination of States, should an attempt be made to break and destroy the yoke of domination and tyranny which it will hereafter set up.[13]

National control of commerce would be another threat to the prosperity of the states and of blocs of states. Some attacks centered on this point. James Winthrop of Massachusetts explained that, since there was diversity of production among the several states, it was commerce, not power, that was the bond of interstate union.[14] But Congressional control of commerce would give to some states—the southern states or the northern states or the large states or particular states, depending upon who was making the point at the moment—the power to throttle and destroy the commerce of other sections of the country. Thus, for example, the eight northern and eastern states, acting in the interests of merchants and carriers, would by Congressional action be able to bring economic ruin to the five southern states.[15]

One version of this argument maintained that commerce and wealth, as well as political favors and preferment, would naturally become concentrated at the seat of the federal government and that commerce and prosperity would wither at the territorial extremes. In regulating trade in a large state, there would "always be a desire of the government to increase the trade of the capital, and to weaken the extremes." [16] In this case, Winthrop was arguing that Massachusetts would suffer. The Virginian, Richard Henry Lee, made the same argument in a more extended form:

---

[13] John Smilie in the Ratifying Convention of Pennsylvania, McMaster and Stone, p. 269.

[14] "Agrippa, VIII" (25 Dec. 1787), Paul Leicester Ford, ed., *Essays on the Constitution of the United States, Published During Its Discussion by the People, 1787–1788* (Brooklyn, N.Y., 1892), pp. 76–78.

[15] "Objections of the Hon. George Mason, to the Proposed Federal Constitution; Assigned as His Reasons for Not Signing the Same," Elliot, I, 495. (Portions of this work appear in this book at p. 65, "Objections to the Proposed Constitution.")

[16] Winthrop, "Agrippa, III" (30 Nov. 1787), Ford, *Essays,* p. 61.

If it were possible to consolidate the states, and preserve the features of a free government, still it is evident that the middle states, the parts of the union, about the seat of government, would enjoy great advantages, while the more remote states would experience the many inconveniences of remote provinces. Wealth, offices, and the benefits of government would collect in the centre . . . .[17]

To add to the danger, the federal government would secure exclusive control of the sword, as well as of the purse and of commerce. The Constitution provided for a standing army, "that engine of arbitrary power, which has so often and so successfully been used for the subversion of freedom." [18] To make matters worse, Congress was given the power to call out the militia of a state to execute national laws, to suppress insurrections, and to repel invasion. Hence Congress would have the power

to march the whole militia of Maryland to the remotest part of the Union, and keep them in service as long as they think proper; [during such service, members of the militia may] be subjected to military law, and tied up and whipped at the halbert, like the meanest of slaves.[19]

This was an extreme and excited statement of the argument. But, in other statements as well, many anti-Federalists took for granted that it would be necessary to execute federal law, not resting upon popular consent, by a standing army or by federal use of state militias.[20]

The anti-Federalists found further evidence of the determination to undermine completely the position of the states. Luther Martin did not doubt that the Congressional power to make or alter regulations concerning "the times, places, and manner of

---

[17] Richard Henry Lee, "The Federal Farmer, Letter II" (9 Oct. 1787), Ford, *Pamphlets,* p. 290.

[18] Luther Martin, "Genuine Information," Elliot, I, 371.

[19] *Ibid.*

[20] See, e.g., elaboration of this point by the Pennsylvania Minority, McMaster and Stone, pp. 479 f.

holding elections for Senators and Representatives" was designed for "the utter extinction and abolition of all state governments."[21] James Wilson patiently explained that the federal structure itself depended both upon the continued existence of state governments and upon a continued relationship between Congress and the people; but he could not convince the Pennsylvania opponents that this provision was intended merely to protect Congress, and not as a threat against the states. As with the question of the jurisdiction of federal courts, there was a great deal of speculation about what Congress might do. Thus George Clinton explained that Congress might establish the place or places of election far from the centers of population and at a time and season when it would be difficult for voters to attend, "and by these means destroy the rights of election."[22]

The proposed Constitution would transform Congress from a confederate debating society with restricted powers and no independent revenue into an effective legislative body with its own source of revenue and with substantial and unclearly defined powers. That was bad enough. Equally bad, and in the opinion of some anti-Federalists still worse, were the proposed powers of the President and of the courts.

The President, elected for a four-year term, eligible without limit for reelection, equipped with powers to nominate judicial officers, to fill vacancies during the recess of the Senate, to pardon for the offense of treason, and with the armed forces at his disposal, would, in fact, be an *"elective king."*[23] "A king in substance," the President would be able, when he chose, to become a *"king in name"* as well; and, if he chose, he would be able to perpetuate the kingship in his family.[24] George Clinton

[21] "Genuine Information," Elliot, I, 361 f.

[22] "Cato, VII," Ford, *Essays,* p. 276.

[23] William Findley, "To the Citizens of Philadelphia" (3 Nov. 1787), McMaster and Stone, p. 181. (Portions of this letter appear in this book at p. 133, "Letter of an Officer of the Late Continental Army.")

[24] Martin, "Genuine Information," Elliot, I, 379.

of New York speculated with gusto about the dissolute ambition, baseness, and perfidy that would characterize the ten square miles of the federal District. Here the President would surround himself with "expectants and courtiers," with "flatterers," "minions and favorites." He would preside over a court that would become an "asylum of the base, idle, avaricious and ambitious," in which the President's power to grant pardons for treason might well be used "to screen from punishment those whom he had secretly instigated to commit the crime." [25] The powers vested in the President, Clinton concluded, would lead to "a vile and arbitrary aristocracy or monarchy." [26] Clinton was not alone in portraying the federal District as a kind of dissolute Versailles of the New World, presided over by an irresponsible, reckless pseudomonarch. The cautious George Mason, writing in more moderate language, expressed similar fears.

A federal judiciary also presented a novel threat of very serious if unpredictable dimensions. Most of the anti-Federalists were inclined to agree that the national judiciary "would eventually absorb and swallow up the state judiciaries, by drawing all business from them to the courts of the general government.[27] This would be both inconvenient and costly since, for example, "an inhabitant of Pittsburgh, on a charge of crime committed on the banks of the Ohio, may be obliged to defend himself at the side of the Delaware, and so *vice versa*." [28] It would also further imperil the liberty of the people, since trial by jury, that "boast of the English constitution" and "palladium of liberty," was not guaranteed in civil cases, nor, it was claimed, even in criminal cases when appealed to the Supreme Court. Furthermore, even where trial by jury was guaranteed, there was no requirement that the jury be drawn from the vicinage. More generally, the

---

[25] "Cato, IV" (8 Nov. 1787) and "Cato, V" (22 Nov. 1787), Ford, *Essays*, pp. 260–269 *passim*.

[26] "Cato, IV," Ford, *Essays*, p. 264.

[27] Martin, "Genuine Information," Elliot, I, 370.

[28] Pennsylvania Minority, McMaster and Stone, p. 475.

constitutional provisions concerning judicial procedure showed clear evidence, it was said, that the common-law traditions were being undermined and that the costly procedure of civil law courts, such as prevailed in the Chancery in England and in the courts of Scotland and France, was being established. Thus the Constitution would impose an alien judicial system upon the healthy indigenous common-law systems of the states. Richard Henry Lee could not detect in the Supreme Court "a spark of freedom or a shadow of our own or the British common law." [29] Legally minded critics expounded these points at great length. They were inclined to dismiss contemptuously James Wilson's attempt to explain that the diversity of judicial procedures in the several states made it difficult, if not impossible, to write more detailed provisions into the Constitution. But, however tedious much of the debate about judicial procedure was, it was not without significant effect. Amendments V through VIII of the Bill of Rights clearly reflect the impact of this part of the anti-Federalist case.

Related to concern about a national system of courts and the assumed threat of an alien system of judicial procedure was the general demand for a comprehensive bill of rights. The anti-Federalists rejected impatiently the argument that a bill of rights, while necessary to protect a people against a monarchic or aristocratic government, was not necessary to protect the people of a republic against themselves; and, in fact, much of the argument of *The Federalist* was inconsistent with this position. Nor were the anti-Federalists impressed by the argument that some of the state constitutions lacked systematic bills of rights. And if, as some of the Federalists pointed out, the question of a bill of rights had not been raised at Philadelphia until near the end of the sessions and if it had received no serious consideration, then, said the anti-Federalists, this in itself was a serious charge against the Philadelphia Convention. The question of a systematic bill of rights should have been seriously

---

[29] "The Federal Farmer, Letter III" (10 Oct. 1787), Ford, *Pamphlets,* p. 309.

and thoroughly explored. By the transformation of the confederacy into a "consolidated government," declared Patrick Henry, the "rights of conscience, trial by jury, liberty of the press, all your immunities and franchises, all pretensions to human rights and privileges, are rendered insecure, if not lost." [30]

Of substantive rights, freedom of the press, another "palladium of freedom," was mentioned most often. Other specific substantive rights, such as freedom of conscience, were occasionally mentioned. The delicate question of slavery was sometimes brought into the debate. But a guarantee of jury trial in civil cases was the most common demand, and the demand for a guarantee of freedom of the press was not far behind.

As long as the liberty of the press continues unviolated, and the people have the right of expressing and publishing their sentiments upon every public measure, it is next to impossible to enslave a free nation. . . . Men of an aspiring and tyrannical disposition, sensible of this truth, have ever been inimical to the press, and have considered the shackling of it as the first step towards the accomplishment of their hateful domination, and the entire suppression of all liberty of public discussion, as necessary to its support. . . . The abolition of that grand palladium of freedom, the liberty of the press, in the proposed plan of government, and the conduct of its authors and patrons, is a striking exemplification of these observations.[31]

The anti-Federalists claimed further that a dangerous blending of powers permeated the Constitution in violation of the "sacred maxim" of separation of powers. Benjamin F. Wright has pointed out that practically all parties to the debate accepted the principle of separation of powers as basic to constitutional government.[32] Among the anti-Federalists, only one apparently opposed the "sacred maxim" and argued the case against the

---

[30] In the Ratifying Convention of Virginia (5 June 1788), Elliot, III, 44.

[31] Samuel Bryan, "Centinel, II" (24 Oct. 1787), McMaster and Stone, p. 576.

[32] "The Federalist on the Nature of Political Man," Ethics, LIX (1949), 1–31.

Constitution on other grounds. It is significant that this one, Samuel Bryan, was a Pennsylvanian.[33] The rest united in hurling the authority of "the celebrated Montesquieu" against the proposed Constitution. The Pennsylvania minority objected to "the undue and dangerous mixture of the powers of government; the same body possessing legislative, executive and judicial powers." The Senate, they observed, had judicial power in cases of impeachment; it had executive power in respect to appointments and treaties; the President, furthermore, was "dangerously connected with the senate." [34]

[This is] inconsistent with all freedom; the celebrated Montesquieu tells us, that "when the legislative and executive powers are united in the same person, or in the same body of magistrates, there can be no liberty, because apprehensions may arise, lest the same monarch or *senate* should enact tyrannical laws, to execute them in a tyrannical manner." [35]

George Mason argued that the Senate, in conjunction with the President, would "destroy any balance in the government"; their extensive powers, their continuity in office, and their connection with the executive would "enable them to accomplish what usurpations they please[d] upon the rights and liberties of the people." [36] In short, as William Findley declared:

The Legislative and Executive powers are not kept separate, as every one of the American constitutions declares they ought to be;

---

[33] In his "Centinel, I" (5 Oct. 1787), McMaster and Stone, at pp. 569 f., Bryan argued against John Adams's theory of balanced government, maintaining: "If you complicate the plan by various orders, the people will be perplexed and divided in their sentiment about the source of abuses, or misconduct . . . . But if, imitating the constitution of Pennsylvania, you vest all the legislative power in one body of men (separating the executive and judicial) . . . , you will create the most perfect responsibility . . . ." It was the direct responsibility of officers to their constituents that would guarantee free government, not a baffling distribution of powers.
[34] McMaster and Stone, pp. 475–477 *passim.*
[35] *Ibid.,* p. 476.
[36] "Objections," Elliot, I, 494 f.

but they are mixed in a manner entirely novel and unknown, even in the constitution of Great Britain . . . .[37]

Intertwined with these specific fears, predictions, and warnings were a number of assumptions that could be said to constitute a general anti-Federalist political theory. The theory was usually invoked piecemeal, rather than presented with any degree of systematic continuity; different elements of it appeared more or less prominently, as the occasion demanded, in different writers and speakers.

First, the anti-Federalists agreed with the Federalists that the primary object of a constitution should be to secure and maintain the advantages of republican government and the liberty of individual persons. By "republican government" they meant government based upon popular consent and responsible to popular control. They meant in other words what we mean today by "democracy"; but the use of that term was exceptional. They then argued that a single government spread over such a large area as that of the thirteen states could not possibly be republican and would consequently be oppressive. Republican government and liberty could be maintained only in small, homogeneous communities. The authority of "the celebrated Montesquieu" was cited endlessly in support of this opinion. The Constitution would produce a "consolidated" rather than a federated system; a "consolidated government" over a large area would necessarily be antirepublican and destructive of liberty.

A "consolidated government" would be despotic since the great diversity of interests among the states would make agreed compromise among competing interests impossible. Laws in the interest of dominant groups would necessarily be imposed upon minority groups against their will and to their grave disadvantage. Furthermore, the differences in morals and habits produced by differences in climate, social institutions, and economic

---

[37] "To the Citizens of Philadelphia" (3 Nov. 1787), McMaster and Stone, p. 181.

systems would make it utterly impossible "for one code of laws to suit Georgia and Massachusetts." Some of the anti-Federalists became quite eloquent on Montesquieu's theme of "the spirit of the laws." The laws must be adapted to the manners of the people, James Winthrop of Massachusetts explained, and the manners of the people differed greatly in many respects.

The idle and dissolute inhabitants of the south require a different regimen from the sober and active people of the north. . . . The unequal distribution of property, the toleration of slavery, the ignorance and poverty of the lower classes, the softness of the climate and dissoluteness of manners [make the people of the southern states quite different from the people of the north, who by their general education, their] small and nearly equal estates, equality of rights, and the severity of the climate, [are made] industrious and sober [and are distinguished also by attention] to religion and good morals . . . .[38]

The idea of an uncompounded republick, on an average one thousand miles in length, and eight hundred in breadth, and containing six millions of white inhabitants all reduced to the same standard of morals, of habits, and of laws, is in itself an absurdity, and contrary to the whole experience of mankind. The attempt made by Great Britain to introduce such a system, struck us with horrour . . . .[39]

The Virginian, Richard Henry Lee, apparently agreed with Winthrop's unflattering New England view of southern as contrasted with northern conditions and manners.

The Eastern states are very democratic, and composed chiefly of moderate freeholders; they have but few rich men and no slaves; the Southern states are composed chiefly of rich planters and slaves; they have but few moderate freeholders, and the prevailing influence, in them is generally a dissipated aristocracy . . . .[40]

---

[38] "Agrippa, XII" (11 Jan. 1788), Ford, *Essays,* pp. 91 f.
[39] "Agrippa, IV" (3 Dec. 1787), Ford, *Essays,* p. 65.
[40] "The Federal Farmer, Letter III" (10 Oct. 1787), Ford, *Pamphlets,* pp. 296 f.

James Winthrop argued in some detail that diversity of interests required diversity of government. Men would always seek their immediate interests and would understand their own interests. "All the states have local advantages, and in a considerable degree separate interests." [41] "It is vain to tell us that we ought to overlook local interests." [42] This concentration on one's immediate local interests was healthy, as well as inevitable. "It is only by protecting local concerns that the interest of the whole is preserved." [43] The diverse interests of the several states were complementary: the plantations of Carolina were important to Massachusetts; the manufacture and commerce of Massachusetts were necessary and important to the planters of Carolina. Pursuit of local interests would promote the economic welfare of the whole and bind the whole together. "A diversity of produce, wants and interests, produces commerce; and commerce, where there is a common, equal and moderate authority to preside, produces friendship." [44] As throughout the rest of the anti-Federalist arguments, the moral once more is clear. Since "one code of laws" could never be made "to suit Georgia and Massachusetts" and since the diverse but complementary interests of the several states were the principal bond of union among them, the states "must, therefore, legislate for themselves." [45]

Second, the anti-Federalists argued, "consolidated government" would necessarily be antirepublican because representation, as they interpreted it, would be impossible in the system they envisioned. The argument at this point went beyond the claim that regionally diverse interests would be irreconcilable, and democratic compromise on a large scale therefore impossible. It involved a conception of democratic representation that goes to the center of the theoretical system of the anti-Federal-

---

[41] "Agrippa, VIII" (25 Dec. 1787), Ford, *Essays*, p. 76.
[42] "Agrippa, VII" (18 Dec. 1787), Ford, *Essays*, p. 73.
[43] *Ibid.*
[44] "Agrippa, VIII" (25 Dec. 1787), Ford, *Essays*, p. 77.
[45] "Agrippa, IV" (3 Dec. 1787), Ford, *Essays*, p. 64.

ists and to the ultimate basis of much of their suspicion of specific arrangements of the new Constitution.

Against the demands made by states'-rights delegates at the Philadelphia Convention for a Congress that would represent the states equally, as under the Articles of Confederation, James Wilson and James Madison had argued vigorously for representation according to population and for direct election of representatives to the House. "As all authority was derived from the people," Wilson declared, "equal numbers of people ought to have an equal number of representatives." [46] Madison argued that proportionate representation and popular election of representatives would give a broad base to the new government, inspire confidence, and "induce the government to sympathize with the people." [47] When it was proposed that the Convention recommend that the Constitution be ratified by specially selected state conventions, Madison reminded the Convention once more that "the people were in fact, the fountain of all power, and by resorting to them, all difficulties were got over." [48] Later, Wilson in the Pennsylvania Convention and Madison in *The Federalist* made much of the argument that all the powers of the new government would, in Wilson's words, derive from "one great and noble source, THE PEOPLE." [49] Wilson insisted that "the supreme, absolute and uncontrollable authority *remains* with the people." [50]

The anti-Federalists could scarcely deny the proposition that the ultimate source of authority was the people; but they did deny some of the conclusions that the Federalists drew from the proposition. There were two anti-Federalist responses to the Federalist appeal to popular sovereignty. The first, developed by Luther Martin at Philadelphia and repeated in his "Genuine

---

[46] (9 June 1787), Farrand, I, 179.
[47] (31 May 1787), Farrand, I, 57.
[48] (31 Aug. 1787), Farrand, II, 476.
[49] (24 Nov. 1787), McMaster and Stone, p. 231.
[50] (4 Dec. 1787), McMaster and Stone, p. 316.

Information," was a rather contrived restatement of the argument for the continuing sovereign independence of the states. In a precivil state of nature, Martin explained, men were equally free and independent. When they enter into civil society, their natural equality dictates that each should have an equal voice in the establishment of government and an equal vote in the government established, regardless of differences "*in personal strength, understanding, or wealth.*" Martin's logic then took a bold leap. He went on to explain:

> Having thus established these principles with respect to the *rights* of *individuals* in a *state of nature,* and what is due to *each* on entering into government,—principles established by every writer on liberty,—[advocates of equal suffrage in the states] proceeded to show that *states,* when *once formed,* are considered, *with respect* to *each other,* as *individuals* in a state of nature; that, like individuals, each *state* is considered *equally free* and *equally independent,* the *one* having no right to exercise authority over the *other,* though *more strong, more wealthy,* or *abounding with more inhabitants. . . .*[51]

Hence, when a number of states enter into a confederation, the principle of equal voting rights for each must prevail, as the principle applies to individuals who have formed a political community.[52]

> [In] a federal government, the parties to the compact are not the *people,* as individuals, but the states, as states; . . . in a federal government over states equally free, sovereign, and independent, every state ought to have an equal share in making the federal laws or regulations, in *deciding* upon them, and in carrying them into execution . . . .[53]

Furthermore, the contracts by which state governments were established were irreversible by the people themselves.

---

[51] "Genuine Information," Elliot, I, 352.
[52] *Ibid.,* pp. 352 f.
[53] *Ibid.,* p. 360.

[When] once the people have *exercised their power* in establishing and forming themselves into a *state government*, it never devolves back to them; nor have they a right to resume or again to exercise that power, until such events take place as will amount to a dissolution of their state government.[54]

In effect, Martin was regarding the states as internationally sovereign units of government and assuming that the principles of international sovereignty were to be applied to the position of the states in the confederation.[55] It should be noted that, whereas Martin of Delaware argued for equal representation of the states as states, anti-Federalists from large states, Pennsylvania and Virginia, for example, continued the Philadelphia debate by objecting to equal representation in the Senate and insisting that representation in both houses should be apportioned according to population.

The second response to the Federalist appeal to popular sovereignty was the widespread anti-Federalist claim that the new Constitution was not and could not be based upon popular representation in any meaningful sense. As a representative body, the House would be utterly deficient for a number of reasons. Having only sixty-five members, it would, in the first place, be too small: "One Representative to thirty thousand inhabitants is a very inadequate representation."[56] Second, Representatives would sit for two years rather than facing their constituents

---

[54] *Ibid.*, pp. 387 f.

[55] This appears to be what Martin had argued in his three-hour speech in the Philadelphia Convention on June 27. Of that speech Yates wrote (Farrand, I, 438 f.): "As his arguments were too diffuse, and in many instances desultory, it was not possible to trace him through the whole, or to methodize his ideas into a systematic argument." Madison summarized the three-hour speech in a page and a half; summarizing the second section of Martin's speech, delivered on June 28, he remarked (Farrand, I, 445): "This was the substance of the residue of his discourse which was delivered with much diffuseness and considerable vehemence." The Convention seems to have paid little attention to Martin's elaborate effort.

[56] Gerry, "Replies to the Strictures of A *Landholder*," Ford, *Pamphlets*, p. 12.

annually. Third, that healthy check to "the overbearing insolence of office" provided by compulsory rotation would be lost; with no limit upon reeligibility, there would be nothing to prevent "the perpetuity of office in the same hands for life." [57] Furthermore, since thirty-three members of the House would constitute a quorum and seventeen of these a majority, and since fourteen Senators would form a quorum and eight of these a majority,

> the liberties, happiness, interests, and great concerns of the whole United States, may be dependent upon the integrity, virtue, wisdom, and knowledge of twenty-five or twenty-six men. How unadequate and unsafe a representation! Inadequate, because the sense and views of three or four millions of people, diffused over so extensive a territory, comprising such various climates, products, habits, interests, and opinions, cannot be collected in so small a body . . . .[58]

Thus the House of Representatives, the only part of the constitutional structure that looked in the direction of democracy, would contain "a mere shred or rag of representation." [59]

The small size of Congress would make adequate representation impossible; to try to make Congress large enough to be truly representative would be too costly and would produce an unwieldy body. But the problem was not really one of size nor of the length of terms of office; it went deeper. Because of the manner of election, because of Congressional control over elections, and because of the small size of the representative body,

> men of the most elevated rank in life will alone be chosen. The other orders in the society, such as farmers, traders, and mechanics, who all ought to have a competent number of their best informed men in the legislature, shall be totally unrepresented. . . . [Congress] will consist of the lordly and high minded; of men who will

---

[57] *Ibid.*, pp. 11 f.

[58] Pennsylvania Minority, McMaster and Stone, p. 472.

[59] Richard Henry Lee, Letter to Edmund Randolph (16 Oct. 1787), Elliot, I, 503.

have no congenial feelings with the people, but a perfect indifference for, and contempt of them; [it] will consist of those harpies of power that prey upon the very vitals, that riot on the miseries of the community.[60]

In consequence, Congress would not have the confidence of the people nor their willing compliance, but would, as noted above, have to rely on the force of a standing army to have its laws enforced.[61]

This extreme statement led to the familiar conclusion: a plot was afoot that would, if successful, end in despotic rule by a distant, self-perpetuating aristocracy, kept in power by force. But the claim that the proposed Congress would not be truly representative was often made even when it was not a part of a closely linked argument that the Constitution necessarily looked toward aristocracy or tyranny; one must conclude that it was also sincerely believed. It was based on a conception of representation that could be possible only for small political units.[62] Whereas *The Federalist* argued that representatives must be able to rise above devotion to limited local interests, the anti-Federalists were firmly convinced of the opposite. They insisted that representatives should represent local sentiments and speak for local interests; that they should mirror as precisely as possible the sentiments of their constituents.

To make representation real and actual, . . . [representatives] ought to mix with the people, think as they think, feel as they feel,—ought to be perfectly amenable to them, and thoroughly acquainted with their interest and condition.[63]

---

[60] Pennsylvania Minority, McMaster and Stone, pp. 472, 479.

[61] *Ibid.*, p. 481.

[62] See Cecelia M. Kenyon's brilliant article, "Men of Little Faith: The Anti-Federalists on the Nature of Representative Government," *William and Mary Quarterly*, XII (1955), 3–43. This analysis owes much to Miss Kenyon's suggestions.

[63] George Mason, In the Ratifying Convention of Virginia (4 June 1788), Elliot, III, 32.

They should be a true picture of the people, possess a knowledge of their circumstances and their wants, sympathize in all their distresses, and be disposed to seek their true interests.[64]

The perennial dispute over the proper role of representatives was hotly waged at this early period in American political history.

For some of the anti-Federalist protesters, this theoretical argument was no doubt mixed with concern about threats to personal power and influence in local politics, which might be engulfed in the larger system. But the argument could not be simply dismissed, as the Federalists were inclined to dismiss it, as merely defensive of personal interests and ambitions. The idea that representatives should precisely represent the sentiments of their constituents and serve their immediate interests reflected the deeply ingrained suspicion of distant authority engendered by colonial experience and strengthened by the theory and practice of the period of the Revolution. The anti-Federalists did not argue for direct democracy; but it seems clear that they regarded representative democracy as a second-best substitute for it. After all, republican government on a large scale was a novel venture; precedent for it could be found neither in American experience nor in the earlier history of constitutional government; the flexible authority of "the celebrated Montesquieu" seemed to run against it. James Madison was well aware of this reasoning when in *The Federalist* he argued at length and so persuasively the advantages of representative over direct democracy.

Incorporated into the anti-Federalist denial of the feasibility of representative government on a large scale was a sharp and persistent emphasis on the class structure of society. "[Every] order of men in the community," Richard Henry Lee explained, "professional men, merchants, traders, farmers, mechanics,"

---

[64] Melancton Smith, In the Ratifying Convention of New York (21 June 1788), Elliot, II, 245.

should be represented. But the House was too small to permit such representation. Consequently, "nine times in ten, men of the elevated classes in the community only can be chosen"; "the middle and lower classes," "the common people of the country," "the men of middling property" would have little or no share in enacting national laws and levying taxes.[65] Melancton Smith developed the same argument at length for the benefit of the Ratifying Convention of New York. "Every society," he said, "naturally divides itself into classes." Distinctions of "birth, education, talents, and wealth" clearly marked out a class that would "command a superior degree of respect." If there were but a few offices to be filled, members of this *natural aristocracy* would be chosen to fill them. "Men in the middling class" would not aspire to such heights of distinction, for they had "been used to walk in the plain and frugal paths of life." [66]

Furthermore, the system would work against representation of the common people because it would be difficult for them to organize support for a candidate in an electoral district containing thirty or forty thousand inhabitants. "The great easily form associations; the poor and middling class form them with difficulty." Hence, "none but the great will be chosen, for they easily unite their interests: the common people will divide, and their divisions will be promoted by the others." There would be little chance of the common people uniting, unless in support of a popular, but unprincipled, demagogue. Under the proposed system, then, control of the government would "fall into the hands of the few and the great"; whereas a healthy government would be one in which a "respectable yeomanry" would make up the principal part of the representative legislature. This class ought to dominate the legislature because it was the largest in the community, because it stood as a bulwark between the rich and the poor, and because it would quickly feel the weight of

---

[65] "The Federal Farmer, Letters II, III, IV" (9, 10, 14 Oct. 1787), Ford, *Pamphlets*, pp. 288–318 *passim.*

[66] (21 June 1788), Elliot, II, 246.

any burden upon the poor and the risk of any insecurity to property. In short, when members of this class "pursue their own interest, they promote that of the public, for it is involved in it." [67] Viewed in the light of these considerations, Melancton Smith declared, the House of Representatives offered a "mere shadow of representation." [68]

It should by now be clear that the anti-Federalist view of human nature was not an especially flattering one. The anti-Federalists were certain that men would pursue their immediate interests and that men's views of their interests were not readily enlarged by enlarged responsibilities. Dreading "the depravity of human nature," Patrick Henry would guard against it by means of every possible check and "trust nothing to accident or chance." [69] "[The] depraved nature of man is well known," he declared. "He has a natural bias towards his own interest, which will prevail over every consideration, unless it be checked." [70] Others, not always so forthright or oratorical as Henry, would have agreed. There would have been general approval of Samuel Adams's later comment: "Few men are contented with less power than they have a right to exercise." [71] The anti-Federalists outdid Alexander Hamilton in their conviction of the corruptibility of human nature and anticipated Lord Acton's opinion on the corrupting influence of power. The only safeguard against the abuse of power was to keep it ever immediately visible before the eyes of the people; this would be impossible in a large territory. The "respectable yeomanry," "the men in the middling class," were safer repositories of the interests they understood, sympathized with, and represented, not because they were essentially better people than those who had scrambled upward

---

[67] *Ibid.*, pp. 246–248 *passim.*

[68] *Ibid.*, p. 249.

[69] In the Ratifying Convention of Virginia (12 June 1788), Elliot, III, 327.

[70] *Ibid.*, p. 326.

[71] To Richard Henry Lee (22 Apr. 1789), Cushing, IV, 327.

in the social, economic, and political order, but primarily because they had not been favored by opportunities to display and exert their antisocial ambitions—in short, because they had not been corrupted by power. Consequently, liberty had more often been destroyed by the "tyranny of rulers" than by "the licentiousness of the people." [72] George Clinton warned the citizens of New York that few of them would have a chance to sit in Congress and that the choice of representatives would be "confined to few." The number of representatives, he declared, would be "too few to resist the influence of corruption, and the temptation to treachery, against which all governments ought to take precautions." [73]

To sum up: The anti-Federalists asserted that Congress would not and could not represent the people; that the President would be a king in all but name; that the courts would be dominated by an aristocratic influence, against which the people would struggle in vain; that the powers of all three agencies would be so great and undefined as to be dangerous to local autonomy, to republican government, and to liberty; and, finally, that the rights of the people would be protected neither by an institutional separation of powers nor by a complete bill of rights. Behind these specific objections and intensifying them were basic assumptions about human nature, about men's commitment to their interests, about the corrupting influence of power, about the advantages possessed by the aristocrats, and consequently about the logically unavoidable dangers of "consolidated government" and of distant government generally.

It is not hard to understand how such arguments easily shaded into an interpretation of the Constitution as the culmination of a long-standing plot by "the aristocrats" against the mass of "the common people." This was, as indicated above, Luther Martin's interpretation of the Philadelphia Convention. Although

---

[72] Patrick Henry, In the Ratifying Convention of Virginia (5 June 1788), Elliot, III, 47.

[73] "Cato, V" (22 Nov. 1787), Ford, *Essays,* p. 269.

the party favoring "monarchy" was small, he said, it was powerful by virtue of its alliance with the larger party that favored the destruction of state governments and with the party that favored the ascendancy of the larger over the smaller states. The party of "monarchy" had, in the end, been decisive in controlling the essential features of the Constitution.[74] A pamphlet attributed to Elbridge Gerry, another dissenting member of the Convention, agreed with Martin's view. It explained that those "aristocrats" who now rushed forth to save the country had been, for the most part, too young or too obscure, or even traitorously uninterested, at the time of the Revolution, when real dangers threatened. Genuine patriots, who at the time of real danger had learned to respect the "unalienable rights" of men and the real nature of popular sovereignty, now beheld with great concern

the insidious arts, and the strenuous efforts of the partisans of arbitrary power, by their vague definitions of the best established truths, endeavoring to envelope the mind in darkness the concomitant of slavery, and to lock the strong chains of domestic despotism on a country . . . but newly emancipated from the spectre of foreign domination. . . . [Some disreputable characters] are endeavouring by all the arts of insinuation, and influence, to betray the people of the United States, into an acceptance of a most complicated system of goverment; marked on the one side with the *dark, secret* and *profound intrigues,* of the statesman, long practised in the purlieus of despotism and on the other, with the ideal projects of *young ambition,* with its wings just expanded to soar to a summit . . . .[75]

"But," it pointed out, "the most sagacious advocates" had failed to produce rational arguments for "this many headed monster; of such motley mixture," in which the opponents could not find "a feature of Democratick or Republican extract" and which its

---

[74] "Genuine Information," Elliot, I, 344–389.
[75] "Observations . . . by a Columbian Patriot," Ford, *Pamphlets,* pp. 6 f.

friends had not the courage to call "a Monarchy, an Aristocracy, or an Oligarchy." [76]

Ad hominem references were not absent from this kind of argument. As the Federalists detected personal ambitions at stake in state politics, so the anti-Federalists detected personal hopes and ambitions among those who supported effective central government. Thus anti-Federalists in Pennsylvania and outside the state often attacked James Wilson, that wily "Caledonian," as one of the ambitious slackers of 1776 who hoped, by deceiving the people, to win prominence for himself and for his efforts of 1787–1788. But, however the anti-Federalists might choose to deal with the strong and informed advocacy of Wilson and Madison, the support given the Constitution by Washington and Franklin raised a very difficult problem. Recognizing their positions of national and international prestige, the extreme anti-Federalists argued either that they had been misled by those who knew more clearly what they were about or that their alleged judicious aloofness from the debates at Philadelphia was a pose assumed to conceal their antirepublican views from the people.

Not all the anti-Federalists wanted to reject the new system completely: most were prepared to acknowledge that changes in the existing system were necessary.[77] Some, in fact, anticipated Hamilton's long catalog of problems that existed or could be anticipated under the Articles of Confederation. Objecting to the Constitution, Edmund Randolph was none the less convinced "that the Confederation must be thrown aside"; he found himself "fatigued" with calling up to his imagination the miseries that might come to the United States under the Articles.[78] Those

---

[76] *Ibid.*, pp. 7 f.

[77] There were, of course, those who were convinced, or at any rate asserted, that there had been great recovery since the Revolution, that problems that the Federalists complained of were rapidly being liquidated, and that matters could scarcely be in a happier state for honest, hardworking Americans.

[78] Letter to the Virginia House of Delegates (10 Oct. 1787), Elliot, I, 486, 488.

who agreed that problems existed argued either that the difficulties could be met by amendments to the Articles, granting Congress authority to deal with such notorious difficulties as revenue and taxation,[79] or that the proposed Constitution should not be approved without a series of amendments to meet numerous specific objections.[80] Other opponents, who saw the Constitution as a deliberate assault upon republican government and liberty, demanded amendments that would have fundamentally changed its character. Such comprehensive demands were meant also to suggest the need for a second constitutional convention. The amendments proposed by the Pennsylvania minority offer a good illustration. Proposals one through six dealt with freedom of conscience, freedom of speech, trial by jury in certain civil cases, and procedural protections in criminal action, and number fourteen defined very specifically the jurisdiction of federal courts. Other proposals dealt with state control over militias; declared for strict interpretation of federal powers, for a strict separation of powers, for a responsible executive council "to advise and assist the President"; declared against standing armies in time of peace; and closely restricted the power of Congress to tax. The thirteenth proposition was, in effect, an anticipation of the proposed Bricker Amendment on the power to make treaties. The eighth guaranteed the residents of the states the right "to fowl and hunt" on their lands and on public lands and "to fish in all navigable waters." Thus, acceptable amendments were mixed with others clearly unacceptable to the supporters of the Constitution, and basically important amendments were mixed with trivial; the whole made a mélange that could scarcely have been acceptable to the most conciliatory Federalist.[81]

---

[79] See, e.g., Yates and Lansing, Elliot, I, 481.

[80] See, e.g., Edmund Randolph's list, Elliot, I, 491, and Winthrop, "Agrippa, IX" (28 Dec. 1787), Ford, *Essays*, pp. 79–81.

[81] "Address and Reasons" (18 Dec. 1787), McMaster and Stone, pp. 461–463. See also Winthrop, "Agrippa, XVIII" (5 Feb. 1788), Ford, *Essays*, pp. 115–121.

It should now be clear that, as Miss Kenyon (see note 62) has so cogently pointed out, the anti-Federalists were far removed from sanguine twentieth-century defenders of absolute majority rule. They were not modern "Progressives" with unlimited confidence in the ability of popular majorities to reduce national problems to simple terms and, if only the complex system would allow them to act, to deal with such problems on a national scale. Their emphasis was consistently and persistently upon closely defining and restraining delegated political power rather than upon making authority effective. They professed a democratic theory, but they were conservative rather than radical democrats. They were far more impressed by the past than concerned about the future of democratic representation. Their own experience, their interpretation of the experience of history, and their literary authorities convinced them that popular government could operate only on a small scale. They declined to face the problem of what would ultimately happen to thirteen separate peoples, each pursuing its own conception of state interests, loosely combined, for limited purposes, with other states. Hence they found a multitude of specific objections to a constitution which was based upon a totally different conception of the necessity and the potentialities of a nationwide system of representative democracy.

THE FEDERALIST DEFENSE

The immediate achievement of the anti-Federalists was historically and theoretically important. They compelled Federalists who had helped defeat the drive to make ratification conditional to sponsor amendments to the Constitution. These amendments included the famous and increasingly important bill of rights, proposed to Congress by James Madison in 1789. If the ultimate result of these amendments was not what advocates of states' rights desired, this does not detract from their importance.[82]

---

[82] On this point see Alpheus T. Mason, *The States Rights Debate: Antifederalism and the Constitution* (Englewood Cliffs, N.J.: Prentice-Hall, Inc., 1964).

Quite as important for the future was the fact that the anti-Federalist criticism forced the Federalists to develop their general theory of republican constitutional government into a system, or at least to make the system explicit. There were, of course, Federalist replies in addition to those by "Publius." Examples of reasoned Federalist responses by John Jay before he became "Publius," by James Wilson, and by Tench Coxe are included in Part II of this book. But the series of letters composing *The Federalist* was the most thorough and systematic of the calm and dispassionate responses. What influence these letters may have had upon the immediate course of the debate remains a moot point,[83] but their importance for constitutional theory generally and for American constitutional theory particularly has long been established.

[83] Contemporary opinion of the letters reflected partisan assessment of the position taken. One critic (*New York Journal,* 14 Feb. 1788, Ford, *Pamphlets,* p. 395) compared Publius to a lawyer "hard pressed, in a bad cause, with a rich client": he frequently said "a great deal, which does not apply; but yet if it will not convince the judge and jury, may perhaps help to make them forget some part of the evidence, embarrass their opponents, and make the audience stare." Samuel Bryan ("Centinel, XI," 16 Jan. 1788, McMaster and Stone, pp. 635 f.) observed caustically that the danger of the states' splitting into rival confederations was a "hobgoblin . . . sprung from the deranged brain of *Publius,* a New York writer, who, mistaking sound for argument, has with Herculean labor accumulated myriads of unmeaning sentences, and *mechanically* endeavored to force conviction by a torrent of misplaced words." Friends of the Constitution naturally made an opposite assessment: "It would be difficult to find a treatise which, in so small a compass, contains so much valuable political information, or in which the true principles of republican government are unfolded with such precision" (*American Magazine,* March 1788, Ford, *Pamphlets,* p. 395). Jefferson's laudatory ultimate assessment appears in this book at p. 123.

Douglass Adair ("The Authorship of the Disputed Federalist Papers, II," *William and Mary Quarterly,* I [1944], 235–264) has suggested that the propaganda value of *The Federalist* "as first published in the newspapers should not be overrated" and that "the essays probably influenced few votes among the general electorate," but that "served up hot in debate" in Virginia and New York, the letters "played an important part in getting the new government ratified." "In the Virginia and New York Conventions," he added, "the bound volumes were enormously valuable."

The authors of *The Federalist* might have dodged many of the theoretical objections by pointing out that the new Constitution simply did not say some of the things attributed to it or by arguing that there was no ground for imaginative speculation. They might simply have ridiculed the quality of the arguments of the opposition and questioned the motivation behind them. In fact, they did all these things. From time to time they denounced their opponents for the shallowness of their arguments or for their lack of perception; at times they impugned their motives. Even though the "charge of a conspiracy against the liberties of the people . . . has something in it too wanton and too malignant, not to excite the indignation of every man who feels in his own bosom a refutation of the calumny," [84] it was necessary for *The Federalist* to deal with those "Gorgons, hydras, and chimeras dire" that had been evoked by the critics. They had to try to straighten out the "ill-written tale or romance" that had presented such "frightful and distorted shapes." [85]

But the level of argument of *The Federalist* seldom sank to simple denunciation, ridicule, or imputation of improper motivation.[86] Nor did the authors of *The Federalist* content themselves with merely describing the provisions of the Constitution, although they spent much time analyzing particular sections and meeting specific objections. They could scarcely have stopped with descriptive rebuttal once their opponents had raised issues of basic principle. Had they done so, *The Federalist* would scarcely have gained the importance it has as a classical American statement of constitutional theory. The enduring significance of *The Federalist* comes from the fact that the specific arguments

---

[84] Alexander Hamilton, James Madison, and John Jay, *The Federalist,* Benjamin F. Wright, ed. (Cambridge, Mass.: Harvard University Press, 1961), No. 85, p. 542.

[85] *Ibid.,* No. 29, p. 230.

[86] As interesting contrasts with the tone of *The Federalist,* note the "Caesar" papers, Ford, *Essays,* pp. 279–291, erroneously attributed to Hamilton, and the diatribe signed "Tar and Feathers" (2 Oct. 1787), McMaster and Stone, p. 138.

were constantly related to general, theoretical propositions, which gave the whole a unity and consistency that was lacking even in the more solid of the writings and speeches on the other side. Hence it is safe to apply to *The Federalist* an analytical approach that in the case of the anti-Federalists could have supported misapprehension. One can isolate a series of basic propositions to which the authors adhered fairly systematically and which from time to time they defended explicitly.

The first proposition that the authors of *The Federalist* appear to have taken for granted was that principles of politics could be discussed and defended rationally, despite men's tendency to rely upon emotions. In this respect, they were still good rationalists, and their book as a whole may be viewed as an elaborate appeal to reason. At times, however, they were quite willing to flatter their readers and incidentally to belittle their opponents. Thus Madison would not scruple to speak plainly to "a people as little blinded by prejudice or corrupted by flattery as those whom" he addressed.[87] Hamilton believed that the "citizens of America have too much discernment to be argued into anarchy." [88] He denounced the arguments of "the credulous votaries of State power" [89] and those who had "not scrupled to draw resources even from the regions of fiction" and to indulge in "deliberate imposture and deception";[90] he must combat those opponents whose "rage for objection . . . disorders their imaginations and judgments"; [91] he would appeal "purely to the dictates of reason and good sense." [92] "[It] is the reason, alone, of the public, that ought to control and regulate the government," Madison declared. "The passions ought to be controlled and regulated by the government." [93] The authors of *The Federalist*

---

[87] *The Federalist*, No. 63, p. 415.
[88] *Ibid.*, No. 26, p. 214.
[89] *Ibid.*, No. 60, p. 401.
[90] *Ibid.*, No. 67, pp. 436 f.
[91] *Ibid.*, No. 78, p. 490.
[92] *Ibid.*, No. 70, p. 453.
[93] *Ibid.*, No. 49, p. 351.

were convinced not only that reason should prevail, but also that it could.

They took perhaps undue pride in the advanced state of the modern science of politics and, as good rationalists, they expressed their willingness to rely upon the modern principles of politics. If men would only learn to follow the dictates of their reason, all would be well. Madison regretted the lack of scientific detachment that too often colored debate on public matters.

It is a misfortune, inseparable from human affairs, that public measures are rarely investigated with that spirit of moderation which is essential to a just estimate of their real tendency to advance or obstruct the public good; and that this spirit is more apt to be diminished than promoted, by those occasions which require an unusual exercise of it.[94]

Hamilton, acknowledging the difficulty of such detachment, expressed his belief in "principles of moral and political knowledge" and was certain that the science of politics was far more advanced in modern than in earlier times.

Though it cannot be pretended that the principles of moral and political knowledge have, in general, the same degree of certainty with those of the mathematics, yet they have much better claims in this respect than, to judge from the conduct of men in particular situations, we should be disposed to allow them. The obscurity is much oftener in the passions and prejudices of the reasoner than in the subject. Men, upon too many occasions, do not give their own understandings fair play; but, yielding to some untoward bias, they entangle themselves in words and confound themselves in subtleties.[95]

The science of politics, however, like most other sciences, has received great improvement. The efficacy of various principles is

---

[94] *Ibid.*, No. 37, pp. 265 f.   [95] *Ibid.*, No. 31, p. 237.

now well understood, which were either not known at all, or imperfectly known to the ancients.[96]

The modern science of government had taught the modern student many principles. Among these were the principles of the separation of powers, of legislative checks and balances, of representation, and of the importance of a permanent judiciary. "[These] are wholly new discoveries, or have made their principal progress towards perfection in modern times." They were, of course, particularly relevant to the debate because they suggested ways in which republican government could be maintained and "its imperfections lessened or avoided"; above all, they opened the possibility of extending republican government over a large area.[97]

Shut your ears to the complaint that the new Constitution involves novelties in government, Madison urged his readers.[98] It was true that "the great principles of the Constitution" were not new; but their expansion and practical application were.[99] But, even if some arrangements were not entirely familiar, that was no reason for Americans to reject them.

> Is it not the glory of the people of America, that, whilst they have paid a decent regard to the opinions of former times and other nations, they have not suffered a blind veneration for antiquity, for custom, or for names, to overrule the suggestions of their own good sense, the knowledge of their own situation, and the lessons of their own experience? [100]

This admonition not to fear novelty blended readily with the theme, popularized later by Jefferson, Emerson, and others, of a special American destiny. Americans had an opportunity, if they would but act decisively, to set an example to the rest of the world. Thus, in the opening paragraph of the first letter, Hamilton observed:

---

[96] *Ibid.*, No. 9, p. 125.   [97] *Ibid.*   [98] *Ibid.*, No. 14, p. 154.
[99] *Ibid.*, No. 40, p. 290.   [100] *Ibid.*, No. 14, p. 154.

It has been frequently remarked that it seems to have been reserved to the people of this country, by their conduct and example, to decide the important question, whether societies of men are really capable or not of establishing good government from reflection and choice, or whether they are forever destined to depend for their political constitutions on accident and force.

Madison went on from the statement quoted above to the prediction:

To this manly spirit, posterity will be indebted for the possession, and the world for the example, of the numerous innovations displayed on the American theatre, in favor of private rights and public happiness.[101]

There was also, especially in Hamilton's letters, a strong emphasis on the advantages of a strong national union to material American interests.

By a steady adherence to the Union, we may hope, erelong, to become the arbiter of Europe in America, and to be able to incline the balance of European competitions in this part of the world as our interest may dictate.[102]

On the other hand, weakness and interstate rivalry would leave American commerce open "to the wanton intermeddlings of all nations at war with each other . . . . A nation, despicable by its weakness, forfeits even the privilege of being neutral." [103]

The Federalist appealed on occasion to the "ablest adepts in political science" [104] and to those "politicians and statesmen who have been the most celebrated for the soundness of their principles and for the justice of their views." [105] But they apparently thought of their principles as a realistic blend of logical deduction and generalization from history and contemporary observation. They did not hesitate to refer to the lessons of

---

[101] *Ibid.*   [102] *Ibid.*, No. 11, p. 138.   [103] *Ibid.*, p. 139.
[104] *Ibid.*, No. 66, p. 431.   [105] *Ibid.*, No. 70, p. 452.

history, but those lessons were more often than not negative warnings rather than positive directives. Modern men, it seemed, could learn from history the mistakes to be avoided more often than the path to be followed. Furthermore, politics was not mathematics. Because of the limitations of reason and of observation, political axioms could not often "be brought to the test of a mathematical demonstration." [106] Hence men who looked for perfection in human institutions were expecting the impossible.

If mankind were to resolve to agree in no institution of government, until every part of it had been adjusted to the most exact standard of perfection, society would soon become a general scene of anarchy, and the world a desert. Where is the standard of perfection to be found? . . . To answer the purpose of the adversaries of the Constitution, they ought to prove, not merely that particular provisions in it are not the best which might have been imagined, but that the plan upon the whole is bad and pernicious.[107]

I never expect to see a perfect work from imperfect man. The result of the deliberations of all collective bodies must necessarily be a compound, as well of the errors and prejudices, as of the good sense and wisdom, of the individuals of whom they are composed.[108]

One thing to be learned from history and observation was the complexity of human nature. The frankness of Madison, as well as Hamilton, in discussing the weakness of human nature, at one time aroused the suspicion of modern democrats. Merriam, J. Allen Smith, Beard, and Parrington were inclined to agree with those anti-Federalists who saw the Philadelphia Convention as a plot against democracy and *The Federalist* as a slick cover-up. Members of this school of thought curiously neglected the opinions that anti-Federalists held of their fellow men. More recently, Wright has pointed out that the realistic Federalist

---

[106] *Ibid.,* No. 85, p. 546.   [107] *Ibid.,* No. 65, p. 430.
[108] *Ibid.,* No. 85, p. 544.

view of men cannot be correctly interpreted as antidemocratic elitism,[109] and Kenyon has demonstrated that the anti-Federalists were in fact more pessimistic in their view of men and the prospects of self-government than were the Federalists.[110]

The Federalist's reiterated praise of republican government would have been a shoddy and patently deceitful performance had Madison and Hamilton held a Hobbesian view of human nature; but they did not. References in *The Federalist* to "the folly and wickedness of mankind," [111] to "the ordinary depravity of human nature," [112] to "the impulses of rage, resentment, jealousy, avarice, and of other irregular and violent propensities," [113] are too familiar to need elaborate documentation. But its authors maintained that selfishness, impulsiveness, and irrational behavior generally could be held under restraint, and that errors in public policy resulting from such causes could be prevented or corrected, given the proper structure of governmental machinery. They believed firmly in the socializing effect of institutions. Traits that balanced the antisocial traits of human nature must be appealed to and must be cultivated, if "the public good," "the national interest," and "the permanent and aggregate interests" of the community were to be served. Although he believed that there is "nothing so apt to agitate the passions of mankind as personal considerations," [114] Hamilton insisted:

> This supposition of universal venality in human nature is little less an error in political reasoning, than the supposition of universal rectitude. The institution of delegated power implies, that there is a portion of virtue and honor among mankind, which may be a reasonable foundation of confidence; and experience justifies the theory.[115]

---

[109] "*The Federalist* on the Nature of Political Man," *Ethics*, LIX (1949), 1–31.

[110] "Men of Little Faith," *William and Mary Quarterly*, XII (1955), 3–43.

[111] *The Federalist*, No. 78, p. 496.

[112] *Ibid.*   [113] *Ibid.*, No. 6, p. 111.

[114] *Ibid.*, No. 76, p. 481.   [115] *Ibid.*, p. 483.

Furthermore, if "the desire of reward is one of the strongest incentives of human conduct," and if "the best security for the fidelity of mankind is to make their interest coincide with their duty," still "the love of fame, the ruling passion of the noblest minds, . . . would prompt a man to plan and undertake extensive and arduous enterprises for the public benefit." [116] Hamilton was speaking in these instances of leaders—the President and Senators; but clearly "virtue and honor," as well as "passion and prejudice," were distributed among people generally. "The people commonly *intend* the PUBLIC GOOD," even when they err about the means to attain it.[117] Anticipating this statement of Hamilton, Jay had written earlier that

the people at large always mean well, and although they may on certain occasions be misled by the counsels, or injured by the efforts of the few who expect more advantage from the wreck, than from the preservation of national prosperity, yet the motives of these few, are by no means to be confounded with those of the community in general.[118]

Demagogues, acting in their own immediate interest, might seek to mislead the people; but that was not an argument against an appeal to reason. Nor was it an argument against the importance of leadership. It was national leaders particularly who could be expected to identify their own ambitions and sense of honor with an enlarged conception of the public good. In short, the authors of *The Federalist* asserted as one of their basic beliefs what is often said of the contemporary American Presidency—that the size and importance of the job impel a man to grow up to it. More generally, they asserted the importance of leadership in democratic government and insisted, as Jefferson

---

[116] *Ibid.,* No. 72, p. 464. [117] *Ibid.,* No. 71, p. 459.

[118] "An Address to the People of the State of New-York, on the Subject of the Constitution, Agreed upon at Philadelphia" (17 Sept. 1787), Ford, *Pamphlets,* pp. 69 f. (Portions of this pamphlet appear in this book at p. 101, "Address to the People of New York.")

did, that the necessary role of a "natural aristocracy" was entirely compatible with popular government.

Publius obviously did not share modern doubts about something that might be labeled "the national interest" or "the public good." [119] If one asks what *The Federalist's* conception of the public good or "the great interests of society" [120] was, the answer appears in generalities which no parties to the controversy would have disputed. The object of all government was "the happiness of the people." [121] For this happiness, liberty was essential, and liberty was necessarily associated with republican government. The new Constitution would give "additional security" to republican government, to liberty, and to property. This was the theme of the opening letter; it was repeated *verbatim* in the last letter.

Assuming that there would be no serious dispute about such general objectives of government, the problem was to adjust the structure of government to human drives in a way best calculated to secure them. This must be done by carefully circumscribing delegated political power and surrounding its holders with numerous checks, said the anti-Federalists. The problem was not so simple, said *The Federalist*. In the first place, those who contented themselves with singing the praises of liberty should remember that stability and energy were important attributes of good government and, in fact, necessary to liberty itself. The Philadelphia Convention, Madison explained, had faced the problem of "combining the requisite stability and energy in government, with the inviolable attention due to liberty and to the republican form." [122] Tracing "the mischievous effects of a mutable government," he wrote, "would fill a volume. . . . The

---

[119] These and similar phrases appear throughout *The Federalist*. See, e.g., No. 10, pp. 130, 132; No. 24, p. 202; No. 37, p. 272.

[120] *Ibid.*, No. 70, p. 454.   [121] *Ibid.*, No. 62, p. 410.

[122] *Ibid.*, No. 37, p. 267.

internal effects of a mutable policy" would poison "the blessing of liberty itself." [123]

A government must have power commensurate with its responsibilities. It was one of the axioms of politics that "the *means* ought to be proportioned to the *end;* the persons, from whose agency the attainment of any *end* is expected, ought to possess the *means* by which it is to be attained." Thus since the "circumstances that endanger the safety of nations are infinite," [124] constitutional shackles should not be imposed upon the power to provide for the common defense. The generalization was often repeated in other contexts; it was obviously very useful especially in defending increased federal power and the independent position of the President. Oliver Ellsworth, who wrote a series of papers in defense of the Constitution, put the case succinctly:

A government capable of controlling the whole, and bringing its force to a point, is one of the prerequisites for national liberty. We combine in society, with an expectation to have our persons and properties defended against unreasonable exactions either at home or abroad. If the public are unable to protest against the unjust impositions of foreigners, in this case we do not enjoy our natural rights, and a weakness of government is the cause. If we mean to have our natural rights and properties protected, we must first create a power which is able to do it. . . . But power when necessary for our good is as much to be desired as the food we eat or the air we breathe. Some men are mightily afraid of giving power lest it should be improved for oppression; this is doubtless possible, but where is the probability[?] . . . [A] power of doing good always implies a power to do evil if the person or party be disposed.[125]

The authors of *The Federalist* agreed with other Federalists on the proposition that there was but one legitimate source of

---

[123] *Ibid.,* No. 62, p. 411.   [124] *Ibid.,* No. 23, p. 200.
[125] *A Landholder,* III (19 Nov. 1787), Ford, *Essays,* p. 147.

political power.[126] In this respect they also agreed fully with their opponents.

> The fabric of American empire ought to rest on the solid basis of THE CONSENT OF THE PEOPLE. The streams of national power ought to flow immediately from that pure, original foundation of all legitimate authority.[127]

Some early twentieth-century commentators on *The Federalist* were so intent upon demonstrating its distrust of democracy that they passed over in silence the repeated assertions by Hamilton and by Madison that popular sovereignty was the necessary foundation of all American government. Such assertions should not surprise a reader familiar with what had been happening in American political thinking. By 1789 the principle of popular sovereignty had become so firmly established as a basic fact of political life that no realistic writer who hoped to influence opinion could have ignored it.

> [No government other than one] strictly republican . . . would be reconcilable with the genius of the people of America; with the fundamental principles of the Revolution; or with that honorable determination . . . to rest all our political experiments on the capacity of mankind for self-government.[128]

Rather than trying to ignore the doctrine of popular sovereignty, the authors of *The Federalist* turned it to their advantage and against their opponents. But one cannot without obvious distortion suppose that they accepted the doctrine as a matter of political expediency. Too much of their serious argument centered upon popular sovereignty and republican government. They took for granted throughout that legitimate authority must come from the people, that officials must use delegated power

---

[126] See above, p. 16.
[127] *The Federalist*, No. 22, p. 199.
[128] *Ibid.*, No. 39, p. 280.

to serve the interests of the people, that officials must be held responsible to the people.

> The genius of republican liberty seems to demand on one side, not only that all power should be derived from the people, but that those intrusted with it should be kept in dependence on the people . . . .[129]

The House of Representatives was the agency through which popular sovereignty would operate most directly and continuously.

> As it is essential to liberty that the government in general should have a common interest with the people, so it is particularly essential that the branch of it under consideration should have an immediate dependence on, and an intimate sympathy with, the people.[130]

Madison explained that popular government operating on a large scale was one of the novelties of the new Constitution, made possible by applying fully the principle of democratic representation within a constitutional system. His repeated insistence upon the difference between "democracy" and "republican government," [131] which has supported modern interpretations of *The Federalist* as a covert defense of antidemocratic aristocracy, is explicable only in the light of the repeated insistence of the anti-Federalists that popular government on a large scale was impossible. What Madison was trying to say should be perfectly clear from his own words. By a "pure democracy" he meant "a society consisting of a small number of citizens, who assemble and administer the government in person." [132] By a "republic" he meant "a government in which the scheme of representation takes place." [133] In a republic, the people

---

[129] *Ibid.*, No. 37, p. 268. [130] *Ibid.*, No. 52, p. 361.
[131] See especially *ibid.*, Nos. 10 and 14.
[132] *Ibid.*, No. 10, p. 133; see also No. 14, p. 150.
[133] *Ibid.*, No. 10, p. 133.

"assemble and administer [the government] by their representatives and agents." [134] In short, by "republican government" he meant what we today mean by democratic government. Madison declared firmly and repeatedly that it was the device of representation that made popular government possible on a national scale and that popular representative government would avoid the instability and turbulence so often attributed to ancient democracies. Hence

the vices and defects of . . . the turbulent democracies of ancient Greece and modern Italy [were not evidence against the new system, since] most of the popular governments of antiquity were of the democratic species; and even in modern Europe, to which we owe the great principle of representation, no example is seen of a government wholly popular, and founded, at the same time, wholly on that principle.[135]

The development of the science of politics and American experience made possible constitutional arrangements, arrangements for popular government on a large scale, that the authority of "the celebrated Montesquieu" had thrown under doubt.

Frequent elections were a principal means of maintaining close association between representatives and constituents and dependence of representatives upon their constituents. But political power must be vested in men who, if unrestrained, were likely to put their own immediate interests above public interests and to push their powers to the limit. "It will not be denied, that power is of an encroaching nature . . . ." [136] Safety against abuse of power was not to be sought in denying representatives or other officers the power to act. "A government ought to contain in itself every power requisite to the full accomplishment of the objects committed to its care, and to the complete execution of the trusts for which it is responsible . . . ." [137] "[Every] POWER ought to be in proportion to its OBJECT . . . ." [138] Hence, since

---

[134] *Ibid.*, No. 14, p. 150. [135] *Ibid.*, p. 151.
[136] *Ibid.*, No. 48, p. 343. [137] *Ibid.*, No. 31, p. 238.
[138] *Ibid.*, No. 30, p. 233.

the effective organization of power was necessary, since power could be delegated only into the hands of men, and since power tended to corrupt, "auxiliary precautions" against the abuse of power were necessary.

To keep representative officials virtuous and attentive to "the common good of the society," "ambition must be made to counteract ambition," vested power must be balanced by restraining power vested elsewhere. From this proposition came the familiar argument for separation of powers and Madison's famous exposition, in Nos. 47 and 48, of the correct meaning of the doctrine. He concluded No. 47 with the summary statement that

the charge brought against the proposed Constitution, of violating the sacred maxim of free government, is warranted neither by the real meaning annexed to that maxim by its author, nor by the sense in which it has hitherto been understood in America.[139]

It is clear, as explained by Wright [140] and as stated by Madison himself, that the debate over separation of powers was not about the importance of the "sacred maxim" itself, but about whether it was or was not embodied in the Constitution. The anti-Federalists' argument had cut two ways inconsistently: it deplored the absence of checks upon the use of vested powers; at the same time, it objected to the fusion of powers that resulted from giving the officers of one department the power to check the other two. Madison had to explain that effective separation of powers required interlocking checks.

It was a basic part of the argument that the federal government must be republican.[141] But it remained true that, whereas in "republican government, the legislative authority necessarily predominates," [142] "the tendency of republican governments is to

---

[139] Ibid., No. 47, p. 342.

[140] "The Federalist on the Nature of Political Man," Ethics, LIX (1949), 1–31.

[141] See especially The Federalist, No. 39, p. 280; No. 46, p. 330; No. 57, pp. 384 f.

[142] Ibid., No. 51, p. 356.

an aggrandizement of the legislative at the expense of the other departments." [143] A republican legislature would need to be checked, as would other parts of the government. Overlegislation and "inconstancy and mutability in the laws [are] the greatest blemish in the character and genius of our governments." [144] "The republican principle demands that the deliberate sense of the community" should govern the actions of representatives, rather than "every sudden breeze of passion, or . . . every transient impulse" to which the people and their representatives might be swayed by demagogic appeals.[145] Hence, in the first place, the need of a second house of the legislature. The Senate would provide a "stable institution in the government";[146] it would double "the security to the people, by requiring the concurrence of two distinct bodies in schemes of usurpation or perfidy, where the ambition or corruption of one would otherwise be sufficient"; [147] it would lessen the danger that the legislature would "yield to the impulse of sudden and violent passions, and . . . be seduced by factious leaders into intemperate and pernicious resolutions"; [148] it would balance the rapidly changing membership of the House by a more experienced group; and "a due sense of national character" would win the respect of foreign powers, hitherto "forfeited by an unenlightened and variable policy." [149] In his defense of the Senate, Madison did not find it necessary to expand the federal argument, by which the equal representation and equal vote of each state was viewed as "at once a constitutional recognition of the portion of sovereignty remaining in the individual States, and an instrument for preserving that residuary sovereignty." [150] Having dealt with the Senate as a check upon the people's representatives, he added that the Senate might also on occasion protect the people themselves "against their own temporary errors and delusions."

---

[143] *Ibid.*, No. 49, p. 350.   [144] *Ibid.*, No. 73, p. 470.
[145] *Ibid.*, No. 71, p. 459.   [146] *Ibid.*, No. 62, p. 411.
[147] *Ibid.*, p. 409.   [148] *Ibid.*, p. 410.
[149] *Ibid.*, No. 63, p. 413.   [150] *Ibid.*, No. 62, p. 408.

As the cool and deliberate sense of the community ought, in all governments, and actually will, in all free governments, ultimately prevail over the views of its rulers; so there are particular moments in public affairs when the people, stimulated by some irregular passion, or some illicit advantage, or misled by the artful misrepresentations of interested men, may call for measures which they themselves will afterwards be the most ready to lament and condemn. In these critical moments, how salutary will be the interference of some temperate and respectable body of citizens, in order to check the misguided career, and to suspend the blow meditated by the people against themselves, until reason, justice, and truth can regain their authority over the public mind? [151]

The Federalist defended the Presidency on the ground that "a vigorous Executive" was necessary to effective republican government.[152] But it also argued that the executive check upon the legislature would add a further guarantee that the "deliberate sense of the community" would prevail. One of Hamilton's most emphatic and famous statements on the people and the public good occurs in his development of the latter argument.[153] The authors of *The Federalist* were also convinced that the proposed method for electing the President would insure that the office would never go to a man not eminently qualified for it.[154]

Replying to numerous anti-Federalist critics, Hamilton asserted that the judiciary would be "the weakest of the three departments of power," rather than an awesome threat to individual liberties.

[From] the nature of its functions, [it] will always be the least dangerous to the political rights of the Constitution; because it will be least in a capacity to annoy or injure them. . . . [It] has no influence over either the sword or the purse: no direction either of the strength or of the wealth of the society; and can take no active resolution whatever. It may truly be said to have neither FORCE nor

---

[151] *Ibid.*, No. 63, p. 415.   [152] *Ibid.*, No. 70.
[153] *Ibid.*, No. 71, p. 459.   [154] *Ibid.*, No. 68, p. 442.

WILL, but merely judgment; and must ultimately depend upon the aid of the executive arm even for the efficacy of its judgments.[155]

From there Hamilton proceeded to his classical statement of the argument for judicial review.

But *The Federalist* insisted that dependence upon and responsibility to the people and the mechanics of constitutional arrangements did not exhaust the list of factors working upon officials to keep them faithful to their trust.

> There is in every breast a sensibility to marks of honor, of favor, of esteem, and of confidence, which, apart from all considerations of interest, is some pledge for grateful and benevolent returns. . . . Duty, gratitude, interest, ambition itself, are the chords by which [Representatives] will be bound to fidelity and sympathy with the great mass of the people.[156]

Thus Madison on members of the House. Considerations of honor, esteem, gratitude, duty, ambition would restrain not only Representatives, but other officials as well. Speaking of Senators, for example, Hamilton remarked: "We may thus far count upon their pride, if not upon their virtue." [157] And Jay, writing of Senators and their role in the making of treaties, explained:

> Every consideration that can influence the human mind, such as honor, oaths, reputations, conscience, the love of country, and family affections and attachments, afford security for their fidelity.[158]

There was, in short, a public spirit or public morality which in a republican community would tend to curb men's antisocial behavior and center their concern upon their reputations as guardians of large public interests. This is another dominant theme that reappears frequently in *The Federalist*. It is not the

---

[155] *Ibid.*, No. 78, p. 490.   [156] *Ibid.*, No. 57, pp. 384 f.
[157] *Ibid.*, No. 66, p. 436.   [158] *Ibid.*, No. 64, p. 425.

special property of Hamilton, but appears with equal emphasis in the other two authors. Their belief in the proposition helps to explain the distinctive attitude of *The Federalist*; but the importance of the proposition has too often been neglected in analyses and interpretations of why they wrote as they did.

If the authors of *The Federalist* were deeply impressed by the need to keep public policy focused, by every possible means, upon national interests or the public good, they were, as already suggested, quite as deeply impressed by the persistent force exerted by partial interest groups or "factions." Much has been written in recent years about the "group theory" of *The Federalist* and especially about Madison's famous tenth letter. But there is a lurking ambivalence in his treatment of groups and group leadership which also deserves more attention than it has usually received.

Madison suggested that interest groups arose naturally from the "diversity in the faculties of men." Their causes were in the nature of men and could not be removed without destroying liberty itself.[159] "Different interests necessarily exist in different classes of citizens."[160] The pursuit of interests appeared to be perfectly legitimate as well as natural and unavoidable. It was from a wide diversity of interests, rather than from enforced, unnatural homogeneity, that safety was to be found for individuals and groups. "[The] society itself will be broken into so many parts, interests and classes of citizens, that the rights of individuals, or of the minority, will be in little danger from interested combinations of the majority."[161] In this section especially, but elsewhere as well, Madison seemed to suggest that, with governmental direction, a common or public interest would arise from the necessary compromising of many particular interests.

---

[159] *Ibid.*, No. 10, pp. 130–132. [160] *Ibid.*, No. 51, p. 358.
[161] *Ibid.*

The regulation of these various and interfering interests forms the principal task of modern legislation, and involves the spirit of party and faction in the necessary and ordinary operations of the government.[162]

But the concept of a composite, fluid, common interest which was simply the result of the necessary compromising of numerous particular interests was not made very explicit.

More explicit was the conception of factions or interest groups as motivated by considerations "adverse to the rights of other citizens, or to the permanent and aggregate interests of the community." [163] From this view, groups or factions did not appear as legitimately representative of particular interests, which must have free and equal opportunity to contribute to an aggregate pattern, while being restrained from destroying other interests. They appeared rather as obstacles in the way of fostering the great and aggregate interests of the whole national community. This interpretation is supported not only by *The Federalist's* reiterated concern about the common interest, but also by its confidence in those "men of talents, and integrity" [164] who would be induced by ambition, honor, and those other qualities already enumerated to rise above the demands of their local communities. Thus, although Madison did not clearly resolve the ambiguity in his theory of groups, the general argument of *The Federalist* leads one to suppose that, had one insisted upon an "either-or" answer, Madison would have said that there was, of course, a common interest that constitutional representative government must serve. But his refusal to put the question in "either-or" form and his constant interest in and concern about the role that groups do in fact play in politics suggest that the ambiguity may be inherent in a realistic analysis of democratic

---

[162] *Ibid.,* No. 10, p. 131.   [163] *Ibid.,* p. 130.

[164] The phrase is Jay's: *ibid.,* No. 64, p. 425. The idea is common to the three.

politics, rather than being a reflection of Madison's loose thinking.[165]

In one sense, *The Federalist* may be considered less "democratic" or more "elitist" than the anti-Federalists. Agreeing with the anti-Federalists that men tended to respond most readily to the pressures of local interests, its authors vigorously denied that a representative body should mirror local interests and local sentiments directly and precisely. Not only would such representation be impossible on a national scale, it would also be entirely undesirable. Representative democracy was not a second-best substitute for direct democracy, impossible even in the states. It was, Madison argued, superior to direct democracy, not only because it could comprehend a broader range of interests, but also because its effect was "to refine and enlarge the public views, by passing them through the medium of a chosen body of citizens, whose wisdom may best discern the true interest of their country." [166] The result of representation, Madison continued, might well be that decisions of the representatives would come closer to the public good than would decisions of the people acting directly. The opposite might also happen if "by intrigue, by corruption, or by other means, . . . [men] of factious tempers, of local prejudices, or of sinister design" got themselves chosen to represent the people. But it was an ad-

---

[165] This is as good a point as any to report that the writer does not find a "split personality" in *The Federalist*. However widely Madison and Hamilton may have differed before and after their collaboration, each seems quite willing in *The Federalist* to accept and build upon a common set of fundamental propositions. There are, of course, differences in emphasis and in style in the letters; but these do not add up to a split in the basic political theory of *The Federalist*. For the opposite interpretation, see Alpheus T. Mason, "*The Federalist*—A Split Personality," *American Historical Review*, LVII (1952), 625–643. See also Wright's Introduction to his edition of *The Federalist*, p. 31, for a much more limited comment on the differences between Hamilton's early letter No. 9 and Madison's No. 10, which was clearly the fruit of much thought on the subject.

[166] *The Federalist*, No. 10, p. 134.

vantage of large republics over small ones that more independent men would be found to represent the larger interests of the people.[167]

The Federalist, then, accepted certain general propositions concerning the role of reason and of experience, the complexity of human nature, the necessity of adequate power to govern, the dangers inherent in power, the consequent necessity of "auxiliary precautions," the popular source of authority, the relations between particular and common interests, and the necessary role of "men of talents, and integrity." The application of these principles to the question of the need for a new Constitution, to the structure of the new government, and to the relations between its parts gave them their answers to the criticisms of the anti-Federalists.

When more specific arguments were not available, *The Federalist* was prepared, on rare occasions, to appeal to natural law, the social contract, and natural rights. Thus, for example, when Madison replied to the complaint that a solemn compact among the states, the Articles of Confederation, could not be superseded by the decision of nine of the states, he appealed

> to the absolute necessity of the case; to the great principle of self-preservation; to the transcendent law of nature and of nature's God, which declares that the safety and happiness of society are the objects at which all political institutions aim, and to which all such institutions must be sacrificed.[168]

In the next letter, he declared:

> Bills of attainder, *ex-post-facto* laws, and laws impairing the obligation of contracts, are contrary to the first principles of the social compact, and to every principle of sound legislation.[169]

Such references are infrequent; but it is clear that *The Federalist* did not reject the general theory of natural law and social

---

[167] *Ibid.*, pp. 134 f.   [168] *Ibid.*, No. 43, p. 316.
[169] *Ibid.*, No. 44, p. 319; cf. Jay, *ibid.*, No. 2, p. 93.

contract. Its authors were arguing the case for a specific instrument of government on the basis of intermediate practical principles, rather than expounding a more basic theory of the ultimate origin and nature of government. As Wright has pointed out, they did not deny the "Spirit of '76"; it was "an assumed basis for the discussion in the Federal Convention and in the ratification controversy." [170]

Although there is some repetition and some backtracking, the general structure of The Federalist is coherent and the arguments are developed systematically. The opening group of letters (Nos. 1–14) deal chiefly with the dangerous conditions that existed under the Confederation and with the need for a more effective general government. Madison summed up the argument in the opening paragraph of No. 14:

> We have seen the necessity of the Union, as our bulwark against foreign danger, as the conservator of peace among ourselves, as the guardian of our commerce and other common interests, as the only substitute for those military establishments which have subverted the liberties of the Old World, and as the proper antidote for the diseases of faction, which have proved fatal to other popular governments, and of which alarming symptoms have been betrayed by our own.[171]

The next group (Nos. 15–36) deal more specifically with the defects of the system of government provided by the Articles of Confederation, review the failures of ancient and modern confederacies, argue the "necessity of a Constitution, at least equally energetic with the one proposed," [172] and examine the general principles involved in a workable federal distribution of powers, particularly the need for federal control of defense and the need for dependable sources of federal revenue.

In Nos. 37–46, Madison, after reviewing the problems that had

---

[170] Wright, Introduction, p. 13; see also his Consensus and Continuity, 1776–1787 (Boston: Boston University Press, 1958).

[171] The Federalist, No. 14, p. 150.

[172] Ibid., No. 23, p. 199.

confronted the Philadelphia Convention and summarizing the major arguments against the new Constitution, took up specific objections. To the argument that the Convention had no authority to draft a new constitution, he responded that

> the charge against the convention of exceeding their powers, except in one instance little urged by the objectors [that is, the recommendation that the new Constitution become effective after ratification by nine states instead of thirteen], has no foundation to support it; that if they had exceeded their powers, they were not only warranted, but required, as the confidential servants of their country, by the circumstances in which they were placed, to exercise the liberty which they assumed; and that finally, if they had violated both their powers and their obligations, in proposing a Constitution, this ought nevertheless to be embraced, if it be calculated to accomplish the views and happiness of the people of America.[173]

In No. 39, Madison sought to quiet the fears about "consolidated government" by explaining that the new Constitution was neither national nor "federal," but a "composition of both." Had present linguistic usage prevailed at the time, his task would have been simpler. What he called "federal" we would today call "confederate." But for the system between a national or unitary government and a confederacy there were neither historical precedents nor current instances. Nor was there a convenient distinguishing term. The federal system was another innovation, supported by American experience and by a clearer understanding of the ways in which the principles of government could be adapted to the needs of an inventive people. The Philadelphia Convention had created a novel system, unfamiliar and naturally frightening to those who did not share *The Federalist's* confidence in the science of politics and in a federalist interpretation of the lessons of history. It was necessary for Madison to explain the system in terms that seem to a modern

---

[173] *Ibid.*, No. 41, p. 293.

reader rather pedantic. In Nos. 41–46, he examined the specific distribution of powers between federal and state governments.

Four separate, but related, themes recurred throughout the discussion of the federal distribution of powers and of the relations between federal and state governments. The first, already mentioned, was the warning that Americans should not fear institutions supported by reason and by their own experience simply because precedents for such institutions could not be found. The second was a reminder that all authority in a popularly based constitutional system would come from a single source: the consent of the people. "The power of the people, Sir, is the great foundation of the proposed system," James Wilson had declared.[174] "[The] people are the only legitimate fountain of power," Madison repeated in *The Federalist*.[175] The critics "must be told that the ultimate authority, wherever the derivative may be found, resides in the people alone . . . . The federal and State governments are in fact but different agents and trustees of the people . . . ."[176] The federal government, as the governments of the states, deriving its power to act from the people, would be equally restrained by responsibility to the people. The third theme was the reminder that the "auxiliary precautions" worked into the Constitution included a separation and balancing of powers within the federal government, as well as a federal distribution of power. The fourth was the reiterated claim that the state governments, being closer to the people and having functions more intimately related to their daily lives, would be a greater danger than the federal government. Thus Madison explained:

The State governments will have the advantage of the Federal government, whether we compare them in respect to the immediate dependence of the one on the other; to the weight of personal

---

[174] In the Ratifying Convention of Pennsylvania, McMaster and Stone, p. 265.

[175] *The Federalist*, No. 49, p. 348; see also Hamilton in No. 28, pp. 224 f.

[176] *Ibid.*, No. 46, p. 330.

influence which each side will possess; to the powers respectively vested in them to the predilection and probable support of the people; to the disposition and faculty of resisting and frustrating the measures of each other.[177]

The powers delegated by the proposed Constitution to the federal government are few and defined. Those which are to remain in the State governments are numerous and indefinite. The former will be exercised principally on external objects, as war, peace, negotiation, and foreign commerce . . . . The powers reserved to the several States will extend to all the objects which, in the ordinary course of affairs, concern the lives, liberties, and properties of the people; and the internal order, improvement, and prosperity of the State.[178]

Thus it might be taken as an axiom in the American constitutional system that "the State governments will, in all possible contingencies, afford complete security against invasions of the public liberty by the national authority." [179]

There follows, in Nos. 47–51, Madison's famous analysis of the true meaning of the doctrine of separation of powers and its general application in the new Constitution. The way was thus prepared for a systematic discussion of the several branches of the new federal government: the House of Representatives (Nos. 52–61), the Senate (Nos. 62–66), the Presidency (Nos. 67–77), and the courts (Nos. 78–83). *The Federalist* discussed each in terms of the general principles already described, and with regard to the detailed criticisms that had been made by the opposition. In No. 84, Hamilton dealt, somewhat equivocally, with the question of the lack of a systematic bill of rights in the Constitution; in the concluding letter, he argued for immediate ratification without amendment.

On a bill of rights, *The Federalist* was at a disadvantage because the authors were unfortunately committed to the error of the Convention. They could not simply yield the argument without acknowledging that the Convention had been grossly

---

[177] *Ibid.*, No. 45, p. 326; see also Hamilton in No. 31, p. 240.
[178] *Ibid.*, No. 45, p. 328.   [179] *Ibid.*, No. 28, p. 225.

negligent on a point regarded by the opposition as of major importance. Nor could they weaken their own case by acknowledging that the proposed arrangements were not in fact sufficient to secure and maintain liberty, including the specific liberties so hotly debated by the anti-Federalists. Perhaps Hamilton made the best of a poor case; but it was not good enough, as Madison and others were later prepared to concede when they gave their support to the first ten amendments, proposed in 1789 and ratified in 1791.

PART I

*Minority Reports from the
Philadelphia Convention*

ROBERT YATES

AND

JOHN LANSING

Letter to Governor George Clinton
on Their Reasons for Leaving the Convention

1787 (?)

Sir:

✸ ✸ ✸ ✸

It is with the sincerest concern we observe that, in the prosecution of the important objects of our mission, we have been reduced to the disagreeable alternative of either exceeding the powers delegated to us, and giving assent to measures which we conceive destructive to the political happiness of the citizens of the United States, or opposing our opinions to that of a body of respectable men, to whom those citizens had given the most unequivocal proofs of confidence. Thus circumstanced, under these impressions, to have hesitated would have been to be culpable. We therefore gave the principles of the Constitution, which has received the sanction of a majority of the Convention, our decided and unreserved dissent; but we must candidly confess that we should have been equally opposed to any system, however modified, which had in object the consolidation of the United States into one government.

From Elliot, I, 480–482. Yates and Lansing left in mid-July.—J.D.L.

We beg leave, briefly, to state some cogent reasons, which, among others, influenced us to decide against a consolidation of the states. These are reducible into two heads:—

1st. The limited and well-defined powers under which we acted, and which could not, on any possible construction, embrace an idea of such magnitude as to assent to a general Constitution, in subversion of that of the state.

2d. A conviction of the impracticability of establishing a general government, pervading every part of the United States, and extending essential benefits to all.

Our powers were explicit, and confined to the sole and express purpose of revising the Articles of Confederation, and reporting such alterations and provisions therein as should render the Federal Constitution adequate to the exigencies of government and the preservation of the Union.

From these expressions, we were led to believe that a system of consolidated government could not, in the remotest degree, have been in contemplation of the legislature of this state; for that so important a trust as the adopting measures which tended to deprive the state government of its most essential rights of sovereignty, and to place it in a dependent situation, could not have been confided by implication; and the circumstance, that the acts of the Convention were to receive a state approbation in the last resort, forcibly corroborated the opinion that our powers could not involve the subversion of a Constitution which, being immediately derived from the people, could only be abolished by their express consent, and not by a legislature possessing authority vested in them for its preservation. Nor could we suppose that, if it had been the intention of the legislature to abrogate the existing Confederation, they would, in such pointed terms, have directed the attention of their delegates to the revision and amendment of it, in total exclusion of every other idea.

Reasoning in this manner, we were of opinion that the leading feature of every amendment ought to be the preservation of the individual states in their uncontrolled constitutional rights; and that, in reserving these, a mode might have been devised of granting to the Confederacy the moneys arising from a general system of revenue, the power of regulating commerce and enforcing the observance of foreign treaties, and other necessary matters of less moment.

Exclusive of our objections originating from the want of power, we entertained an opinion that a general government, however guarded by declarations of rights, or cautionary provisions, must unavoidably, in a short time, be productive of the destruction of the civil liberty of such citizens who could be effectually coerced by it, by reason of the extensive territory of the United States, the dispersed situation of its inhabitants, and the insuperable difficulty of controlling or counteracting the views of a set of men (however unconstitutional and oppressive their acts might be) possessed of all the powers of government, and who, from their remoteness from their constituents, and necessary permanency of office, could not be supposed to be uniformly actuated by an attention to their welfare and happiness; that, however wise and energetic the principles of the general government might be, the extremities of the United States could not be kept in due submission and obedience to its laws, at the distance of many hundred miles from the seat of government; that, if the general legislature was composed of so numerous a body of men as to represent the interests of all the inhabitants of the United States, in the usual and true ideas of representation, the expense of supporting it would become intolerably burdensome; and that, if a few only were vested with a power of legislation, the interests of a great majority of the inhabitants of the United States must necessarily be unknown; or, if known, even in the first stages of the operations of the new government, unattended to.

❊   ❊   ❊   ❊

. . . [We] cannot forbear to declare that we have the strongest apprehensions that a government so organized as that recommended by the Convention cannot afford that security to equal and permanent liberty which we wished to make an invariable object of our pursuit.

We were not present at the completion of the new Constitution; but before we left the Convention, its principles were so well established as to convince us that no alteration was to be expected, to conform it to our ideas of expediency and safety. A persuasion, that our further attendance would be fruitless and unavailing, rendered us less solicitous to return.

✽   ✽   ✽   ✽

ROBERT YATES
JOHN LANSING, Jun.

EDMUND RANDOLPH, GEORGE MASON,

AND

ELBRIDGE GERRY

☆☆☆

In the Convention

☆☆☆

15 SEPTEMBER 1787

Mr. Randolph animadverting on the indefinite and dangerous power given by the Constitution to Congress, expressing the pain he felt at differing from the body of the Convention, on the close of the great & awful subject of their labours, and anxiously wishing for some accommodating expedient which would relieve him from his embarrassments, made a motion importing "that amendments to the plan might be offered by the State Conventions, which should be submitted to and finally decided on by another general Convention[.]" Should this proposition be disregarded, it would he said be impossible for him to put his name to the instrument. Whether he should oppose it afterwards he would not then decide but he would not deprive himself of the freedom to do so in his own State, if that course should be prescribed by his final judgment—

Col[.] Mason 2ded. & followed Mr. Randolph in animadversions on the dangerous power and structure of the Government, concluding that it would end either in monarchy, or a tyrannical aristocracy; which, he was in doubt[,] but one or other, he was

---

From Documentary History of the Constitution of the United States of America, 1786–1870, *III, 759, 760–711. The* Documentary History *indicates emendations and corrections. What is given here is only the language of the finished document.*

63

sure. This Constitution had been formed without the knowledge or idea of the people. A second Convention will know more of the sense of the people, and be able to provide a system more consonant to it. It was improper to say to the people, take this or nothing. As the Constitution now stands, he could neither give it his support or vote in Virginia; and he could not sign here what he could not support there. With the expedient of another Convention as proposed, he could sign.

Mr. Gerry, stated the objections which determined him to withhold his name from the Constitution. 1. the duration and re-eligibility of the Senate. 2. the power of the House of Representatives to conceal their journals. 3— the power of Congress over the places of election. 4 the unlimited power of Congress over their own compensations. 5 Massachusetts has not a due share of Representatives allotted to her. 6. $\frac{3}{5}$ of the Blacks are to be represented as if they were freemen 7. Under the power over commerce, monopolies may be established. 8. The vice president being made head of the Senate. He could however he said get over all these, if the rights of the Citizens were not rendered insecure 1. by the general power of the Legislature to make what laws they may please to call necessary and proper. 2. raise armies and money without limit. 3. to establish a tribunal without juries, which will be a Star-chamber as to Civil cases. Under such a view of the Constitution, the best that could be done he conceived was to provide for a second general Convention.

GEORGE MASON

Objections to the Proposed Constitution

OCTOBER 1787

There is no declaration of rights; and, the laws of the general government being paramount to the laws and constitutions of the several states, the declarations of rights in the separate states are no security. Nor are the people secured even in the enjoyment of the benefit of the common law, which stands here upon no other foundation than its having been adopted by the respective acts forming the constitutions of the several states.

In the House of Representatives there is not the substance, but the shadow only, of representation, which can never produce proper information in the legislature, or inspire confidence in the people. The laws will, therefore, be generally made by men little concerned in, and unacquainted with, their effects and consequences.

The Senate have the power of altering all money bills, and of originating appropriations of money, and the salaries of the officers of their own appointment, in conjunction with the President of the United States, although they are not the representatives of the people, or amenable to them. These, with their other great powers, (viz., their powers in the appointment of ambassadors, and all public officers, in making treaties, and in

From Elliot, I, 494–496.

65

trying all impeachments;) their influence upon, and connection with, the supreme executive from these causes; their duration of office; and their being a constant existing body, almost continually sitting, joined with their being one complete branch of the legislature,—will destroy any balance in the government, and enable them to accomplish what usurpations they please upon the rights and liberties of the people.

The judiciary of the United States is so constructed and extended as to absorb and destroy the judiciaries of the several states; thereby rendering laws as tedious, intricate, and expensive, and justice as unattainable, by a great part of the community, as in England; and enabling the rich to oppress and ruin the poor.

The President of the United States has no constitutional council, (a thing unknown in any safe and regular government.) He will therefore be unsupported by proper information and advice, and will generally be directed by minions and favorites; or he will become a tool to the Senate; or a council of state will grow out of the principal officers of the great departments— the worst and most dangerous of all ingredients for such a council, in a free country; for they may be induced to join in any dangerous or oppressive measures, to shelter themselves, and prevent an inquiry into their own misconduct in office. Whereas, had a constitutional council been formed (as was proposed) of six members, viz., two from the Eastern, two from the Middle, and two from the Southern States, to be appointed by vote of the states in the House of Representatives, with the same duration and rotation of office as the Senate, the executive would always have had safe and proper information and advice: the president of such a council might have acted as Vice-President of the United States, *pro tempore*, upon any vacancy or disability of the chief magistrate; and long-continued sessions of the Senate would in a great measure have been prevented. From this fatal defect of a constitutional council has arisen the improper power of the Senate in the appointment of the public officers, and the alarming dependence and connection between that branch of the legislature and the supreme executive. Hence, also, sprang that unnecessary officer, the Vice-President, who, for want of other employment, is made president of the Senate; thereby dangerously blending the executive and legislative powers, besides always giving to some one of the states an unnecessary and unjust preëminence over the others.

The President of the United States has the unrestrained power of granting pardon for treason; which may be sometimes exercised to screen from punishment those whom he had secretly instigated to commit the crime, and thereby prevent a discovery of his own guilt. By declaring all treaties supreme laws of the land, the executive and the Senate have, in many cases, an exclusive power of legislation, which might have been avoided, by proper distinctions with respect to treaties, and requiring the assent of the House of Representatives, where it could be done with safety.

By requiring only a majority to make all commercial and navigation laws, the five Southern States (whose produce and circumstances are totally different from those of the eight Northern and Eastern States) will be ruined; for such rigid and premature regulations may be made, as will enable the merchants of the Northern and Eastern States not only to demand an exorbitant freight, but to monopolize the purchase of the commodities, at their own price, for many years, to the great injury of the landed interest, and the impoverishment of the people; and the danger is the greater, as the gain on one side will be in proportion to the loss on the other. Whereas, requiring two thirds of the members present in both houses, would have produced mutual moderation, promoted the general interest, and removed an insuperable objection to the adoption of the government.

Under their own construction of the general clause at the end of the enumerated powers, the Congress may grant monopolies in trade and commerce, constitute new crimes, inflict unusual and severe punishments, and extend their power as far as they shall think proper; so that the state legislatures have no security for the powers now presumed to remain to them, or the people for their rights. There is no declaration of any kind for preserving the liberty of the press, the trial by jury in civil cases, nor against the danger of standing armies in time of peace.

The state legislatures are restrained from laying export duties on their own produce; the general legislature is restrained from prohibiting the further importation of slaves for twenty-odd years, though such importations render the United States weaker, more vulnerable, and less capable of defence. Both the general legislature and the state legislatures are expressly prohibited making *ex post facto* laws, though there never was, nor can be, a legislature but must and will make such laws, when necessity and the public safety require them, which will hereafter be a breach of all the constitutions in the Union, and afford precedents for other innovations.

This government will commence in a moderate aristocracy; it is at present impossible to foresee whether it will, in its operation, produce a monarchy or a corrupt oppressive aristocracy; it will most probably vibrate some years between the two, and then terminate in the one or the other.

GEO. MASON

EDMUND RANDOLPH

★★

Letter to the Virginia House of Delegates

★★

10 OCTOBER 1787

Sir:

❀   ❀   ❀   ❀

Before my departure for the Convention, I believed that the Confederation was not so eminently defective as it had been supposed. But after I had entered into a free communication with those who were best informed of the condition and interest of each state; . . . I became persuaded that the Confederation was destitute of every energy which a constitution of the United States ought to possess.

For the objects proposed by its institution were, that it should be a shield against foreign hostility, and a firm resort against domestic commotion; that it should cherish trade, and promote the prosperity of the states under its care.

But these are not among the attributes of our present union. Severe experience under the pressure of war, a ruinous weakness manifested since the return of peace, and the contemplation of those dangers which darken the future prospect, have condemned the hope of grandeur and safety under the auspices of the Confederation.

From Elliot, I, 482–491. The letter was addressed to the Speaker of the House.—J. D. L.

In the exigencies of war, indeed, the history of its effects is but short; the final ratification having been delayed until the beginning of the year 1781. But however short, this period is distinguished by melancholy testimonies of its inability to maintain in harmony the social intercourse of the states, to defend Congress against encroachments on their rights, and to obtain, by requisitions, supplies to the federal treasury, or recruits to the federal armies. . . .

In the season of peace, too, not many years have elapsed; and yet each of them has produced fatal examples of delinquency, and sometimes of pointed opposition to federal duties. To the various remonstrances of Congress I appeal for a gloomy but unexaggerated narrative of the injuries which our faith, honor, and happiness, have sustained by the failure of the states.

But these evils are past; and some may be led by an honest zeal to conclude that they cannot be repeated. Yes, sir, they will be repeated as long as the Confederation exists, and will bring with them other mischiefs springing from the same source, which cannot yet be foreseen in their full array of terror.

If we examine the constitution and laws of the several states, it is immediately discovered that the law of nations is unprovided with sanctions in many cases which deeply affect public dignity and public justice. The letter, however, of the Confederation does not permit Congress to remedy these defects; and such an authority, although evidently deducible from its spirit, cannot without violation of the second article, be assumed. Is it not a political phenomenon, that the head of the confederacy should be doomed to be plunged into war, from its wretched impotency to check offences against this law, and sentenced to witness, in unavailing anguish, the infraction of their engagements to foreign sovereigns?

And yet this is not the only grievous point of weakness. After a war shall be inevitable, the requisitions of Congress for quotas of men or money will again prove unproductive and fallacious. Two causes will always conspire to this baneful consequence.

1. No government can be stable which hangs on human inclination alone, unbiased by coercion; and, 2, from the very
connection between states bound to proportionate contributions,
jealousies and suspicions naturally arise, which at least chill the
ardor, if they do not excite the murmurs, of the whole. . . .

* * * *

. . . [The] requisitions for money will not be more cordially
received; for, besides the distrust which would prevail with respect to them also, besides the opinion entertained by each
state of its own liberality and unsatisfied demands against the
United States, there is another consideration, not less worthy of
attention—the first rule for determining each quota by the value
of all lands granted or surveyed, and of the buildings and improvements thereon. It is no longer doubted that an equitable,
uniform mode of estimating that value is impracticable; and
therefore twelve states have substituted the number of inhabitants, under certain limitations, as the standard according to
which money is to be furnished. But under the subsisting articles
of the Union, the assent of the thirteenth state is necessary, and
has not yet been given. This does itself lessen the hope of procuring a revenue for federal uses; and the miscarriage of the impost
almost rivets our despondency.

Amidst these disappointments, it would afford some consola-
tion, if, when rebellion shall threaten any state, an ultimate
asylum could be found under the wing of Congress. But it is
at least equivocal whether they can intrude forces into a state
rent asunder by civil discord, even with the purest solicitude for
our federal welfare, and on the most urgent entreaties of the
state itself. Nay, the very allowance of this power would be
pageantry alone, from the want of money and of men.

To these defects of congressional power, the history of man
has subjoined others, not less alarming. I earnestly pray that the
recollection of common sufferings, which terminated in common
glory, may check the sallies of violence, and perpetuate mutual

friendship between the states. But I cannot presume that we are superior to those unsocial passions which, under like circumstances, have infested more ancient nations. . . .

In the prosecution of this inquiry, we shall find the general prosperity to decline under a system thus unnerved. No sooner is the merchant prepared for foreign ports, with the treasures which this new world kindly offers to his acceptance, than it is announced to him that they are shut against American shipping, or opened under oppressive regulations. He urges Congress to a counter-policy, and is answered only by a condolence on the general misfortune. He is immediately struck with the conviction that, until exclusion shall be opposed to exclusion, and restriction to restriction, the American flag will be disgraced; for who can conceive that thirteen legislatures, viewing commerce under different points of view, and fancying themselves discharged from every obligation to concede the smallest of their commercial advantages for the benefit of the whole, will be wrought into a concert of action, and defiance of every prejudice? . . .

I have not exemplified the preceding remarks by minute details, because they are evidently fortified by truth and the consciousness of the United States of America. I shall, therefore, no longer deplore the unfitness of the Confederation to secure our peace, but proceed . . . to examine what order of powers the government of the United States ought to enjoy; how they ought to be defended against encroachments; whether they can be interwoven in the Confederation, without an alteration of its very essence, or must be lodged in new hands;—showing, at the same time, the convulsions which seem to await us, from a dissolution of the Union, or partial confederacies.

To mark the kind and degree of authority which ought to be confided to the government of the United States, is no more than to reverse the description which I have already given of the defects of the Confederation.

. . . Let us . . . substitute the same process by which individuals are compelled to contribute to the government of their own states. Instead of making requisitions to the legislatures, it would appear more proper that taxes should be imposed by the federal head, under due modification and guards; that the collectors should demand from the citizens their respective quotas, and be supported as in the collection of ordinary taxes.

It follows, too, that, as the general government will be responsible to foreign nations, it ought to be able to annul any offensive measure, or enforce any public right. Perhaps, among the topics on which they may be aggrieved or complain, the commercial intercourse, and the manner in which contracts are discharged, may constitute the principal articles of clamor.

It follows, too, that the general government ought to be the supreme arbiter for adjusting every contention among the states. In all their connections, therefore, with each other, and particularly in commerce, which will probably create the greatest discord, it ought to hold the reins.

It follows, too, that the general government ought to protect each state against domestic as well as external violence.

And, lastly, it follows that through the general government alone can we ever assume the rank to which we are entitled by our resources and situation.

Should the people of America surrender these powers, they can be paramount to the constitutions and ordinary acts of legislation only by being delegated by them. . . .

This will be one security against encroachment. But another, not less effectual, is, to exclude the individual states from any agency in the national government, as far as it may be safe, and their interposition may not be absolutely necessary.

. . . [The] powers by which alone the blessings of a general government can be accomplished, cannot be interwoven in the Confederation without a change in its very essence; or, in other words, that the Confederation must be thrown aside. . . .

1. The legislative and executive are concentrated in the same persons. This, where real power exists, must eventuate in tyranny.

2. The representation of the states bears no proportion to their

importance. This is an unreasonable subjection of the will of the majority to that of the minority.

3. The mode of election, and the liability of being recalled, may too often render the delegates rather partisans of their own states than representatives of the Union.

4. Cabal and intrigue must consequently gain an ascendency in a course of years.

5. A single house of legislation will sometimes be precipitate, perhaps passionate.

6. As long as seven states are required for the smallest, and nine for the greatest votes, may not foreign influence, at some future day, insinuate itself, so as to interrupt every active exertion?

7. To crown the whole, it is scarce within the verge of possibility that so numerous an assembly should acquire that secrecy, despatch, and vigor, which are the test of excellence in the executive department.

My inference from these facts and principles is, that the new powers must be deposited in a new body, growing out of a consolidation of the Union, as far as the circumstances of the states will allow. Perhaps, however, some may meditate its dissolution, and others, partial confederacies.

❋   ❋   ❋   ❋

But dreadful as the total dissolution of the Union is to my mind, I entertain no less horror at the thought of partial confederacies. I have not the least ground for supposing that an overture of this kind would be listened to by a single state; and the presumption is, that the politics of the greater part of the states flow from the warmest attachment to a union of the whole. If, however, a lesser confederacy could be obtained by Virginia, let me conjure my countrymen well to weigh the probable consequences, before they attempt to form it.

On such an event, the strength of the Union would be divided in two, or perhaps three parts. Has it so increased, since the war, as to be divisible, and yet remain sufficient for our happiness?

The utmost limit of any partial confederacy, which Virginia could expect to form, would comprehend the three Southern States, and her nearest northern neighbor. But they, like ourselves, are diminished in their real force, by the mixture of an unhappy species of population.

Again may I ask, whether the opulence of the United States has been augmented since the war? This is answered in the negative, by a load of debt, and the declension of trade.

At all times must a southern confederacy support ships of war and soldiery? As soon would a navy move from the forest, and an army spring from the earth, as such a confederacy, indebted, impoverished in its commerce, and destitute of men, could, for some years at least, provide an ample defence for itself.

Let it not be forgotten that nations, which can enforce their rights, have large claims against the United States, and that the creditor may insist upon payment from any of them. Which of them would probably be the victim? The most productive and the most exposed. When vexed by reprisals of war, the Southern States will sue for alliance on this continent or beyond the sea. If for the former, the necessity of a union of the whole is decided; if for the latter, America will, I fear, react the scenes of confusion and bloodshed exhibited among most of those nations, which have, too late, repented the folly of relying on auxiliaries.

Two or more confederacies cannot but be competitors for power. The ancient friendship between the citizens of America being thus cut off, bitterness and hostility will succeed in its place. In order to prepare against surrounding danger, we shall be compelled to vest, somewhere or other, power approaching near to military government.

The annals of the world have abounded so much with instances of a divided people being a prey to foreign influence, that I shall not restrain my apprehensions of it, should our Union be torn asunder. The opportunity of insinuating it will be multiplied in proportion to the parts into which we may be broken.

In short, sir, I am fatigued with summoning up to my imagination the miseries which will harass the United States, if torn from each other, and which will not end until they are superseded by fresh mischiefs under the yoke of a tyrant.

I come, therefore, to the last, and perhaps only refuge in our difficulties,—a consolidation of the Union, as far as circumstances will permit. To fulfil this desirable object, the Constitution was framed by the Federal Convention. A quorum of eleven states, and the only member from the twelfth, have subscribed it; *Mr. Mason, of Virginia, Mr. Gerry, of Massachusetts,* and myself, having refused to subscribe; also *Robert Yates, and John Lansing, of New York.*

Why I refused will, I hope, be solved to the satisfaction of those who know me, by saying that a sense of duty commanded me thus to act. . . . To subscribe seemed to offer no inconsiderable gratification, since it would have presented me to the world as a fellow-laborer with the learned and zealous statesmen of America.

✿   ✿   ✿   ✿

It would have been a peculiar pleasure to me to have ascertained, before I left Virginia, the temper and genius of my fellow-citizens, considered relatively to a government so substantially differing from the Confederation as that which is now submitted. But this was, for many obvious reasons, impossible; and I was thereby deprived of what I thought the necessary guides.

I saw, however, that the Confederation was tottering from its own weakness, and that the sitting of the Convention was a signal of its total insufficiency. I was, therefore, ready to assent to a scheme of government which was proposed, and which went beyond the limits of the Confederation, believing that, without being too extensive, it would have preserved our tranquillity until that temper and that genius should be collected.

But when the plan which is now before the General Assembly was on its passage through the Convention, I moved that the state conventions should be at liberty to amend, and that a second General Convention should be holden, to discuss the amendments which should be suggested by them. . . . But it [the motion] was negatived. I then expressed my unwillingness to sign. My reasons were the following:—

1. It is said, in the resolutions which accompany the Constitution, that it is to be submitted to a convention of delegates chosen in each state by the people thereof, for their assent and ratification. The meaning of these terms is universally allowed to be, that the convention must either adopt the Constitution in the whole, or reject it in the whole, and is positively forbidden to amend. If, therefore, I had signed, I should have felt myself bound to be silent as to amendments, and to endeavor to support the Constitution without the correction of a letter. . . .

2. My opinion always was, and still is, that every citizen of America, let the crisis be what it may, ought to have a full opportunity to propose, through his representatives, any amendment which, in his apprehension, tends to the public welfare. . . .

3. A constitution ought to have the hearts of the people on its side. But if, at a future day, it should become burdensome after having been adopted in the whole, and they should insinuate that it was in some measure forced upon them by being confined to the single alternative of taking or rejecting it altogether, . . . I should not be able to justify myself, had I signed.

4. I was always satisfied, as I have now experienced, that this great subject would be placed in new lights and attitudes by the criticism of the world, and that no man can assure himself how a constitution will work for a course of years, until at least he shall have the observations of the people at large. I also fear more from inaccuracies in a constitution, than from gross errors in any other composition; because our dearest interests are to be regulated by it, and power, if loosely given, especially where it will be interpreted with great latitude, may bring sorrow in its execu-

tion. Had I signed with these ideas, I should have virtually shut my ears against the information which I ardently desired.

5. I was afraid that, if the Constitution was to be submitted to the people, to be wholly adopted or wholly rejected by them, they would not only reject it, but bid a lasting farewell to the Union. This formidable event I wished to avert, by keeping myself free to propose amendments, and thus, if possible, to remove the obstacles to an effectual government. . . .

Again, may I be asked why the mode pointed out in the Constitution, for its amendment, may not be sufficient security against its imperfections, without now arresting its progress? My answers are—1. That it is better to amend, while we have the Constitution in our power, while the passions of designing men are not yet enlisted, and while a bare majority of the states may amend, than to wait for the uncertain assent of three fourths of the states. 2. That a bad feature in government becomes more and more fixed every day. 3. That frequent changes of a constitution, even if practicable, ought not to be wished, but avoided as much as possible. And, 4. That in the present case, it may be questionable whether, after the particular advantages of its operation shall be discerned, three fourths of the states can be induced to amend.

. . . Many expedients have occurred to me, but none of them appear less exceptionable than this; that if our convention should choose to amend, another federal convention be recommended; that, in that federal convention, the amendments proposed by this or any other state be discussed; and if incorporated in the Constitution, or rejected,—or if a proper number of the other states should be unwilling to accede to a second convention,— the Constitution be again laid before the same state conventions, which shall again assemble on the summons of the executives, and it shall be either wholly adopted, or wholly rejected, without a further power of amendment. I count such a delay as nothing, in comparison with so grand an object; especially, too, as the privilege of amending must terminate after the use of it once.

. . . I shall content myself with enumerating certain heads in which the Constitution is most repugnant to my wishes:—

The two first points are the equality of suffrage in the Senate, and the submission of commerce to a mere majority in the legislature, with no other check than the revision of the President. I conjecture that neither of these things can be corrected, and particularly the former, without which we must have risen perhaps in disorder.

But I am sanguine in hoping that, in every other justly obnoxious cause, Virginia will be seconded by a majority of the states. I hope that she will be seconded; 1. In causing all ambiguities of expression to be precisely explained; 2. In rendering the President ineligible after a given number of years; 3. In taking from him the power of nominating to the judiciary offices, or of filling up vacancies which may there happen during the recess of the Senate, by granting commissions which shall expire at the end of their next session; 4. In taking from him the power of pardoning for treason, at least before conviction; 5. In drawing a line between the powers of Congress and individual states; and in defining the former, so as to leave no clashing of jurisdictions nor dangerous deputies; and to prevent the one from being swallowed up by the other, under cover of general words and implication; 6. In abridging the power of the Senate to make treaties supreme laws of the land; 7. In incapacitating the Congress to determine their own salaries; and, 8. In limiting and defining the judicial power.

✿   ✿   ✿   ✿

EDMUND RANDOLPH

ELBRIDGE GERRY

☆☆

Letter to the Legislature of Massachusetts

☆☆

18 OCTOBER 1787

Gentlemen:

❋   ❋   ❋   ❋

My principal objections to the plan are, that there is no adequate provision for a representation of the people; that they have no security for the right of election; that some of the powers of the legislature are ambiguous, and others indefinite and dangerous; that the executive is blended with, and will have an undue influence over, the legislature; that the judicial department will be oppressive; that treaties of the highest importance may be formed by the President, with the advice of two thirds of a quorum of the Senate; and that the system is without the security of a bill of rights. These are objections which are not local, but apply equally to all the states.

As the Convention was called for "the sole and express purpose of revising the Articles of Confederation, and reporting to Congress, and the several legislatures, such alterations and provisions as shall render the Federal Constitution adequate to the exigencies of government, and the preservation of the Union," I did not conceive that these powers extend to the formation of the

From Elliot, I, 492–494.

80

plan proposed; but the Convention being of a different opinion, I acquiesced in it, being fully convinced that, to preserve the Union, an efficient government was indispensably necessary, and that it would be difficult to make proper amendments to the Articles of Confederation.

The Constitution proposed has few, if any, federal features, but is rather a system of national government. Nevertheless, in many respects, I think it has great merit, and, by proper amendments, may be adapted to the "exigencies of government, and preservation of liberty."

The question on this plan involves others of the highest importance: 1. Whether there shall be a dissolution of the federal government; 2. Whether the several state governments shall be so altered as in effect to be dissolved; 3. Whether, in lieu of the federal and state governments, the national Constitution now proposed shall be substituted without amendment. Never, perhaps, were a people called on to decide a question of greater magnitude. Should the citizens of America adopt the plan as it now stands, their liberties may be lost; or should they reject it altogether, anarchy may ensue. It is evident, therefore, that they should not be precipitate in their decisions; that the subject should be well understood;—lest they should refuse to support the government after having hastily accepted it.

If those who are in favor of the Constitution, as well as those who are against it, should preserve moderation, their discussions may afford much information, and finally direct to a happy issue.

It may be urged by some, that an implicit confidence should be placed in the Convention; but, however respectable the members may be who signed the Constitution, it must be admitted that a free people are the proper guardians of their rights and liberties; that the greatest men may err, and that their errors are sometimes of the greatest magnitude.

Others may suppose that the Constitution may be safely adopted, because therein provision is made to amend it. But cannot this object be better attained before a ratification than after it? And should a free people adopt a form of government under conviction that it wants amendment?

And some may conceive that, if the plan is not accepted by the people, they will not unite in another. But surely, while they have the power to amend, they are not under the necessity of rejecting it.

＊　　＊　　＊　　＊

I shall only add that, as the welfare of the Union requires a better Constitution than the Confederation, I shall think it my duty, as a citizen of Massachusetts, to support that which shall be finally adopted, sincerely hoping it will secure the liberty and happiness of America.

＊　　＊　　＊　　＊

E. GERRY

LUTHER MARTIN

****

Genuine Information,
to the Legislature of Maryland

****

DECEMBER 1787–FEBRUARY 1788

❈   ❈   ❈   ❈

The members of the Convention from the states came there under different powers; the greatest number, I believe, under powers nearly the same as those of the delegates of this state. Some came to the Convention under the former appointment, authorizing the meeting of delegates merely to regulate trade. Those of Delaware were expressly instructed to agree to no system which should take away from the states that equality of suffrage secured by the original Articles of Confederation. . . .

You have heard, sir, the resolutions which were brought forward by the honorable member from Virginia. Let me call the attention of this house to the conduct of Virginia when our Confederation was entered into. That state then proposed, and obstinately contended, *contrary to the sense of, and unsupported by, the other states, for an inequality of suffrage,* founded on *numbers, or some such scale,* which should give *her,* and certain other states, *influence in the Union over the rest.* . . .

The object of *Virginia* and *other large states, to increase their*

From Elliot, I, 345–346, 348–353, 356–357.

power and influence over the others, did not escape observation. . . .

* * * *

. . . [Under the Virginia plan, fifteen] senators were to be a quorum to proceed to business; those *three states* [Virginia, Pennsylvania, and Massachusetts] would, therefore, have *thirteen* out of that quorum. Having this inequality *in each branch* of the legislature, it must be evident, sir, that *they would make what laws they pleased, however injurious or disagreeable to the other states,* and that *they would always prevent the other states from making any laws, however necessary and proper, if not agreeable to the views of those three states.* They were not only, sir, by this system, to have such an undue superiority in making laws and regulations for the Union, but to have the same superiority in the *appointment* of the *President,* the *judges,* and all *other officers* of government.

* * * *

. . . [On] our meeting in Convention, it was soon found there were among us three parties of very different sentiments and views:—

One party, whose object and wish it was to abolish and annihilate all state governments, and to bring forward one general government over this extensive continent, of a monarchical nature, under certain restrictions and limitations. Those who openly avowed this sentiment were . . . but few; . . . there was a considerable number who did not openly avow it, who were . . . considered as being in reality favorers of that sentiment, and, acting upon those principles, covertly endeavoring to carry into effect what they well knew openly and avowedly could not be accomplished. The second party was not for the abolition of the state governments, nor for the introduction of a monarchical government under any form; but they wished to establish such a system as could give their own states undue power and influence, in the government, over the other states.

A third party was what I considered truly federal and republican. This party was nearly equal in number with the other two, and was composed of the delegations from Connecticut, New York, New Jersey, Delaware, and in part from Maryland; also of some individuals from other representations. . . .

＊ ＊ ＊ ＊

But, sir, the favorers of monarchy, and those who wished the total abolition of state governments,—well knowing that a government founded on *truly federal principles,* the bases of which were the *thirteen state governments preserved in full force and energy,* would be destructive of their views; and knowing they were too weak in numbers openly to bring forward their system; conscious, also, that the people of America would reject it if proposed to them,—joined their interest with that party who wished a system giving *particular states* the *power* and *influence over the others,* procuring, in return, mutual sacrifices from them, in giving the government *great* and *undefined powers* as to its *legislative* and *executive;* well knowing that, by *departing from a federal system,* they paved the way for their favorite object—the *destruction of the state governments,* and the introduction of *monarchy.* . . .

. . . They said no state ought to wish to have influence in government, except in proportion to what it contributes to it; . . . that, if one state had *sixteen times as many inhabitants* as another, or was *sixteen times as wealthy,* it ought to have *sixteen times as many votes* . . . .

. . . Those who advocated the *equality of suffrage* . . . urged that all men, considered in a state of nature, before any government is formed, are equally free and independent, no one having any right or authority to exercise power over another, and this *without any regard to difference in personal strength,*

understanding, or wealth—that, when such individuals enter
into government, they have *each* a *right* to an *equal voice* in its
first formation, and afterwards have *each* a right to an *equal vote*
in every matter which relates to their government . . . .

❖   ❖   ❖   ❖

Having thus established these principles with respect to the
rights of *individuals* in a *state of nature,* and what is due to
each on entering into government,—principles established by
every writer on liberty,—they proceeded to show that *states,*
when *once formed,* are considered, *with respect* to *each other,*
as *individuals* in a state of nature; that, like individuals, each
state is considered *equally free* and *equally independent,* the
one having no right to exercise authority over the *other,* though
more strong, more wealthy, or *abounding with more inhabitants*
—that, when a number of *states* unite themselves under a *federal
government,* the *same principles apply* to *them* as when a *number of individual men* unite themselves under a *state government*—that every argument which shows *one man* ought not to
have *more votes* than *another,* because he is *wiser, stronger,* or
wealthier, proves that *one state* ought not to have *more votes*
than *another,* because it is *stronger, richer,* or *more populous;*
and that, by *giving one state,* or *one or two states, more votes*
than the *others,* the *others* thereby are *enslaved to such state or
states,* having the *greater number of votes,* in the *same manner*
as in the case before put of *individuals,* when *one* has *more
votes than the others* . . . .

❖   ❖   ❖   ❖

. . . The *one side* insisted on the *inequality* of suffrage in both
branches; the *other side, equality* in both. . . . When it was
found that nothing could induce us to yield the inequality in
both branches, they at length proposed, by way of compromise,
if *we* would accede to their wishes as to the *first* branch, *they*
would agree to an equal representation in the *second.* To this

it was answered, that . . . it was only consenting, after they had struggled to put both their feet on our necks, to take one of them off, provided we would consent to let them keep the other on . . . .

❀   ❀   ❀   ❀

PART II

General Defenses of the Constitution

JAMES WILSON

✧✧

Defense, in the State House of Pennsylvania

✧✧

9 OCTOBER 1787

Mr. Chairman and Fellow Citizens:
. . . [The] insidious attempts which are clandestinely and in-
dustriously made to pervert and destroy the new plan, induce
me the more readily to engage in its defence; and the impressions of four months' constant attention to the subject, have not
been so easily effaced as to leave me without an answer to the
objections which have been raised.

. . . When the people established the powers of legislation
under their separate governments, they invested their representatives with every right and authority which they did not in
explicit terms reserve; and therefore upon every question respecting the jurisdiction of the House of Assembly, if the frame of
government is silent, the jurisdiction is efficient and complete.
But in delegating federal powers, another criterion was necessarily introduced, and the congressional power is to be
collected, not from tacit implication, but from the positive grant
expressed in the instrument of the union. Hence, it is evident,
that in the former case everything which is not reserved is given;
but in the latter the reverse of the proposition prevails, and
everything which is not given is reserved.

From McMaster and Stone, pp. 143–149.

This distinction being recognized, will furnish an answer to those who think the omission of a bill of rights a defect in the proposed constitution; for it would have been superfluous and absurd to have stipulated with a federal body of our own creation, that we should enjoy those privileges of which we are not divested, either by the intention or the act that has brought the body into existence. For instance, the liberty of the press, which has been a copious source of declamation and opposition—what control can proceed from the Federal government to shackle or destroy that sacred palladium of national freedom? If, indeed, a power similar to that which has been granted for the regulation of commerce had been granted to regulate literary publications, it would have been as necessary to stipulate that the liberty of the press should be preserved inviolate, as that the impost should be general in its operation. . . . In truth, then, the proposed system possesses no influence whatever upon the press, and it would have been merely nugatory to have introduced a formal declaration upon the subject—nay, that very declaration might have been construed to imply that some degree of power was given, since we undertook to define its extent.

Another objection that has been fabricated against the new constitution, is expressed in this disingenuous form—"The trial by jury is abolished in civil cases." . . . Let it be remembered . . . that the business of the Federal Convention was not local, but general—not limited to the views and establishments of a single State, but co-extensive with the continent, and comprehending the views and establishments of thirteen independent sovereignties. When, therefore, this subject was in discussion, we were involved in difficulties which pressed on all sides, and no precedent could be discovered to direct our course. The cases open to a trial by jury differed in the different States. It was therefore impracticable, on that ground, to have made a general rule. The want of uniformity would have rendered any reference to the practice of the States idle and useless; and it could not with any propriety be said that, "The trial by jury shall be as heretofore," since there has never existed any federal system of jurisprudence, to which the declaration could relate. Besides, it is not in all cases that the trial by jury is adopted in civil questions . . . . How, then was the line of discrimination to be drawn? The Convention found the task too difficult for them, and they left the business as it stands, in the fullest confidence that no danger could possibly ensue, since the proceedings of the Supreme Court are to be regulated by the Congress, which is a faithful representation of the people; and the oppression of government is effectually barred, by declaring that in all criminal cases the trial by jury shall be perserved.

This constitution, it has been further urged, is of a pernicious tendency, because it tolerates a standing army in the time of peace. This has always been a topic of popular declamation; and yet I do not know a nation in the world which has not found it necessary and useful to maintain the appearance of strength in a season of the most profound tranquility. Nor is it a novelty with us; for under the present articles of confederation, Congress certainly possesses this reprobated power, and the exercise of that power is proved at this moment by her cantonments along the banks of the Ohio. But what would be our national situation were it otherwise? Every principle of policy must be subverted, and the government must declare war, before they are prepared to carry it on. Whatever may be the provocation, however important the object in view, and however necessary dispatch and secrecy may be, still the declaration must precede the preparation, and the enemy will be informed of your intention, not only before you are equipped for an attack, but even before you are fortified for a defence. . . . [No] man who regards the dignity and safety of his country can deny the necessity of a military force, under the control and with the restrictions which the new constitution provides.

Perhaps there never was a charge made with less reasons than that which predicts the institution of a baneful aristocracy in the federal Senate. This body branches into two characters, the one legislative and the other executive. In its legislative character it can effect no purpose, without the co-operation of the House of Representatives, and in its executive character it can accomplish no object without the concurrence of the President. Thus fettered, I do not know any act which the Senate can of itself perform, and such dependence necessarily precludes every idea of influence and superiority. But I will confess that in the organization of this body a compromise between contending interests is descernible; and when we reflect how various are the laws, commerce, habits, population and extent of the confederated States, this evidence of mutual concession and accommodation ought rather to command a generous applause, than to excite jealousy and reproach. . . .

The next accusation I shall consider is that which represents the federal constitution, as not only calculated, but designedly framed, to reduce the State governments to mere corporations, and eventually to annihilate them. . . . But upon what pretence can it be alleged that it was designed to annihilate the State governments? For I will undertake to prove that upon their existence depends the existence of the Federal plan. For this purpose, permit me to call your attention to the manner in which the President, Senate and House of Representatives are proposed to be appointed. The President is to be chosen by electors, nominated in such manner as the legislature of each State may direct; so that if there is no legislature there can be no electors, and consequently the office of President cannot be supplied.

The Senate is to be composed of two Senators from each State, chosen by the Legislature; and, therefore, if there is no Legislature, there can be no Senate. The House of Representatives is to be composed of members chosen every second year by the people of the several States, and the electors in each State shall have the qualifications requisite for electors of the most numerous branch of the State Legislature; unless, therefore, there is a State Legislature, that qualification cannot be ascertained, and the popular branch of the federal constitution must be extinct.

From this view, then, it is evidently absurd to suppose that the annihilation of the separate governments will result from their union; or, that having that intention, the authors of the new system would have bound their connection with such indissoluble ties. . . .

The power of direct taxation has likewise been treated as an improper delegation to the federal government; but when we consider it as the duty of that body to provide for the national safety, to support the dignity of the union, and to discharge the debts contracted upon the collected faith of the States for their common benefit, it must be acknowledged that those upon whom such important obligations are imposed, ought in justice and in policy to possess every means requisite for a faithful performance of their trust. But why should we be alarmed with visionary evils? I will venture to predict that the great revenue of the United States must, and always will, be raised by impost, for, being at once less obnoxious and more productive, the interest of the government will be best promoted by the accommodation of the people. Still, however, the objects of direct taxation should be within reach in all cases of emergency; and there is no more reason to apprehend oppression in the mode of collecting a revenue from this resource, than in the form of an impost, which, by universal assent, is left to the authority of the federal government. In either case, the force of civil institutions will be adequate to the purpose; and the dread of military violence, which has been assiduously disseminated, must eventually prove the mere effusion of a wild imagination or a factious spirit. But the salutary consequences that must flow from thus enabling the government to receive and support the credit of the union, will afford another answer to the objections upon this ground. The State of Pennsylvania particularly, which has encumbered itself with the assumption of a great proportion of the public debt, will derive considerable relief and advantage . . . .

After all, my fellow-citizens, it is neither extraordinary or unexpected that the constitution offered to your consideration should meet with opposition. It is the nature of man to pursue his own interest in preference to the public good, and I do not mean to make any personal reflection when I add that it is the interest of a very numerous, powerful and respectable body to counteract and destroy the excellent work produced by the late convention. All the officers of government and all the appointments for the administration of justice and the collection of the public revenue, which are transferred from the individual to the aggregate sovereignty of the States, will necessarily turn the stream of influence and emolument into a new channel. Every person, therefore, who enjoys or expects to enjoy a place of profit under the present establishment, will object to the proposed innovation; not, in truth, because it is injurious to the liberties of his country, but because it affects his schemes of wealth and consequence. I will confess, indeed, that I am not a blind admirer of this plan of government, and that there are some parts of it which, if my wish had prevailed, would certainly have been altered. But, when I reflect how widely men differ in their opinions, and that every man (and the observation applies likewise to every State) has an equal pretension to assert his own, I am satisfied that anything nearer to perfection could not have been accomplished. If there are errors, it should be remembered that the seeds of reformation are sown in the work itself, and the concurrence of two-thirds of the Congress may at any time introduce alterations and amendments. Regarding it, then, in every point of view, with a candid and disinterested mind, I am bold to assert that it is the best form of government which has ever been offered to the world.

JAMES WILSON

✩✩

In the Ratifying Convention of Pennsylvania

✩✩

24 NOVEMBER 1787

. . . To frame a government for a single city or State, is a business both in its importance and facility, widely different from the task entrusted to the Federal Convention . . . .

. . . But the magnitude of the object was equalled by the difficulty of accomplishing it, when we considered the uncommon dexterity and address that were necessary to combat and reconcile the jarring interests that seemed naturally to prevail, in a country which, presenting a coast of 1500 miles to the Atlantic, is composed of 13 distinct and independent States, varying essentially in their situation and dimensions, and in the number and habits of their citizens—their interests too, in some respects really different, and in many apparently so . . . . Can it then be a subject for surprise that with the sensations indispensably excited by so comprehensive and so arduous an undertaking, we should . . . resort to mutual concession, as the only means to obtain the great end for which we were convened? . . .

❖   ❖   ❖   ❖

In this dilemma, a Federal Republic naturally presented itself to our observation, as a species of government which secured all

From McMaster and Stone: remarks of 24 November 1787, pp. 218–223, 226, 230–231; remarks of 4 December 1787, pp. 316–317.

the internal advantages of a republic, at the same time that it maintained the external dignity and force of a monarchy. The definition of this form of government may be found in Montesquieu, who says, I believe, that it consists in assembling distinct societies which are consolidated into a new body, capable of being increased by the addition of other members—an expanding quality peculiarly fitted to the circumstances of America.

But while a federal republic removed one difficulty, it introduced another, since there existed not any precedent to assist our deliberations; for, though there are many single governments, both ancient and modern, the history and principles of which are faithfully preserved and well understood, a perfect confederation of independent states is a system hitherto unknown. . . .

Government, indeed, taken as a science, may yet be considered in its infancy; and with all its various modifications, it has hitherto been the result of force, fraud, or accident. For, after the lapse of six thousand years since the creation of the world, America now presents the first instance of a people assembled to weigh deliberately and calmly, and to decide leisurely and peaceably, upon the form of government by which they will bind themselves and their posterity. Among the ancients, three forms of government seem to have been correctly known—the monarchical, aristocratical, and democratical; but their knowledge did not extend beyond those simple kinds . . . . It is surprising, indeed, how very imperfectly, at this day, the doctrine of representation is understood in Europe. Even Great Britain, which boasts a superior knowledge of the subject, and is generally supposed to have carried it into practice, falls far short of its true and genuine principles. . . . [The] vital principle of the British constitution is confined to a narrow corner, and the world has left to America the glory and happiness of forming a government where representation shall at once supply the basis and the cement of the superstructure. For representation, Sir, is the true chain between the people and those to whom they entrust the administration of the government . . . .

❖   ❖   ❖   ❖

. . . [The] Convention did right in proposing a single confederated Republic. But in proposing it they were necessarily led, not only to consider the situation, circumstances, and interests of one, two, or three States, but of the collective body; and as it is essential to society, that the welfare of the whole should be preferred to the accommodation of a part, they followed the same rule in promoting the national advantages of the Union, in preference to the separate advantages of the States. . . .

❄   ❄   ❄   ❄

. . . The advantages of a monarchy are strength, dispatch, and unity; its disadvantages are expense, tyranny, and war. The advantages of an aristocracy are experience, and the wisdom resulting from education; its disadvantages are the dissension of the governors, and the oppression of the people. The advantages of a democracy are liberty, caution, industry, fidelity, and an opportunity of bringing forward the talents and abilities of the citizens, without regard to birth or fortune; its disadvantages are dissension and imbecility, for the assent of many being required, their exertions will be feeble, and their counsels too soon discovered.

To obtain all the advantages, and to avoid all the inconveniences of these governments, was the leading object of the late convention. . . . In its principles, Sir, it is purely democratical; varying indeed, in its form, in order to admit all the advantages, and to exclude all the disadvantages which are incidental to the known and established constitutions of government. But when we take an extensive and accurate view of the streams of power that appear through this great and comprehensive plan, . . . however numerous and wide their courses, however diversified and remote the blessings they diffuse, we shall be able to trace them all to one great and noble source, THE PEOPLE.

4 DECEMBER 1787

. . . [The] truth is, that the supreme, absolute and uncontrollable authority, *remains* with the people. . . .

. . . [Mr. Findley's] position is, that the supreme power resides in the States, as governments; and mine is, that it *resides* in the PEOPLE, as the fountain of government; that the people have not —that the people mean not—and that the people ought not, to part with it to any government whatsoever. . . . They can delegate it in such proportions, to such bodies, on such terms, and under such limitations, as they think proper. I agree with the members in opposition, that there cannot be two sovereign powers on the same subject.

I consider the people of the United States as forming one great community, and I consider the people of the different States as forming communities again on a lesser scale. . . .

. . . I view the States as made *for* the people as well as *by* them, and not the people as made for the States. The people, therefore, have a right, whilst enjoying the undeniable powers of society, to form either a general government, or state governments, in what manner they please; or to accommodate them to one another, and by this means preserve them all. . . .

JOHN JAY

☆☆☆

Address to the People of New York

☆☆☆

17 SEPTEMBER 1787

Friends and Fellow Citizens:

❉   ❉   ❉   ❉

. . . It is unquestionably true, that the great body of the people love their country, and wish it prosperity; and this observation is particularly applicable to the people of a *free* country, for they have more and stronger reasons for loving it than others. It is not therefore to vicious motives that the unhappy divisions which sometimes prevail among them are to be imputed; the people at large always mean well, and although they may on certain occasions be misled by the counsels, or injured by the efforts of the few who expect more advantage from the wreck, than from the preservation of national prosperity, yet the motives of these few, are by no means to be confounded with those of the community in general.

❉   ❉   ❉   ❉

That glorious war [the Revolution] was succeeded by an advantageous peace. When danger disappeared, ease, tranquility,

---

From Ford, Pamphlets, *pp. 69–86. Ford's indication of the pagination in the original pamphlet has been omitted.*

101

and a sense of security loosened the bands of union; and Congress and soldiers and good faith depreciated with their apparent importance. . . . The spirit of private gain expelled the spirit of public good, and men became more intent on the means of enriching and aggrandizing themselves, than of enriching and aggrandizing their country. Hence the war-worn veteran, whose reward for toils and wounds existed in written promises, found Congress without the means, and too many of the States without the disposition, to do him justice. Hard necessity compelled him, and others under similar circumstances, to sell their honest claims on the public for a little bread; and thus unmerited misfortunes and patriotic distresses became articles of speculation and commerce.

These and many other evils, too well known to require enumeration, imperceptibly stole in upon us, and acquired an unhappy influence on our public affairs. . . .

It is a pity that the expectations which actuated the authors of the existing confederation, neither have nor can be realized: —accustomed to see and admire the glorious spirit which moved all ranks of people in the most gloomy moments of the war, observing their steadfast attachment to Union, and the wisdom they so often manifested both in choosing and confiding in their rulers, those gentlemen were led to flatter themselves that the people of America only required to know what ought to be done, to do it. This amiable mistake induced them to institute a national government in such a manner, as though very fit to give advice, was yet destitute of power, and so constructed as to be very unfit to be trusted with it. They seem not to have been sensible that mere advice is a sad substitute for laws; nor to have recollected that the advice even of the allwise and best of Beings, has been always disregarded by a great majority of all the men that ever lived.

✻   ✻   ✻   ✻

By the Confederation as it now stands, the direction of general and national affairs is committed to a single body of men, viz.

the Congress. They may make war, but are not empowered to raise men or money to carry it on. They may make peace, but without power to see the terms of it observed—They may form alliances, but without ability to comply with the stipulations on their part—They may enter into treaties of commerce, but without power to enforce them at home or abroad—They may borrow money, but without having the means of repayment—They may partly regulate commerce, but without authority to execute their ordinances—They may appoint ministers and other officers of trust, but without power to try or punish them for misdemeanors —They may resolve, but cannot execute either with dispatch or with secrecy—In short, they may consult, and deliberate, and recommend, and make requisitions, and they who please, may regard them.

From this new and wonderful system of Government, it has come to pass, that almost every national object of every kind, is at this day unprovided for; and other nations taking the advantage of its imbecility, are daily multiplying commercial restraints upon us. Our fur trade is gone to Canada, and British garrisons keep the keys of it. Our shipyards have almost ceased to disturb the repose of the neighborhood by the noise of the axe and hammer; and . . . the American Stars seldom do more than shed a few feeble rays about the humble masts of river sloops and coasting schooners. The greater part of our hardy seaman, are plowing the ocean in foreign pay; and not a few of our ingenious shipwrights are now building vessels on alien shores. Although our increasing agriculture and industry extend and multiply our productions, yet they constantly diminish in value; and although we permit all nations to fill our country with their merchandises, yet their best markets are shut against us. Is there an English, or a French, or a Spanish island or port in the West-Indies, to which an American vessel can carry a cargo of flour for sale? Not one. The Algerines exclude us from the Mediterranean, and adjacent countries; and we are neither able to purchase, nor to command the free use of those seas. Can our little towns or larger cities consume the immense productions of our fertile country? or will they without trade be able to pay a good price for the proportion which they do consume? . . . To how much below the former price, is our corn, and wheat and flour and lumber rapidly falling? Our debts remain undiminished, and the interest on them accumulating—our credit abroad is nearly extinguished, and at home unrestored—they who had money have sent it beyond the reach of our laws, and scarcely any man can borrow of his neighbor. Nay, does not experience also tell us, that it is as difficult to pay as to borrow? That even our houses and lands cannot command money—that law suits and usurious contracts abound—that our farms sell on executions for less than half their value, and that distress in various forms, and in various ways, is approaching fast to the doors of our best citizens.

These things have been gradually coming upon us ever since the peace—they have been perceived and proclaimed, but the universal rage and pursuit of private gain conspired with other causes, to prevent any proper efforts being made to meliorate our condition by due attention to our national affairs, until the late Convention was convened for that purpose. . . .

The Convention concurred in opinion with the people, that a national government, *competent to every national object,* was indispensably necessary; and it was as plain to them, as it now is to all America, that the present confederation does not provide for such a government. These points being agreed, they proceeded to consider how and in what manner such a government could be formed, as on the one hand, should be sufficiently energetic to raise us from our prostrate and distressed situation, and on the other be perfectly consistent with the liberties of the people of every State. Like men to whom the experience of other ages and countries had taught wisdom, they not only determined that it should be erected by, and depend on the people; but remembering the many instances in which governments vested solely in one man, or one body of men, had degenerated into tyrannies, they judged it most prudent that the three great branches of power should be committed to different hands, and therefore that the executive should be separated from the legislative, and the judicial from both. . . .

The next question was, what particular powers should be given to these three branches? Here the different views and interests of the different states, as well as the different abstract opinions of their members on such points, interposed many difficulties. Here the business became complicated, and presented a wide field for investigation; too wide for every eye to take a quick and comprehensive view of it.

* * * *

The difficulties before mentioned occupied the Convention a long time and it was not without mutual concessions that they were at last surmounted. These concessions serve to explain to us the reason why some parts of the system please in some states, which displease in others; and why many of the objections which have been made to it, are so contradictory and inconsistent with one another. It does great credit to the temper and talents of the Convention, that they were able so to reconcile the different views and interests of the different States, and the clashing opinions of their members as to unite with such singular and almost perfect unanimity in any plan whatever, on a subject so intricate and perplexed. . . .

. . . The objections made to it are almost without number, and many of them without reason—some of them are real and honest, and others merely ostensible. . . .

We are told, among other strange things, that the liberty of the press is left insecure by the proposed Constitution, and yet that Constitution says neither more nor less about it, than the Constitution of the State of New York does. We are told that it deprives us of trial by jury, whereas the fact is, that it expressly secures it in certain cases, and takes it away in none—it is absurd to construe the silence of this, or of our own constitution, relative to a great number of our rights, into a total extinction of them— silence and blank paper neither grant nor take away anything. Complaints are also made that the proposed constitution is not accompanied by a bill of rights; and yet they who would make these complaints, know and are content that no bill of rights accompanied the Constitution of this State. In days and countries, where Monarchs and their subjects were frequently disputing about prerogative and privileges, the latter often found it necessary, as it were to run out the line between them, and oblige the former to admit by solemn acts, called bills of rights, that certain enumerated rights belonged to the people, and were not comprehended in the royal prerogative. But thank God we have no such disputes—we have no Monarchs to contend with, or demand admission from—the proposed Government is to be the government of the people—all its officers are to be their officers, and to exercise no rights but such as the people commit to them. The Constitution only serves to point out that part of the people's business, which they think proper by it to refer to the management of the persons therein designated—those persons are to receive that business to manage, not for themselves and as their own, but as agents and overseers for the people to whom they are constantly responsible, and by whom only they are to be appointed.

. . . Let it be admitted that this plan, like everything else devised by man, has its imperfections: That it does not please every body is certain and there is little reason to expect one that will. It is a question of great moment to you, whether the probability of your being able seasonably to obtain a better, is such as to render it prudent and advisable to reject this, and run the risque. . . .

*   *   *   *

The question now before us . . . naturally leads to *three* enquiries:

1. Whether it is probable that a better plan can be obtained?

2. Whether, if attainable, it is likely to be in season?

3. What would be our situation, if after rejecting this, all our efforts to obtain a better should prove fruitless?

The men, who formed this plan are Americans, who had long deserved and enjoyed our confidence, and who are as much interested in having a good government as any of us are, or can be. . . . Although well persuaded that nothing but a good national government could oppose and divert the tide of evils that was flowing in upon us, yet those gentlemen met in Convention with minds perfectly unprejudiced in favour of any particular plan. The minds of their Constituents were at that time equally unbiased, cool and dispassionate. All agreed in the necessity of doing something, but no one ventured to say decidedly what precisely ought to be done . . . .

The impossibility of agreeing upon any plan that would exactly quadrate with the local policy and objects of every State, soon became evident; and they wisely thought it better mutually to concede, and accommodate, and in that way to fashion their system as much as possible by the circumstances and wishes of different States, than by pertinaciously adhering, each to his own ideas, oblige the Convention to rise without doing anything. They were sensible that obstacles arising from local circumstances, would not cease while those circumstances continued to exist; and so far as those circumstances depended on differences of climate, productions, and commerce, that no change was to be expected. They were likewise sensible that on a subject so comprehensive, and involving such a variety of points and questions, the most able, the most candid, and the most honest men will differ in opinion. . . . Although many weeks were passed in these discussions, some points remained, on which a unison of opinions could not be effected. Here again that same happy disposition to unite and conciliate, induced them to meet each other; and enabled them, by mutual concessions, finally to complete and agree to the plan they have recommended, and that too with a degree of unanimity which, considering the variety of discordant views and ideas, they had to reconcile, is really astonishing.

They tell us very honestly that this plan is the result of accommodation—they do not hold it up as the best of all possible ones, but only as the best which they could unite in, and agree to. If such men, appointed and meeting under such auspicious circumstances, and so sincerely disposed to conciliation, could go no further in their endeavors to please every State, and every body, what reason have we at present to expect any system that would give more general satisfaction?

Suppose this plan to be rejected, what measures would you propose for obtaining a better? Some will answer, let us appoint another Convention, and as everything has been said and written that can well be said and written on the subject, they will be better informed than the former one was, and consequently be better able to make and agree upon a more eligible one.

This reasoning is fair, and as far as it goes has weight; but it nevertheless takes one thing for granted, which appears very doubtful; for although the new Convention might have more information, and perhaps equal abilities, yet it does not from thence follow that they would be equally *disposed to agree.* The contrary of this position is the most probable. . . . We have unhappily become divided into parties; and this important subject has been handled with such indiscreet and offensive acrimony, and with so many little unhandsome artifices and misrepresentations, that pernicious heats and animosities have been kindled, and spread their flames far and wide among us. When therefore it becomes a question who shall be deputed to the new Convention; we cannot flatter ourselves that the talents and integrity of the candidates will determine who shall be elected. Federal electors will vote for Fœderal deputies, and anti-Fœderal electors for anti-Fœderal ones. Nor will either party prefer the most moderate of their adherents, for as the most staunch and active partizans will be the most popular, so the men most willing and able to carry points, to oppose, and divide, and embarrass their opponents, will be chosen. A Convention formed at such a season, and of such men, would be but too exact an epitome of the great body that named them. . . . Each deputy would recollect *who* sent him, and *why* he was sent; and be too apt to consider himself bound in honor, to contend and act vigorously under the standard of his party, and not hazard their displeasure by prefering compromise to victory. . . . The utmost efforts of that excellent disposition were necessary to enable the late Convention to perform their task; . . . to expect that discord and animosity should produce the fruits of confidence and agreement, is to expect "grapes from thorns, and figs from thistles."

The States of Georgia, Delaware, Jersey, and Connecticut, have adopted the present plan with unexampled unanimity; they are content with it as it is, and consequently their deputies, being apprized of the sentiments of their Constituents, will be little inclined to make alterations, and cannot be otherwise than averse to changes which they have no reason to think would be agreeable to their people—some other States, tho' less unanimous, have nevertheless adopted it by very respectable majorities; and for reasons so evidently cogent, that even the minority in one of them, have nobly pledged themselves for its promotion and support. From these circumstances, the new Convention would derive and experience difficulties unknown to the former. Nor are these the only additional difficulties they would have to encounter. Few are ignorant that there has lately sprung up a sect of politicians who teach and profess to believe that the extent of our nation is too great for the superintendance of one national Government, and on that principle argue that it ought to be divided into two or three. This doctrine, however mischievous in its tendency and consequences, has its advocates; and, should any of them be sent to the Convention, it will naturally be their policy rather to cherish than to prevent divisions; for well knowing that the institution of any national Government, would blast their favourite system, no measures that lead to it can meet with their aid or approbation.

Nor can we be certain whether or not any and what foreign

influence would, on such an occasion, be indirectly exerted, nor for what purposes—delicacy forbids an ample discussion of this question. . . .

These considerations merit much attention, and candid men will judge how far they render it probable that a new Convention would be able either to agree in a better plan, or with tolerable unanimity, in any plan at all. Any plan forcibly carried by a slender majority, must expect numerous opponents among the people, who, especially in their present temper, would be more inclined to reject than adopt any system so made and carried. We should in such case again see the press teeming with publications for and against it; for as the minority would take pains to justify their dissent, so would the majority be industrious to display the wisdom of their proceedings. Hence new divisions, new parties, and new distractions would ensue, and no one can foresee or conjecture when or how they would terminate.

Let those who are sanguine in their expectations of a better plan from a new Convention, also reflect on the delays and risque to which it would expose us. Let them consider whether we ought, by continuing much longer in our present humiliated condition, to give other nations further time to perfect their restrictive systems of commerce, to reconcile their own people to them, and to fence and guard and strengthen them by all those regulations and contrivances in which a jealous policy is ever fruitful. Let them consider whether we ought to give further opportunities to discord to alienate the hearts of our citizens from one another, and thereby encourage new Cromwells to bold exploits. Are we certain that our foreign creditors will continue patient, and ready to proportion their forbearance to our delays? Are we sure that our distresses, dissentions and weakness will neither invite hostility nor insult? If they should, how ill prepared shall we be for defence! without Union, without Government, without money, and without credit!

❀   ❀   ❀   ❀

But if for the reasons already mentioned, and others that we cannot now perceive, the new Convention, instead of producing a better plan, should give us only a history of their disputes, or should offer us one still less pleasing than the present, where should we be then? The old Confederation has done its best, and cannot help us; and is now so relaxed and feeble, that in all probability it would not survive so violent a shock. Then "to your tents Oh Israel!" would be the word. Then every band of union would be severed. Then every State would be a little nation, jealous of its neighbors, and anxious to strengthen itself by foreign alliances, against its former friends. . . .

❃   ❃   ❃   ❃

. . . Reflect that the present plan comes recommended to you by men and fellow citizens who have given you the highest proofs that men can give, of their justice, their love for liberty and their country, of their prudence, of their application, and of their talents. They tell you it is the best that they could form; and that in their opinion, it is necessary to redeem you from those calamities which already begin to be heavy upon us all. . . . You find that whole States concur in the sentiment, and among them are your next neighbors; both whom have shed much blood in the cause of liberty, and have manifested as strong and constant a predilection for a free Republican Government as any State in the Union, and perhaps in the world. They perceive not those latent mischiefs in it, with which some double-sighted politicians endeavor to alarm you. You cannot but be sensible that this plan or constitution will always be in the hands and power of the people, and that if on experiment, it should be found defective or incompetent, they may either remedy its defects, or substitute another in its room. The objectionable parts of it are certainly very questionable, for otherwise there would not be such a contrariety of opinions about them. Experience will better determine such questions than theoretical arguments, and so far as the danger of abuses is urged against the institution of a Government, remember that a power to do good, always involves a power to do harm. We must in the business of Government as well as in all other business, have some degree of confidence, as well as a great degree of caution. . . .

*   *   *   *

A CITIZEN OF NEW YORK

TENCH COXE

★★★

An Examination of the Constitution, IV

★★★

SEPTEMBER–OCTOBER 1787

✿   ✿   ✿   ✿

The United States guarantee to every state in the union a separate republican form of government. From thence it follows, that any man or body of men . . . who shall make an alteration in the form of government of any state, whereby the powers thereof shall be attempted to be taken out of the hands of the people at large, will stand guilty of high treason . . . .

No religious test is ever to be required of any officer or servant of the United States. The people may employ any wise or good citizen in the execution of the various duties of the government. In Italy, Spain, and Portugal, no protestant can hold a public trust. In England every Presbyterian, and other person not of their established church, is incapable of holding an office. No such impious deprivation of the rights of men can take place under the new fœderal constitution. . . .

No qualification in monied or landed property is required by the proposed plan; nor does it admit any preference from the preposterous distinctions of birth and rank. The office of the President, a Senator, and a Representative, and every other place

---

From Ford, Pamphlets, *pp. 145–150, 152–154. Ford's indication of the pagination in the original pamphlet has been omitted.*

113

of power or profit, are therefore open to the whole body of the people. . . .

The importation of slaves from any foreign country is, by a clear implication, held up to the world as equally inconsistent with the dispositions and the duties of the people of America. A solid foundation is laid for exploding the principles of negro slavery, in which many good men of all parties in Pennsylvania, and throughout the union, have already concurred. . . .

The people will remain, under the proposed constitution, the fountain of power and public honour. The President, the Senate, and the House of Representatives, will be the channels through which the stream will flow—but it will flow from the people, and from them only. Every office, religious, civil and military will be either their immediate gift, or it will come from them through the hands of their servants. . . .

The people of those states which have faithfully discharged their duty to the union will be no longer subjected alone to the weight of the public debts. Proper arrangements will call forth the just proportion of their sister states, and our national character will again be as unstained as it was once exalted. . . .

❊   ❊   ❊   ❊

The destruction of the ancient republics was occasioned in every instance by their being ignorant of a great political position, which was left for America to discover and establish. Self-evident as the truth appears, we find no friend to liberty in ancient Greece or Rome asserting, that taxation and representation were inseparable. . . . When America asserted the novel truth, Great Britain, though boasting herself as alone free among the modern nations, denied it by her legislature, and endeavoured to refute it by her arms—the reasoning of tyrants. But the attempt was vain . . . . Henceforth the people of the earth will consider this position as the only rock on which they can found the temple of liberty, that taxation and representation are inseparable. Our new constitution carries it into execution on the most enlarged and liberal scale . . . .

The old fœderal constitution contained many of the same things, which from error or disingenousness are urged against the new ones. Neither of them have a bill of rights, nor does either notice the liberty of the press, because they are already provided for by the state constitutions . . . .

Both the old and new fœderal constitutions, and indeed the constitution of Pennsylvania, admit of courts in which no use is made of a jury. . . . Trial by jury will therefore be in the express words of the Pennsylvania constitution, "as heretofore,"— almost always used, though sometimes omitted. . . . But when a dispute arises between the citizens of any state about lands lying out of the bounds thereof, or when a trial is to be had between the citizens of any state and those of another, or the government of another, the private citizen will not be obliged to go into a court constituted by the state, with which, or with the citizens of which, his dispute is. He can appeal to a disinterested fœderal court. This is surely a great advantage, and promises a fair trial, and an impartial judgment. The trial by jury is not excluded in these fœderal courts. In all criminal cases, where the property, liberty or life of the citizen is at stake, he has the benefit of a jury. . . . [The] sphere of jurisdiction for the fœderal courts is limited, and that sphere only is subject to the regulations of our fœderal government. The known principles of justice, the attachment to trial by jury whenever it can be used, the instructions of the state legislatures, the instructions of the people at large, the operation of the fœderal regulations on the property of a president, a senator, a representative, a judge, as well as on that of a private citizen, will certainly render those regulations as favorable as possible to property; for life and liberty are put more than ever into the hands of the juries. . . .

❋   ❋   ❋   ❋

Besides the securities for the liberties of the people arising out of the fœderal government, they are guarded by their state constitutions, and by the nature of things in the separate states. The Governor or President in each commonwealth, the Councils,

Senates, Assemblies, Judges, Sheriffs, Grand and Pettit Juries, Officers of Militia, . . . Burgesses of towns, Commissioners of counties, County Lieutenants, and many other officers of power and influence, will still be chosen within each state, without any possible interference of the fœderal Government. The separate states will also choose all the members of the legislative and executive branches of the United States. The people at large in each state will choose their fœderal representative, and, unless ordered otherwise by state legislatures, may choose the electors of the President and Vice-President of the Union. And lastly, the legislature of the state will have the election of the senate, as they have heretofore had of the Members of Congress. Let us then, with a candor worthy of the subject, ask ourselves, whether it can be feared, that a majority of the Representatives . . . can betray their country?—Whether a majority of the Senate, each of whom will be chosen by the legislature of a free, sovereign and independent state, . . . can destroy our liberties, controuled as they are too by the house of representatives? or whether a temporary, limited, executive officer, watched by the fœderal Representatives, by the Senate, by the state legislatures, by his personal enemies among the people of his own state, by the jealousy of the people of rival states, and by the whole of the people of the Union, can ever endanger our Freedom.[1]

*   *   *   *

AN AMERICAN CITIZEN

---

[1] There is one grand operation of the new fœderal constitution, favorable to general liberty, which I do not remember to have heard from any of its friends. It is well known, that in most of the states the members of their Houses of Representatives are chosen in equal numbers from each county, and in the eastern states, in equal numbers from each town, without any regard to the number of taxable inhabitants, or the number of souls. Hence it is very frequent for a county, with ten thousand souls, to send only the same number of members to the state house of representatives, as a county

with two thousand souls, by which each person in the least populous county has five times as great a voice in electing representatives, as his fellow citizen of the most populous county. This is clearly a departure from the principles of equal liberty, and ought to be altered in the several states. . . . Now the new constitution expressly declares, that the fœderal Representatives shall be in the proportion of one to every thirty thousand, which accords with reason and the true principles of liberty. This house, therefore, so far as national matters go, will remedy the evil spoken of in the several states, and is one more great step towards the perfection of equal liberty and genuine republicanism in America. . . .

THOMAS JEFFERSON

✮✮✮

Letters on the Constitution

✮✮✮

TO JAMES MADISON

20 DECEMBER 1787

Dear Sir,

❖　　❖　　❖　　❖

. . . I like much the general idea of framing a government
which should go on of itself peaceably, without needing continual recurrence to the state legislatures. I like the organization
of the government into Legislative, Judiciary & Executive. I like
the power given the Legislature to levy taxes, and for that
reason solely approve of the greater house being chosen by
the people directly. For tho' I think a house chosen by them will
be very illy qualified to legislate for the Union, for foreign
nations &c. yet this evil does not weigh against the good of
preserving inviolate the fundamental principle that the people

---

From Ford, The Writings of Thomas Jefferson: *To James Madison, from IV,
473, 475–479; To George Washington, from V, 7–8; To Francis Hopkinson,
from V, 75–78; To David Humphreys, from V, 86, 89–90.*

*Jefferson was in Paris at the time and was not directly a participant in
the public debate. His opinions, expressed in private letters, indicate clearly
that, in spite of his original reservations and his wish for amendments,
he supported the Constitution, which he described in March 1789 as "unquestionably the wisest ever yet presented to men."—J.D.L.*

are not to be taxed but by representatives chosen immediately by themselves. I am captivated by the compromise of the opposite claims of the great & little states, of the latter to equal, and the former to proportional influence. I am much pleased too with the substitution of the method of voting by persons, instead of that of voting by states: and I like the negative given to the Executive with a third of either house, though I should have liked it better had the Judiciary been associated for that purpose, or invested with a similar and separate power. There are other good things of less moment. I will now add what I do not like. First the omission of a bill of rights providing clearly & without the aid of sophisms for freedom of religion, freedom of the press, protection against standing armies, restriction against monopolies, the eternal & unremitting force of the habeas corpus laws, and trials by jury in all matters of fact triable by the laws of the land & not by the law of nations. To say, as Mr. Wilson does that a bill of rights was not necessary because all is reserved in the case of the general government which is not given, while in the particular ones all is given which is not reserved, might do for the audience to whom it was addressed, but is surely a gratis dictum, opposed by strong inferences from the body of the instrument, as well as from the omission of the clause of our present confederation which had declared that in express terms. It was a hard conclusion to say because there has been no uniformity among the states as to the cases triable by jury, because some have been so incautious as to abandon this mode of trial, therefore the more prudent states shall be reduced to the same level of calamity. It would have been much more just & wise to have concluded the other way that as most of the states had judiciously preserved this palladium, those who had wandered should be brought back to it, and to have established general right instead of general wrong. Let me add that a bill of rights is what the people are entitled to against every government on earth, general or particular, & what no just government should refuse, or rest on inferences. The second feature I dislike, and greatly dislike, is the abandonment in every instance of the necessity of rotation in office, and most particularly in the case of the President. Experience concurs with reason in concluding that the first magistrate will always be re-elected if the Constitution permits it. He is then an officer for life. This once observed, it becomes of so much consequence to certain nations to have a friend or a foe at the head of our affairs that they will interfere with money & with arms. A Galloman or an Angloman will be supported by the nation he befriends. If once elected, and at a second or third election out voted by one or two votes, he will pretend false votes, foul play, hold possession of the reins of government, be supported by the States voting for him, especially if they are the central ones lying in a compact body themselves & separating their opponents: and they will be aided by one nation of Europe, while the majority are aided by another. . . . It may be said that if elections are to be attended with these disorders, the seldomer they are renewed the better. But experience shews that the only way to prevent disorder is to render them uninteresting by frequent changes. An incapacity to be elected a second time would have been the only effectual preventative. . . . After all, it is my principle that the will of the majority should always prevail. If they approve the proposed Convention in all it's parts, I shall concur in it chearfully, in hopes that they will amend it whenever they shall find it work wrong. . . .

TO GEORGE WASHINGTON

2 MAY 1788

Sir,

＊　　＊　　＊　　＊

I had intended to have written a word to your Excellency on the subject of the new constitution . . . . I will just observe therefore that according to my ideas there is a great deal of good in it. There are two things however which I dislike strongly. 1. The want of a declaration of rights. I am in hopes the opposition of Virginia will remedy this, & produce such a declaration. 2. The perpetual re-eligibility of the President. This I fear will make an office for life first, & then hereditary. I was much an enemy to monarchy before I came to Europe. I am ten thousand times more so since I have seen what they are. There is scarcely an evil known in these countries which may not be traced to their king as it's source, nor a good which is not derived from the small fibres of republicanism existing among them. . . .

TO FRANCIS HOPKINSON

13 MARCH 1789

Dear Sir,— * * * You say that I have been dished up to you as an antifederalist, and ask me if it be just. . . . I am not a Federalist, because I never submitted the whole system of my opinions to the creed of any party of men whatever in religion, in philosophy, in politics, or in anything else where I was capable of thinking for myself. Such an addiction is the last degradation of a free and moral agent. If I could not go to heaven but with a party, I would not go there at all. Therefore I protest to you I am not of the party of federalists. But I am much farther from that of the Antifederalists. I approved, from the first moment, of the great mass of what is in the new constitution, the consolidation of the government, the organization into Executive legislative & judiciary, the subdivision of the legislative, the happy compromise of interests between the great & little states by the different manner of voting in the different houses, the voting by persons instead of states, the qualified negative on laws given to the Executive which however I should have liked better if associated with the judiciary also as in New York, and the power of taxation. I thought at first that the latter might have been limited. A little reflection soon convinced me it ought not to be. What I disapproved from the first moment also was the want of a bill of rights to guard liberty against the legislative as well as executive branches of the government, that is to say to secure freedom in religion, freedom of the press, freedom from monopolies, freedom from unlawful imprisonment, freedom from a permanent military, and a trial by jury in all cases determinable by the laws of the land. I disapproved also the perpetual re-eligibility of the President. To these points of disapprobation I adhere. My first wish was that the 9. first conventions might accept the constitution, as the means of securing to use the great mass of good it contained, and that the 4. last might reject it, as the means of obtaining amendments. But I was corrected in this wish the moment I saw the much better plan of Massachusetts and which had never occurred to me. With respect to the declaration of rights I suppose the majority of the United states are of my opinion: for I apprehend all the antifederalists, and a very respectable proportion of the federalists think that such a declaration should now be annexed. The enlightened part of Europe have given us the greatest credit for inventing this instrument of security for the rights of the people, and have been not a little surprised to see us so soon give it up. With respect to the re-eligibility of the president, I find myself differing from the majority of my countrymen, for I think there are but three states out of the 11. which have desired an alteration of this. And indeed, since the thing is established, I would wish it not to be altered during the life of our great leader, whose executive talents are superior to those I believe of any man in the world, and who alone by the authority of his name and the confidence reposed in his perfect integrity, is fully qualified to put the new government so under way as to secure it against the efforts of opposition. But having derived from our error all the good there was in it I hope we shall correct it the moment we can no longer have the same name at the helm. These, my dear friend, are my sentiments, by which you will see I was right in saying I am neither federalist nor antifederalist; that I am of neither party, nor yet a trimmer between parties. . . .

TO DAVID HUMPHREYS

18 MARCH 1789

Dear Sir,

✵   ✵   ✵   ✵

The operations which have taken place in America lately, fill me with pleasure. In the first place they realize the confidence I had that whenever our affairs go obviously wrong the good sense of the people will interpose and set them to rights. The example of changing a constitution by assembling the wise men of the State, instead of assembling armies, will be worth as much to the world as the former examples we had given them. The constitution too which was the result of our deliberations, is unquestionably the wisest ever yet presented to men, and some of the accommodations of interest which it has adopted are greatly pleasing to me who have before had occasions of seeing how difficult those interests were to accommodate. A general concurrence of opinion seems to authorize us to say it has some defects. I am one of those who think it a defect that the important rights, not placed in security by the frame of the constitution itself were not explicitly secured by a supplementary declaration. There are rights which it is useless to surrender to the government, and which governments have yet always been fond to invade. These are the rights of thinking, and publishing our thoughts by speaking or writing; the right of free commerce; the right of personal freedom. . . . The general voice has legitimated this objection. It has not however authorized me to consider as a real defect what I thought and still think one, the perpetual re-eligibility of the president. But three states out of 11. having declared against this, we must suppose we are wrong according to the fundamental law of every society, the *lex majoris partis,* to which we are bound to submit. . . .

❋ ❋ ❋ ❋

PART III

The Debate over Ratification:

Anti-Federalist Arguments

****

Reasons of Dissent

****

18 DECEMBER 1787

It was not until after the termination of the late glorious contest, which made the people of the United States an independent nation, that any defect was discovered in the present confederation. It was formed by some of the ablest patriots in America. It carried us successfully through the war, and the virtue and patriotism of the people, with their disposition to promote the common cause, supplied the want of power in Congress.

❊   ❊   ❊   ❊

. . . The [Philadelphia] convention sat upwards of four months. The doors were kept shut, and the members brought under the most solemn engagements of secrecy.[1] Some of those who opposed their going so far beyond their powers, retired, hopeless, from the convention; others had the firmness to refuse signing the plan altogether; and many who did sign it, did it not as a system they wholly approved, but as the best that could be then obtained . . . .

Whilst the gilded chains were forging in the secret conclave,

---

[1] The Journals of the conclave are still concealed.

From McMaster and Stone, pp. 454–455, 457, 459, 461–466, 470, 481.

the meaner instruments of the despotism without were busily employed in alarming the fears of the people with dangers which did not exist, and exciting their hopes of greater advantages from the expected plan than even the best government on earth could produce. The proposed plan had not many hours issued forth from the womb of suspicious secrecy, until such as were prepared for the purpose, were carrying about petitions for people to sign, signifying their approbation of the system, and requesting the legislature to call a convention. . . .

*   *   *   *

In this situation of affairs were the subscribers elected members of the Convention of Pennsylvania—a Convention called by a legislature in direct violation of their duty, and composed in part of members who were compelled to attend for that purpose, to consider of a Constitution proposed by a Convention of the United States, who were not appointed for the purpose of framing a new form of government, but whose powers were expressly confined to altering and amending the present articles of confederation. . . .

*   *   *   *

. . . We offered our objections to the [Pennsylvania] convention, and opposed those parts of the plan which, in our opinion, would be injurious to you, . . . and closed our arguments by offering the following propositions to the convention.

1. The right of conscience shall be held inviolable; and neither the legislative, executive nor judicial powers of the United States shall have authority to alter, abrogate or infringe any part of the constitution of the several States, which provide for the preservation of liberty in matters of religion.

2. That in controversies respecting property, and in suits between man and man, trial by jury shall remain as heretofore, as well in the federal courts as in those of the several States.

3. That in all capital and criminal prosecutions, a man has a

right to demand the cause and nature of his accusation, as well in the federal courts as in those of the several States; to be heard by himself and his counsel; to be confronted with the accusers and witnesses; to call for evidence in his favor, and a speedy trial by an impartial jury of his vicinage, without whose unanimous consent he cannot be found guilty, nor can he be compelled to give evidence against himself; and, that no man be deprived of his liberty, except by the law of the land or the judgment of his peers.

4. That excessive bail ought not to be required, nor excessive fines imposed, nor cruel nor unusual punishments inflicted.

5. That warrants unsupported by evidence, whereby any officer or messenger may be commanded or required to search suspected places; or to seize any person or persons, his or their property not particularly described, are grievous and oppressive, and shall not be granted either by the magistrates of the federal government or others.

6. That the people have a right to the freedom of speech, of writing and publishing their sentiments; therefore the freedom of the press shall not be restrained by any law of the United States.

7. That the people have a right to bear arms for the defence of themselves and their own State or the United States, or for the purpose of killing game; . . . and as standing armies in the time of peace are dangerous to liberty they ought not to be kept up . . . .

8. The inhabitants of the several States shall have liberty to fowl and hunt in seasonable time on the lands they hold, and on all other lands in the United States not inclosed, and in like manner to fish in all navigable waters . . . .

9. That no law shall be passed to restrain the legislatures of the several States from enacting laws for imposing taxes, except imposts and duties on goods imported or exported, and that no taxes, except imposts and duties upon goods imported and exported, and postage on letters, shall be levied by the authority of Congress.

10. That the house of representatives be properly increased in number; that elections shall remain free; that the several States shall have power to regulate the elections for senators and representatives, without being controlled either directly or indirectly by any interference on the part of the Congress; and that the elections of representatives be annual.

11. That the power of organizing, arming and disciplining the militia . . . remain with the individual States, and that Congress shall not have authority to call or march any of the militia out of their own State, without the consent of such State, and for such length of time only as such State shall agree.

That the sovereignty, freedom and independency of the several States shall be retained, and every power, jurisdiction and right which is not by this Constitution expressly delegated to the United States in Congress assembled.

12. That the legislative, executive and judicial powers be kept separate; and to this end that a constitutional council be appointed to advise and assist the President, who shall be responsible for the advice they give—hereby the senators would be relieved from almost constant attendance; and also that the judges be made completely independent.

13. That no treaty which shall be directly opposed to the existing laws of the United States in Congress assembled, shall be valid until such laws shall be repealed or made conformable to such treaty; neither shall any treaties be valid which are in contradiction to the Constitution of the United States, or the constitution of the several States.

14. That the judiciary power of the United States shall be confined to cases affecting ambassadors, other public ministers and consuls, to cases of admiralty and maritime jurisdiction; to controversies to which the United States shall be a party; to controversies between two or more States—between a State and citizens of different States—between citizens claiming lands under grants of different States, and between a State or the citizens thereof and foreign States; and in criminal cases of such only as are expressly enumerated in the constitution; and that

. . . Congress . . . shall not have power to enact laws which shall alter the laws of descent and distribution of the effects of deceased persons, the titles of lands or goods, or the regulation of contracts in the individual States.

. . . [We] declared our willingness to agree to the plan, provided it was so amended as to meet those propositions or something similar to them, and finally moved the convention to adjourn, to give the people of Pennsylvania time to consider the subject and determine for themselves; but these were all rejected . . . .

❋   ❋   ❋   ❋

We dissent, first, because it is the opinion of the most celebrated writers on government, and confirmed by uniform experience, that a very extensive territory cannot be governed on the principles of freedom, otherwise than by a confederation of republics, possessing all the powers of internal government, but united in the management of their general and foreign concerns.

❋   ❋   ❋   ❋

We dissent, secondly, because the powers vested in Congress by this constitution, must necessarily annihilate and absorb the legislative, executive, and judicial powers of the several States, and produce from their ruins one consolidated government, which from the nature of things will be *an iron handed despotism,* as nothing short of the supremacy of despotic sway could connect and govern these United States under one government.

❋   ❋   ❋   ❋

The powers of Congress under the new constitution are complete and unlimited over the *purse* and the *sword,* and are perfectly independent of and supreme over the State governments, whose intervention in these great points is entirely destroyed. . . .

❋   ❋   ❋   ❋

In short, consolidation pervades the whole constitution. It begins with an annunciation that such was the intention. The main pillars of the fabric correspond with it, and the concluding paragraph is a confirmation of it. . . .

*   *   *   *

3. We dissent, thirdly, because if it were practicable to govern so extensive a territory as these United States include, on the plan of a consolidated government, consistent with the principles of liberty and the happiness of the people, yet the construction of this Constitution is not calculated to attain the object; for independent of the nature of the case, it would of itself necessarily produce a despotism, and that not by the usual gradations, but with the celerity that has hitherto only attended revolutions effected by the sword.

*   *   *   *

As this government will not enjoy the confidence of the people, but be executed by force, it will be a very expensive and burthensome government. The standing army must be numerous, and as a further support, it will be the policy of this government to multiply officers in every department; judges, collectors, tax-gatherers, excisemen and the whole host of revenue officers, will swarm over the land, devouring the hard earnings of the industrious—like the locusts of old, impoverishing and desolating all before them.

*   *   *   *

WILLIAM FINDLEY

Letter of an Officer
of the Late Continental Army

3 NOVEMBER 1787

To the Citizens of Philadelphia.

Friends, countrymen, brethren and fellow-citizens: The important day is drawing near when you are to elect delegates to represent you in a convention, on the result of whose deliberations will depend in a great measure your future happiness.

* * * *

. . . Notwithstanding the splendor of names which has attended the publication of the new constitution, notwithstanding the sophistry and vain reasonings that have been urged to support its principles, alas! you must at least have concluded that great men are not always infallible, and that patriotism itself may be led into essential errors.

The objections that have been made to the new constitution are these:

1. It is not merely (as it ought to be) a Confederation of States, but a Government of individuals.

From McMaster and Stone, pp. 179–187.

133

2. The powers of Congress extend to the lives, the liberties and the property of every citizen.

3. The sovereignty of the different States is *ipso facto* destroyed in its most essential parts.

4. What remains of it will only tend to create violent dissension between the State government and the Congress, and terminate in the ruin of the one or the other.

5. The consequence must therefore be, either that the union of the States will be destroyed by a violent struggle, or that their sovereignty will be swallowed up by silent encroachments into a universal aristocracy; because it is clear, that if two different sovereign powers have a coëqual command over the purses of the citizens, they will struggle for the spoils, and the weakest will be in the end obliged to yield to the efforts of the strongest.

6. Congress being possessed of these immense powers, the liberties of the States and of the people are not secured by a bill or Declaration of Rights.

7. The sovereignty of the States is not expressly reserved; the form only, and not the substance of the government, is guaranteed to them by express words.

8. Trial by Jury, that sacred bulwark of liberty, is abolished in civil cases, and Mr. W—— [James Wilson], one of the convention, has told you, that not being able to agree as to the form of establishing this point, they have left you deprived of the substance. Here are his own words: "The subject was involved in difficulties. The convention found the task too difficult for them, and left the business as it stands."

9. The Liberty of the Press is not secured, and the powers of Congress are fully adequate to its destruction, as they are to have the trial of libels, or pretended libels against the United States, and may by a cursed abominable Stamp Act (as the Bowdoin administration has done in Massachusetts) preclude you effectually from all means of information. Mr. W—— has given no answer to these arguments.

10. Congress have the power of keeping up a standing army

in time of peace, and Mr. W—— has told you that it was *necessary*.

11. The Legislative and Executive powers are not kept separate, as every one of the American constitutions declares they ought to be; but they are mixed in a manner entirely novel and unknown, even in the constitution of Great Britain; because,

12. In England the king only has a nominal negative over the proceedings of the legislature, which he has never dared to exercise since the days of King William, whereas by the new constitution, both the President-General and the Senate, two executive branches of Government, have that negative, and are intended to support each other in the exercise of it.

13. The representation of the lower house is too small, consisting only of 65 members.

14. That of the Senate is so small that it renders its extensive powers extremely dangerous; it is to consist only of 26 members, two-thirds of whom must concur to conclude any treaty or alliance with foreign powers. Now we will suppose that five of them are absent, sick, dead, or unable to attend; twenty-one will remain, and eight of these (one-third, and one over) may prevent the conclusion of any treaty, even the most favorable to America. Here will be a fine field for the intrigues and even the bribery and corruption of European powers.

15. The most important branches of the executive department are to be put into the hands of a single magistrate, who will in fact be an *elective king*. The military, the land and naval forces, are to be entirely at his disposal, and therefore,

16. Should the senate, by the intrigues of foreign powers, become devoted to foreign influence, as was the case of late in Sweden, the people will be obliged, as the Swedes have been, to seek their refuge in the arms of the monarch or President-General.

17. Rotation, that noble prerogative of liberty, is entirely excluded from the new system of government, and the great men may and probably will be continued in office during their lives.

18. Annual elections are abolished, and the people are not to re-assume their rights until the expiration of two, four and six years.

19. Congress are to have the power of fixing the time, place and manner of holding elections, so as to keep them forever subjected to their influence.

20. The importation of slaves is not to be prohibited until the year 1808, and *slavery* will probably resume its empire in Pennsylvania.

21. The militia is to be under the immediate command of Congress, and men conscientiously scrupulous of bearing arms may be compelled to perform military duty.

22. The new government will be *expensive* beyond any we have ever experienced; the judicial department alone, with its concomitant train of judges, justices, chancellors, clerks, sheriffs, coroners, escheators, State attorneys and solicitors, constables, etc., in every State and in every county in each State, will be a burden beyond the utmost abilities of the people to bear, and upon the whole,

23. A government partaking of *monarchy* and aristocracy will be fully and firmly established, and liberty will be but a name to adorn the short historic page of the halcyon days of America.

These, my countrymen, are the objections that have been made to the new proposed system of government, and if you read the system itself with attention you will find them all to be founded in truth. But what have you been told in answer?

I pass over the sophistry of Mr. W——, in his equivocal speech at the state-house. His pretended arguments have been echoed and re-echoed by every retailer of politics, and victoriously refuted by several patriotic pens. Indeed, if you read this famous speech in a cool dispassionate moment, you will find it to contain no more than a train of pitiful sophistry and evasions, unworthy of the man who spoke them. . . . Mr. W—— is a man of sense, learning and extensive information; unfortunately for him, he has never sought the more solid frame of patriotism. During the late war he narrowly escaped the effects of popular rage, and the people seldom arm themselves against a citizen in vain. The whole tenor of his political conduct has always been strongly tainted with the spirit of *high aristocracy;* he has never been known to join in a truly popular measure, and his talents have ever been devoted to the patrician interest. . . . He sees at a distance the pomp and pageantry of courts, he sighs after those stately palaces and that apparatus of human greatness which his vivid fancy has taught him to consider as the supreme good. Men of sublime minds, he conceives, were born a different race from the rest of the sons of men; to them and them only, he imagines, high heaven intended to commit the reins of earthly government; the remaining part of mankind he sees at an immense distance; they, he thinks, were born to serve, to administer food to the ambition of their superiors and become the footstool of their power. Such is Mr. W——, and fraught with these high ideas, it is no wonder that he should exert all his talents to support a form of government so admirably contrived to carry them into execution. But when the people, who possess collectively a mass of knowledge superior to his own, inquire into the principles of that government on the establishment or rejection of which depend their dearest concerns, when he is called upon by the voice of thousands to come and explain that favorite system which he holds forth as an object of their admiration, he comes—he attempts to support by reasoning what reason never dictated, and finding the attempt vain, his great mind, made for nobler purposes, is obliged to stoop to mean evasions and pitiful sophistry; himself not deceived, he strives to deceive the people, and the treasonable attempt delineates his true character . . . .

❋   ❋   ❋   ❋

But where argument entirely failed, nothing remained for the supporters of the new constitution but to endeavor to inflame your passions. . . . The great names of *Washington* and *Frank-*

lin have been taken in vain and shockingly prostituted to effect the most infamous purposes. What! because our august chieftain has subscribed his name in his capacity of president of the convention to the plan offered by them to the States, and because the venerable sage of Pennsylvania has testified by his signature that the majority of the delegates of this State assented to the same plan, will any one infer from this that it has met with their entire approbation, and that they consider it as the masterpiece of human wisdom? I am apt to think the contrary, and I have good reason to ground my opinion on.

❖　　❖　　❖　　❖

Now then my fellow-citizens, my brethren, my friends; if the sacred flame of liberty be not extinguished in your breasts, if you have any regard for the happiness of yourselves, and your posterity, let me entreat you, earnestly entreat you by all that is dear and sacred to freemen, to consider well before you take an awful step which may involve in its consequences the ruin of millions yet unborn. You are on the brink of a dreadful precipice—in the name therefore of holy liberty, for which I have fought and for which we have all suffered, I call upon you to make a solemn pause before you proceed. One step more, and perhaps the scene of freedom is closed forever in America. Let not a set of aspiring despots, who make us *slaves,* and tell us 'tis our charter, wrest from you those invaluable blessings, for which the most illustrious sons of America have bled and died—but exert yourselves, like men, like freemen, and like Americans, to transmit unimpaired to your latest posterity those rights, those liberties, which have ever been dear to you, and which it is yet in your power to preserve.

AN OFFICER OF THE LATE CONTINENTAL ARMY

SAMUEL BRYAN

Letters of Centinel

CENTINEL, I

5 OCTOBER 1787

To the FREEMEN of PENNSYLVANIA. *Friends, Countrymen and Fellow Citizens.*

* * * *

I am fearful that the principles of government inculcated in Mr. [John] Adams' treatise, and enforced in the numerous essays and paragraphs in the newspapers, have misled some well designing members of the late Convention. But it will appear in the sequel, that the construction of the proposed plan of government is infinitely more extravagant.

I have been anxiously expecting that some enlightened patriot would, ere this, have taken up the pen to expose the futility, and counteract the baneful tendency of such principles. Mr. Adams' *sine qua non* of a good government is three balancing powers; whose repelling qualities are to produce an equilibrium of interests, and thereby promote the happiness of the whole community. He asserts that the administrators of every government, will ever be actuated by views of private interest and

From McMaster and Stone: Centinel, I, pp. 565, 567–570; Centinel, II, pp. 576–577; Centinel, IV, pp. 601–603; Centinel, V, pp. 608–613; Centinel, IX, pp. 626–628; Centinel, XI, pp. 633–636 (footnote omitted).

ambition, to the prejudice of the public good; that therefore the only effectual method to secure the rights of the people and promote their welfare, is to create an opposition of interests between the members of two distinct bodies, in the exercise of the powers of government, and balanced by those of a third. This hypothesis supposes human wisdom competent to the task of instituting three co-equal orders in government, and a corresponding weight in the community to enable them respectively to exercise their several parts, and whose views and interests should be so distinct as to prevent a coalition of any two of them for the destruction of the third. Mr. Adams, although he has traced the constitution of every form of government that ever existed, as far as history affords materials, has not been able to adduce a single instance of such a government; he indeed says that the British constitution is such in theory, but this is rather a confirmation that his principles are chimerical and not to be reduced to practice. If such an organization of power were practicable, how long would it continue? Not a day—for there is so great a disparity in the talents, wisdom and industry of mankind, that the scale would presently preponderate to one or the other body, and with every accession of power the means of further increase would be greatly extended. The state of society in England is much more favorable to such a scheme of government than that of America. There they have a powerful hereditary nobility, and real distinctions of rank and interests; but even there, for want of that perfect equality of power and distinction of interests in the three orders of government, they exist but in name; the only operative and efficient check upon the conduct of administration, is the sense of the people at large.

Suppose a government could be formed and supported on such principles, would it answer the great purposes of civil society? If the administrators of every government are actuated by views of private interest and ambition, how is the welfare and happiness of the community to be the result of such jarring adverse interests?

Therefore, as different orders in government will not produce the good of the whole, we must recur to other principles. I believe it will be found that the form of government, which holds those entrusted with power in the greatest responsibility to their constituents, the best calculated for freemen. A republican, or free government, can only exist where the body of the people are virtuous, and where property is pretty equally divided. In such a government the people are the sovereign and their sense or opinion is the criterion of every public measure; for when this ceases to be the case, the nature of the government is changed, and an aristocracy, monarchy or despotism will rise on its ruin. The highest responsibility is to be attained in a simple structure of government, for the great body of the people never steadily attend to the operations of government, and for want of due information are liable to be imposed on. If you complicate the plan by various orders, the people will be perplexed and divided in their sentiment about the source of abuses or misconduct; some will impute it to the senate, others to the house of representatives, and so on, that the interposition of the people may be rendered imperfect or perhaps wholly abortive. But if, imitating the constitution of Pennsylvania, you vest all the legislative power in one body of men (separating the executive and judicial) elected for a short period, and necessarily excluded by rotation from permanency, and guarded from precipitancy and surprise by delays imposed on its proceedings, you will create the most perfect responsibility; for then, whenever the people feel a grievance, they cannot mistake the authors, and will apply the remedy with certainty and effect, discarding them at the next election. This tie of responsibility will obviate all the dangers apprehended from a single legislature, and will the best secure the rights of the people.

*   *   *   *

CENTINEL

CENTINEL, II

24 OCTOBER 1787

To the PEOPLE of PENNSYLVANIA. *Friends, Countrymen, and Fellow Citizens.*

As long as the liberty of the press continues unviolated, and the people have the right of expressing and publishing their sentiments upon every public measure, it is next to impossible to enslave a free nation. The state of society must be very corrupt and base indeed, when the people, in possession of such a monitor as the press, can be induced to exchange the heaven-born blessings of liberty for the galling chains of despotism. Men of an aspiring and tyrannical disposition, sensible of this truth, have ever been inimical to the press, and have considered the shackling of it as the first step towards the accomplishment of their hateful domination, and the entire suppression of all liberty of public discussion, as necessary to its support. For even a standing army, that grand engine of oppression, if it were as numerous as the abilities of any nation could maintain, would not be equal to the purposes of despotism over an enlightened people.

The abolition of that grand palladium of freedom, the liberty of the press, in the proposed plan of government, and the conduct of its authors and patrons, is a striking exemplification of these observations. The reason assigned for the omission of a *bill of rights,* securing the *liberty of the press,* and *other invaluable personal rights,* is an insult on the understanding of the people.

✻   ✻   ✻   ✻

CENTINEL

CENTINEL, IV

30 NOVEMBER 1787

To the PEOPLE of PENNSYLVANIA. *Friends, Countrymen and Fellow Citizens,*

That the present confederation is inadequate to the objects of the union, seems to be universally allowed. The only question is, what additional powers are wanting to give due energy to the federal government? . . . Taxation is in every government a very delicate and difficult subject; hence it has been the policy of all wise statesmen, as far as circumstances permitted, to lead the people by small beginnings and almost imperceptible degrees, into the habits of taxation; where the contrary conduct has been pursued, it has ever failed of full success, not unfrequently proving the ruin of the projectors. The imposing of a burdensome tax at once on a people, without the usual gradations, is the severest test that any government can be put to; despotism itself has often proved unequal to the attempt. . . . [How] then can we impute the difficulties of the people to a due compliance with the requisitions of Congress, to a defect in the confederation? for any government, however energetic, in similar circumstances, would have experienced the same fate. If we review the proceedings of the States, we shall find that they gave every sanction and authority to the requisitions of Congress that their laws could confer, that they attempted to collect the sums called for in the same manner as is proposed to be done in future by the general government, instead of the State legislatures.

❋   ❋   ❋   ❋

. . . [The] present inefficacy of the requisitions of Congress is not owing to a defect in the confederation, but the peculiar circumstances of the times.

❋   ❋   ❋   ❋

CENTINEL

CENTINEL, V

4 DECEMBER 1787

To the PEOPLE of PENNSYLVANIA. *Friends, Countrymen, and Fellow Citizens.*

Mr. Wilson in a speech delivered in our Convention on Saturday the 24th instant, has conceded, nay forcibly proved, that one consolidated government will not answer for so extensive a territory as the United States includes, that slavery would be the necessary fate of the people under such a government. . . .

This great point having been now confirmed by the concession of Mr. Wilson, though indeed it was self-evident before, and the writers against the proposed plan of government having proved to demonstration, that the powers proposed to be vested in Congress will necessarily annihilate and absorb the State Legislatures and judiciaries, and produce from their wreck one consolidated government, the question is determined. Every man therefore who has the welfare of his country at heart, every man who values his own liberty and happiness, in short, every description of persons, except those aspiring despots who hope to benefit by the misery and vassalage of their countrymen, must now concur in rejecting the proposed system of government, must now unite in branding its authors with the stigma of eternal infamy. . . .

❖　　❖　　❖　　❖

The Legislature is the highest delegated power in government; all others are subordinate to it. The celebrated Montesquieu established it as a maxim, that legislation necessarily follows the power of taxation. By the 8th sect. of article the 1st, of the proposed government, "the Congress are to have power to lay and collect taxes, duties, imposts, and excises, to pay the debts and provide for the common defence and *general welfare* of the United States." Now what can be more comprehensive than these words? . . . Whatever taxes, duties, and excises that the Congress may deem necessary to the *general welfare* may be imposed on the citizens of these states, and levied by their officers. The Congress are to be the absolute judges of the propriety of such taxes; in short, they may construe every purpose for which the state legislatures now lay taxes, to be for the *general welfare;* they may seize upon every source of taxation, and thus make it impracticable for the states to have the smallest revenue, and if a state should presume to impose a tax or excise that would interfere with a federal tax or excise, Congress may soon terminate the contention by repealing the state law, by virtue of the following section: "To make all laws which shall be necessary and proper for carrying into execution the foregoing powers and all other powers vested by this constitution in the government of the United States, or in any department thereof." Indeed, every law of the states may be controlled by this power. The legislative power granted for these sections is so unlimited in its nature, may be so comprehensive and boundless in its exercise, that this alone would be amply sufficient to carry the coup de grace to the state governments, to swallow them up in the grand vortex of general empire. But the legislative has an able auxiliary in the judicial department, for . . . this may be made greatly instrumental in effecting a consolidation; as the federal judiciary would absorb all others. Lest the foregoing powers should not suffice to consolidate the United States into one empire, the Convention, as if determined to prevent the possibility of a doubt, . . . as if to preclude all struggle for state importance, as if to level all obstacles to the supremacy of universal sway, which in so extensive a territory would be an iron-handed despotism, have ordained by article the 6th, "That this constitution, and the laws of the United States which shall be made in pursuance thereof, and all treaties made, or which shall be made, under the authority of the United States, shall be the *supreme law of the land; and the judges in every state shall be bound thereby, anything in the constitution or laws of any state to the contrary notwithstanding."*

The words "pursuant to the constitution" will be no restriction to the authority of Congress; for the foregoing sections give them unlimited legislation; their unbounded power of taxation does alone include all others, as whoever has the purse-strings will have full dominion. But the convention has superadded another power, by which the Congress may stamp with the sanction of the constitution every possible law; it is contained in the following clause: "To make all laws which shall be necessary and proper for carrying into execution the foregoing powers, and all other powers vested by this constitution in the government of the United States or in any department or officer thereof." Whatever law Congress may deem necessary and proper for carrying into execution any of the powers vested in them may be enacted; and by virtue of this clause, they may control and abrogate any and every of the laws of the State governments, on the allegation that they interfere with the execution of any of their powers, and yet these laws will "be made in pursuance of the constitution," and of course will "be the supreme law of the land, and the judges in every State shall be bound thereby, anything in the *constitution* or *laws* of any state to the contrary notwithstanding."

✿   ✿   ✿   ✿

What restriction does Mr. Wilson pretend there is in the new constitution to the supremacy of despotic sway over the United States? What barrier does he assign for the security of the State governments? Why truly, a mere cobweb of a limit! by interposing the shield of what will become mere *form,* to check the *reality* of power. He says, that the existence of the State governments is essential to the organization of Congress, that the former is made the necessary basis of the latter, for the federal senators and President are to be appointed by the State legislatures; and that hence all fears of a consolidation are groundless and imaginary. . . . Mr. Wilson has displayed much ingenuity on this occasion; he has involved the subject in all the mazes of sophistry, and by subtil distinctions, he has established principles and positions, that exist only in his own fertile imagination. It is a solecism in politics for two co-ordinate sovereignties to exist together; you must separate the sphere of their jurisdiction or after running the race of dominion for some time, one would necessarily triumph over the other, but in the meantime the subject of it would be harassed with double impositions to support the contention; however, the strife between Congress and the States could not be of long continuance, for the former has a decisive superiority in the outset, and has moreover the power by the very constitution itself to terminate it when expedient.

❊ ❊ ❊ ❊

CENTINEL

CENTINEL, IX

8 JANUARY 1788

To the PEOPLE of PENNSYLVANIA. *Fellow Citizens,*

You have the peculiar felicity of living under the most perfect system of local government in the world; prize then this invaluable blessing as it deserves. Suffer it not to be wrested from you, and the scourge of despotic power substituted in its place, under the specious pretence of vesting the general government of the United States with necessary power; that this would be the inevitable consequence of the establishment of the new constitution, the least consideration of its nature and tendency is sufficient to convince every unprejudiced mind. . . .

The highest illustration of the excellence of the constitution of this commonwealth, is, that from its first establishment, the ambitious and profligate have been united in a constant con-

spiracy to destroy it; so sensible are they that it is their great
enemy, that it is the great palladium of equal liberty, and the
property of the people from the rapacious hand of power. The
annals of mankind do not furnish a more glorious instance of the
triumph of patriotism over the lust of ambition aided by most of
the wealth of the State. The few generally prevail over the many
by uniformity of council, unremitted and persevering exertion,
and superior information and address; but in Pennsylvania the
reverse has happened; here the *well-born* have been baffled in
all their efforts to prostrate the altar of liberty for the purpose
of substituting their own insolent sway that would degrade the
freemen of this State into servile dependence upon the *lordly*
and *great*. However it is not the nature of ambition to be dis-
couraged; it is ever ready to improve the first opportunity to
rear its baneful head and with irritated fury to wreak its ven-
geance on the votaries of liberty. The present conspiracy is a
continental exertion of the *well-born* of America to obtain that
darling domination, which they have not been able to accomplish in their respective States. . . .

These conspirators have come forward at a most favorable
conjuncture, when the state of public affairs has lulled all jealousy of power: Emboldened by the sanction of the august name
of a *Washington,* that they have prostituted to their purpose,
they have presumed to overleap the usual gradations to absolute
power, and have attempted to seize at once upon the supremacy
of dominion. The new instrument of government does indeed
make a fallacious parade of some remaining privileges, and insults the understandings of the people with the semblance of
liberty in some of its artful and deceptive clauses, which form
but a flimsy veil over the reality of tyranny, so weakly endeavored to be concealed from the eye of freedom. . . .

✻   ✻   ✻   ✻

CENTINEL

CENTINEL, XI

16 JANUARY 1788

To the PEOPLE of PENNSYLVANIA. *Fellow Citizens.*

The arguments upon which the advocates of the new constitution the most dwell, are the distresses of the community, the evils of anarchy, and the horrible consequences that would ensue from the dissolution of the union of the States, and the institution of separate confederacies or republics . . . . [This] is not the criterion whereby to determine the merits of the new constitution; . . . notwithstanding the reality of the distresses of the people, the new constitution may not only be inadequate as a remedy, but destructive of liberty, and the completion of misery. . . .

The evils of anarchy have been portrayed with all the imagery of language in the glowing colors of eloquence; the affrighted mind is thence led to clasp the new Constitution as the instrument of deliverance, as the only avenue to safety and happiness. To avoid the possible and transitory evils of one extreme, it is seduced into the certain and permanent misery necessarily attendant on the other. A state of anarchy from its very nature can never be of long continuance; the greater its violence the shorter the duration; order and security are immediately sought by the distracted people beneath the shelter of equal laws and the salutary restraints of regular government, and if this be not attainable absolute power is assumed by the *one,* or a *few,* who shall be the most enterprising and successful. If anarchy, therefore, were the inevitable consequence of rejecting the new Constitution, it would be infinitely better to incur it, for even then there would be at least the chance of a good government rising out of licentiousness; but to rush at once into despotism because there is a bare possibility of anarchy ensuing from the rejection, or from what is yet more visionary, the small delay that would be occasioned by a revision and correction of the proposed system of government is so superlatively weak, so fatally blind, that it is astonishing any person of common understanding should suffer such an imposition to have the least influence on his judgment; still more astonishing that so flimsy and deceptive a doctrine should make converts among the enlightened freemen of America, who have so long enjoyed the blessings of liberty . . . .

The source of the apprehensions of this so much dreaded anarchy would upon investigation be found to arise from the artful suggestions of designing men, and not from a rational probability grounded on the actual state of affairs . . . .

The other specter that has been raised to terrify and alarm the people out of the exercise of their judgment on this great occasion, is the dread of our splitting into separate confederacies or republics, that might become rival powers and consequently liable to mutual wars . . . . This is an event still more improbable than the foregoing; it is a presumption unwarranted, either by the situation of affairs, or the sentiments of the people; no disposition leading to it exists; the advocates of the new constitution seem to view such a separation with horror, and its opponents are strenuously contending for a confederation that shall embrace all America under its comprehensive and salutary protection. This hobgoblin appears to have sprung from the deranged brain of *Publius,* a New York writer, who, mistaking sound for argument, has with Herculean labor accumulated myriads of unmeaning sentences, and *mechanically* endeavored to force conviction by a torrent of misplaced words; he might have spared his readers the fatigue of wading through his long-winded disquisitions on the direful effects of the contentions of inimical states, as totally inapplicable to the subject he was *professedly* treating; this writer has devoted much time, and wasted more paper in combating chimeras of his own creation. . . . [Yet] ought such an apprehension, if well founded, to drive us into the fangs of despotism? Infinitely preferable would be

occasional wars to such an event; the former, although a severe
scourge, is transient in its continuance, and in its operation partial, but a small proportion of the community are exposed to its
greatest horrors, and yet fewer experience its greatest evils; the
latter is permanent and universal misery, without remission or
exemption: as passing clouds obscure for a time the splendor of
the sun, so do wars interrupt the welfare of mankind; but despotism is a settled gloom that totally extinguishes happiness, not a
ray of comfort can penetrate to cheer the dejected mind; the
goad of power with unabating rigor insists upon the utmost ex-
action, like a merciless taskmaster, is continually inflicting the
lash, and is never satiated with the feast of unfeeling domination, or the most abject servility.

                        *   *   *   *

                                                    CENTINEL

Letter of a Democratic Federalist

23 OCTOBER 1787

The arguments of the Honorable Mr. Wilson, expressed in the speech that he made at the State House on the Saturday preceding the general election, although extremely *ingenious,* and the best that could be adduced in support of so bad a cause, are yet extremely *futile,* and will not stand the test of investigation.

In the first place, Mr. Wilson pretends to point out a leading discrimination between the State constitution and the constitution of the United States. In the former, he says, every power which is not *reserved* is *given,* and in the latter, every power which is not *given* is *reserved.* And this may furnish an answer, he adds, to those who object that a bill of rights has not been introduced in the proposed federal constitution. If this doctrine is true, and since it is the only security that we are to have for our natural rights, it ought at least to have been clearly expressed in the plan of government. The second section of the present articles of confederation says: *Each State retains its sovereignty, freedom and independence, and every power, jurisdiction and right which is not by this confederation expressly delegated to the United States in Congress assembled.*

From *McMaster and Stone, pp. 150–156.*

152

This declaration (for what purpose I know not) is entirely omitted in the proposed constitution. And yet there is a material difference between this constitution and the present confederation, for Congress in the latter are merely an executive body; it has no power to raise money, it has no *judicial jurisdiction*. In the other, on the contrary, the federal rulers are vested with each of the three essential powers of government—their laws are to be *paramount* to the laws of the different States: what then will there be to oppose to their encroachments? Should they ever pretend to tyrannize over the people, their *standing army* will silence every popular effort; it will be theirs to explain the powers which have been granted to them; Mr. Wilson's distinction will be forgot, denied or explained away, and the liberty of the people will be no more.

It is said in the second section of the third article of the federal plan: "The judicial power shall extend to all cases in law and equity arising under this constitution." It is very clear that under this clause, the tribunal of the United States may claim a right to the cognizance of all offences against the general government, and libels will not probably be excluded. Nay, those offences may be by them construed, or by law declared, misprision of treason, an offence which comes literally under their express jurisdiction. Where is then the safety of our boasted liberty of the press? And in case of a conflict of jurisdiction between the courts of the United States, and those of the several commonwealths, is it not easy to foresee which of the two will obtain the advantage?

Under the enormous power of the new confederation, which extends to the individuals as well as to the States of America, a thousand means may be devised to destroy effectually the liberty of the press. There is no knowing what corrupt and wicked judges may do in process of time, when they are not restrained by express laws. The case of John Peter Zenger, of New York, ought still to be present to our minds, to convince us how displeasing the liberty of the press is to men in high power. At any rate, I lay it down as a general rule, that wherever the powers of a government extend to the lives, the persons and properties of the subject, all of their rights ought to be clearly and expressly defined; otherwise, they have but a poor security for their liberties.

The second and most important objection to the federal plan, which Mr. Wilson pretends to be made in a disingenuous form, is the entire abolition of the trial by jury in civil cases. It seems to me that Mr. Wilson's pretended answer is much more disingenuous than the objection itself, which I maintain to be strictly founded in fact. He says, "that the cases open to trial by jury differing in the different States, it was therefore impracticable to have made a general rule." This answer is extremely futile, because a reference might easily have been made to the common law of England, which obtains through every State, and cases in the maritime and civil law courts would, of course, be excepted. . . .

. . . [Under] the proposed federal constitution, *the trial of facts in civil cases by a jury of the vicinage* is entirely and effectually abolished, and will be absolutely impracticable. I wish the learned gentleman had explained to us what is meant by the appellate jurisdiction as to law and fact which is vested in the superior court of the United States? . . . The word *appeal,* if I understand it right, in its proper legal signification includes the fact as well as the law, and precludes every idea of a trial by jury. It is a word of foreign growth, and is only known in England and America in those courts which are governed by the civil or ecclesiastical law of the Romans. Those courts have always been considered in England as a grievance, and have all been established by the usurpations of the ecclesiastical over the civil power. It is well known that the courts of chancery in England were formerly entirely in the hands of ecclesiastics, who took advantage of the strict forms of the common law, to introduce a foreign mode of jurisprudence under the specious name of equity. Pennsylvania, the freest of the American States, has wisely rejected this establishment, and knows not even the name of a court of chancery. And, in fact, there cannot be anything more absurd than a distinction between *law* and *equity*. It might perhaps have suited those barbarous times when the law of England, like almost every other science, was perplexed with quibbles and Aristotelian distinctions, but it would be shameful to keep up in these more enlightened days. At any rate, it seems to me that there is much more equity in a trial by jury than in an appellate jurisdiction from the fact.

An appeal, therefore, is a thing unknown to the common law. Instead of an appeal from facts, it admits of a second or even third trial by different juries, and mistakes in points of law are rectified by superior courts in the form of a writ of error; and to a mere common lawyer, unskilled in the forms of the civil law courts, the words appeal from law and fact are mere nonsense and unintelligible absurdity.

But, even supposing that the superior court of the United States had the authority to try facts by juries of the vicinage, it would be impossible for them to carry it into execution. It is well known that the supreme courts of the different States, at stated times in every year, go round the different counties of their respective States to try issues of fact, which is called riding the circuits. Now, how is it possible that the supreme continental court, which we will suppose to consist at most of five or six judges, can travel at least twice in every year through the different counties of America, from New Hampshire to Kentucky and from Kentucky to Georgia, to try facts by juries of the vicinage? Common sense will not admit of such a supposition. I am therefore right in my assertion, that *trial by jury in civil cases is by the proposed constitution entirely done away and effectually abolished.*

Let us now attend to the consequences of this enormous innovation and daring encroachment on the liberties of the citizens. Setting aside the oppression, injustice and partiality that may take place in the trial of questions of property between man and man, we will attend to one single case, which is well worth our consideration. Let us remember that all cases arising under the new constitution and all matters between *citizens of different States* are to be submitted to the new jurisdiction. Suppose, therefore, that the military officers of Congress, by a wanton abuse of power, imprison the free citizens of the United States of America; suppose . . . that a constable, having a warrant to search for stolen goods, pulled down the clothes of a bed in which there was a woman and searched under her shift—suppose, I say, that they commit similar or greater indignities, in such cases a trial by jury would be our safest resource, heavy damage would at once punish the offender and deter others from committing the same; but what satisfaction can we expect from a lordly court of justice, always ready to protect the officers of government against the weak and helpless citizens, and who will perhaps sit at the distance of many hundred miles from the place where the outrage was committed? What refuge shall we then have to shelter us from the iron hand of arbitrary power? O! my fellow-citizens, think of this while it is yet time, and never consent to part with the glorious privilege of trial by jury but with your lives.

But Mr. Wilson has not stopped here. He has told us that a standing army, that great support of tyrants, not only was not dangerous, but was absolutely necessary. O, my much respected fellow citizens! and are you then reduced to such a degree of insensibility, that assertions like these will not rouse your warmest resentment and indignation? Are we then, after the experience of past ages, and the result of the enquiries of the best and most celebrated patriots have taught us to dread a standing army above all earthly evils—are we then to go over all the threadbare, common-place arguments that have been used without success by the advocates of tyranny, and which have been for a long time past so gloriously refuted? . . . Even Mr. Hume, an aristocratical writer, has candidly confessed that *an army is a moral distemper in a government, of which it must at last inevitably perish* (2d Burgh, 349), and the Earl of Oxford (Oxford the friend of France and the Pretender, the attainted Oxford), said in the British parliament, in a speech on the mutiny bill, that, "While he had breath he would speak for the liberties of his country, and against courts martial and a standing army in peace, as dangerous to the Constitution." (Ibid., page 455.) Such were the speeches even of the enemies of liberty when Britain had yet a right to be called free. But, says Mr. Wilson, "It is necessary to maintain the appearance of strength even in times of the most profound tranquillity." And what is this more than a thread-bare hackneyed argument . . . ? Had we a standing army when the British invaded our peaceful shores? Was it a standing army that gained the battles of Lexington and Bunker Hill, and took the ill-fated Burgoyne? Is not a well-regulated militia sufficient for every purpose of internal defence? And which of you, my fellow citizens, is afraid of any invasion from foreign powers that our brave militia would not be able immediately to repel?

Mr. Wilson says, that he does not know of any nation in the world which has not found it necessary to maintain the appearance of strength in a season of the most profound tranquillity. If by this equivocal assertion he has meant to say that there is no nation in the world without *a standing army in time of peace,* he has been mistaken. I need only adduce the example of Switzerland, which, like us, is a republic, whose thirteen cantons, like our thirteen States, are under a federal government, and which besides is surrounded by the most powerful nations in Europe, all jealous of its liberty and prosperity. And yet that nation has preserved its freedom for many ages, with the sole help of a militia, and has never been known to have a standing army, except when in actual war. Why should we not follow so glorious [an] example, and are we less able to defend our liberty without an army, than that brave but small nation, which, with its militia alone has hitherto defied all Europe?

It is said likewise, that a standing army is not a new thing in

America—Congress even at this moment have a standing army on foot. I answer that *precedent* is not *principle.* Congress have no right to keep up a standing army in time of peace. If they do, it is an infringement of the liberties of the people—wrong can never be justified by wrong: but it is well known that the assertion is groundless—the few troops that are on the banks of the Ohio, were sent for the express purpose of repelling the invasion of the savages and protecting the inhabitants of the frontiers. . . . [As] soon as the danger is over, there is no doubt but Congress will disband their handful of soldiers; it is therefore not true that Congress keep up a standing army in a time of peace and profound security.

The objection to the enormous powers of the President and Senate is not the least important of all, but it requires a full discussion and ample investigation. . . . [It] is an established principle in America, which pervades every one of our State constitutions, that the legislative and executive powers ought to be kept forever separate and distinct from each other; and yet in this new constitution we find there are two executive branches, each of which has more or less control over the proceedings of the Legislature. This is an innovation of the most dangerous kind upon every known principle of government, and it will be easy for me to convince my fellow citizens that it will, in the first place, create a Venetian aristocracy, and, in the end, produce an absolute monarchy.

✿   ✿   ✿   ✿

A DEMOCRATIC FEDERALIST

SAMUEL ADAMS

✮✮✮✮✮✮✮✮✮✮✮✮✮✮✮✮✮✮✮ ✮✮

Letter to Richard Henry Lee

✮✮✮✮✮✮✮✮✮✮✮✮✮✮✮✮✮✮✮ ✮✮

3 DECEMBER 1787

My dear Sir

❀   ❀   ❀   ❀

I confess, as I enter the Building I stumble at the Threshold. I meet with a National Government, instead of a Federal Union of Sovereign States. I am not able to conceive why the Wisdom of the Convention led them to give the Preference to the former before the latter. If the several States in the Union are to become one entire Nation, under one Legislature, the Powers of which shall extend to every Subject of Legislation, and its Laws be supreme & controul the whole, the Idea of Sovereignty in these States must be lost. Indeed I think, upon such a Supposition, those Sovereignties ought to be eradicated from the Mind; for they would be Imperia in Imperio justly deemd a Solecism in Politicks, & they would be highly dangerous, and destructive of the Peace Union and Safety of the Nation. And can this National Legislature be competent to make Laws for the *free* internal Government of one People, living in Climates so remote and whose "Habits & particular Interests" are and probably always will be so different. Is it to be expected that General Laws can

---

From Cushing, The Writings of Samuel Adams, *IV, 323–325.*

be adapted to the Feelings of the more Eastern and the more Southern Parts of so extensive a Nation? It appears to me difficult if practicable. Hence then may we not look for Discontent, Mistrust, Disaffection to Government and frequent Insurrections, which will require standing Armies to suppress them in one Place & another where they may happen to arise. Or if Laws could be made, adapted to the local Habits, Feelings, Views & Interests of those distant Parts, would they not cause Jealousies of Partiality in Government which would excite Envy and other malignant Passions productive of Wars and fighting. But should we continue distinct sovereign States, confederated for the Purposes of mutual Safety and Happiness, each contributing to the federal Head such a Part of its Sovereignty as would render the Government fully adequate to those Purposes and *no more*, the People would govern themselves more easily, the Laws of each State being well adapted to its own Genius & Circumstances, and the Liberties of the United States would be more secure than they can be, as I humbly conceive, under the proposed new Constitution. You are sensible, Sir, that the Seeds of Aristocracy began to spring even before the Conclusion of our Struggle for the natural Rights of Men, Seeds which like a Canker Worm lie at the Root of free Governments. So great is the Wickedness of some Men, & the stupid Servility of others, that one would be almost inclined to conclude that Communities cannot be free. The few haughty Families, think *They* must govern. The Body of the People tamely consent & submit to be their Slaves. This unravels the Mystery of Millions being enslaved by the few! . . .

JAMES WINTHROP

☆☆

Letters of Agrippa

☆☆

AGRIPPA, II

27 NOVEMBER 1787

To the People of Massachusetts.

In the Gazette of the 23d instant, I ascertained from the state of other countries and the experience of mankind, that free countries are most friendly to commerce and to the rights of property. This produces greater internal tranquility. For every man, finding sufficient employment for his active powers in the way of trade, agriculture and manufactures, feels no disposition to quarrel with his neighbour, nor with the government which protects him, and of which he is a constituent part. Of the truth of these positions we have abundant evidence in the history of our own country. . . .

❋   ❋   ❋   ❋

During the last year,[1] we had decisive evidences of the vigour of this kind of government. In Connecticut, the treason was re-

---

[1] Referring to Shay's rebellion.—*Ed.* [Ford]

From Ford, Essays: *Agrippa, II, pp. 56–58; Agrippa, III, pp. 59–62 (footnotes omitted); Agrippa, IV, pp. 63–65; Agrippa, V, pp. 66–68; Agrippa, VIII, pp. 76–78; Agrippa, XII, pp. 91–92; Agrippa, XIII, pp. 93–95; Agrippa, XVII, pp. 110, 113–114; Agrippa, XVIII, pp. 115–121.*

strained while it existed only in the form of conspiracy. In Vermont, the conspirators assembled in arms, but were suppressed by the exertions of the militia, under the direction of their sheriffs. In New-Hampshire, the attack was made on the legislature, but the insurrection was in a very few hours suppressed, and has never been renewed. In Massachusetts, the danger was by delay suffered to increase. One judicial court after another was stopped, and even the capital trembled. Still, however, when the supreme executive gave the signal, a force of many thousands of active, resolute men, took the field, during the severities of winter, and every difficulty vanished before them. Since that time we have been continually coalescing. . . . Agriculture has been improved, manufactures multiplied, and trade prodigiously enlarged. These are the advantages of freedom in a growing country. While our resources have been thus rapidly increasing, the courts have set in every part of the commonwealth, without any guard to defend them; have tried causes of every kind, whether civil or criminal, and the sheriffs, have in no case been interrupted in the execution of their office. In those cases indeed, where the government was more particularly interested, mercy has been extended; but in civil causes, and in the case of moral offences, the law has been punctually executed. Damage done to individuals, during the tumults, has been repaired, by judgment of the courts of law, and the award has been carried into effect. This is the present state of affairs, when we are asked to relinquish that freedom which produces such happy effects.

The attempt has been made to deprive us of such a beneficial system, and to substitute a rigid one in its stead, by criminally alarming our fears, exalting certain characters on one side, and villifying them on the other. I wish to say nothing of the merits or demerits of individuals; such arguments always do hurt. But assuredly my countrymen cannot fail to consider and determine who are the most worthy of confidence in a business of this magnitude.

Whether they will trust persons, who have from their cradles been incapable of comprehending any other principles of government, than those of absolute power, and who have, in this very affair, tried to deprive them of their constitutional liberty, by a pitiful trick. They cannot avoid prefering those who have uniformly exerted themselves to establish a limited government, and to secure to individuals all the liberty that is consistent with justice, between man and man, and whose efforts, by the smiles of Providence, have hitherto been crowned with the most splendid success. After the treatment we have received, we have a right to be jealous, and to guard our present constitution with the strictest care. It is the right of the people to judge, and they will do wisely to give an explicit instruction to their delegates in the proposed convention, not to agree to any proposition that will in any degree militate with that happy system of government under which Heaven has placed them.

AGRIPPA

AGRIPPA, III

30 NOVEMBER 1787

To the People.

It has been proved from the clearest evidence, in two former papers, that a free government, I mean one in which the power frequently returns to the body of the people, is in principle the most stable and efficient of any kind; that such a government affords the most ready and effectual remedy for all injuries done to persons and the rights of property. . . . Let any man look round his own neighbourhood, and see if the people are not, with a very few exceptions, peaceable and attached to the government; if the country had ever within their knowledge more appearance of industry, improvement and tranquillity; if there was ever more of the produce of all kinds together for the market; if their stock does not rapidly increase; if there was ever a more ready vent for their surplus; and if the average of prices is not about as high as was usual in a plentiful year before the war. These circumstances all denote a general prosperity. Some classes of citizens indeed suffer greatly. Two descriptions I at present recollect. The publick creditors form the first of these classes, and they ought to, and will be provided for.

. . . The embarrassments consequent upon a war, and the usual reduction of prices immediately after a war, necessarily occasioned a want of punctuality in publick payments. Still, however, the publick debt has been very considerably reduced, not by the dirty and delusive scheme of depreciation, but the nominal sum. Applications are continually making for purchases in our eastern and western lands. Great exertions are making for clearing off the arrears of outstanding taxes, so that the certificates for interest on the state debt have considerably increased in value. This is a certain indication of returning credit. Congress this year disposed of a large tract of their lands towards paying the principal of their debt. Pennsylvania has discharged the whole of their part of the continental debt. New York has nearly cleared its state debt, and has located a large part of their new lands towards paying the continental demands. Other states have made considerable payments. Every day from these considerations the publick ability and inclination to satisfy their creditors increases. . . . The prospect therefore of the publick creditors is brightening under the present system. If the new system should take effect without amendments, which however is hardly probable, the increase of expense will be death to the hopes of all creditors, both of the continental and of the state. With respect, however, to our publick delays of payment we have the precedent of the best established countries in Europe.

The other class of citizens to which I alluded was the ship-carpenters. All agree that their business is dull; but as nobody objects against a system of commercial regulations for the whole continent, that business may be relieved without subverting all the ancient foundations and laws which have the respect of the people. It is a very serious question whether giving to Congress the unlimited right to regulate trade would not injure them still further. It is evidently for the interest of the state to encourage our own trade as much as possible. But in a very large empire, as the whole states consolidated must be, there will always be a desire of the government to increase the trade of the capital, and to weaken the extremes. We should in that case be one of the extremes, and should feel all the impoverishment incident to that situation. Besides, a jealousy of our enterprising spirit, would always be an inducement to cramp our exertions. We must then be impoverished or we must rebel. The alternative is dreadful. . . . The same objections are made in all the states, that the civil government which they have adopted and which secures their rights will be subverted. All the defenders of this system undertake to prove that the rights of the states and of the citizens are kept safe. The opposers of it agree that they will receive the least burdensome system which shall defend those rights.

Both parties therefore found their arguments on the idea that these rights ought to be held sacred. With this disposition is it not in every man's mind better to recommit it to a new convention, or to Congress, which is a regular convention for the purpose, and to instruct our delegates to confine the system to the general purposes of the union, than the endeavour to force it through in its present form, and with so many opposers as it must have in every state on the continent? The case is not of such pressing necessity as some have represented. Europe is engaged, and we are tranquil. Never therefore was an happier time for deliberation. The supporters of the measure are by no means afraid of insurrections taking place, but they are afraid that the present government will prove superiour to their assaults.

AGRIPPA

AGRIPPA, IV

3 DECEMBER 1787

To the People.

Having considered some of the principal advantages of the happy form of government under which it is our peculiar good fortune to live, we find by experience, that it is the best calculated of any form hitherto invented, to secure to us the rights of our persons and of our property, and that the general circumstances of the people shew an advanced state of improvement never before known. We have found the shock given by the war, in a great measure obliterated, and the public debt contracted at that time to be considerably reduced in the nominal sum. The Congress lands are full adequate to the redemption of the principal of their debt, and are selling and populating very fast. The lands of this state, at the west, are, at the moderate price of eighteen pence an acre, worth near half a million pounds in our money. . . . Our resources are daily augmenting.

We find, then, that after the experience of near two centuries our separate governments are in full vigor. They discover, for all the purposes of internal regulation, every symptom of strength, and none of decay. The new system is, therefore, for such purposes, useless and burdensome.

. . . It is the opinion of the ablest writers on the subject, that no extensive empire can be governed upon republican principles, and that such a government will degenerate to a despotism, unless it be made up of a confederacy of smaller states, each having the full powers of internal regulation. This is precisely the principle which has hitherto preserved our freedom. No instance can be found of any free government of considerable extent which has been supported upon any other plan. . . .

The reason is obvious. In large states the same principles of legislation will not apply to all the parts. The inhabitants of warmer climates are more dissolute in their manners, and less industrious, than in colder countries. A degree of severity is, therefore, necessary with one which would cramp the spirit of the other. We accordingly find that the very great empires have always been despotick. They have indeed tried to remedy the inconveniences to which the people were exposed by local regulations; but these contrivances have never answered the end. The laws not being made by the people, who felt the inconveniences, did not suit their circumstances. . . . To promote the happiness of the people it is necessary that there should be local laws; and it is necessary that those laws should be made by the representatives of those who are immediately subject to the want of them. By endeavouring to suit both extremes, both are injured.

It is impossible for one code of laws to suit Georgia and Massachusetts. They must, therefore, legislate for themselves. Yet there is, I believe, not one point of legislation that is not surrendered in the proposed plan. . . . The idea of an uncompounded republick, on an average one thousand miles in length, and eight hundred in breadth, and containing six millions of white inhabitants all reduced to the same standard of morals, of habits, and of laws, is in itself an absurdity, and contrary to the whole experience of mankind. The attempt made by Great Britain to introduce such a system, struck us with horrour, and when it was proposed by some theorist that we should be represented in parliament, we uniformly declared that one legislature could not represent so many different interests for the purposes of legislation and taxation. This was the leading principle of the revolution, and makes an essential article in our creed. All that part, therefore, of the new system, which relates to the internal government of the states, ought at once to be rejected.

AGRIPPA

AGRIPPA, V

11 DECEMBER 1787

To the People.

*   *   *   *

Causes of all kinds, between citizens of different states, are to be tried before a continental court. This court is not bound to try it according to the local laws where the controversies happen; for in that case it may as well be tried in a state court. The rule which is to govern the new courts, must, therefore, be made by the court itself, or by its employers, the Congress. If by the former, the legislative and judicial departments will be blended; and if by the Congress, though these departments will be kept separate, still the power of legislation departs from the state in all those cases. The Congress, therefore, have the right to make rules for trying all kinds of questions relating to property between citizens of different states. The sixth article of the new constitution provides, that the continental laws shall be the supreme law of the land, and that all judges in the separate states shall be bound thereby, anything in the constitution or laws of any state to the contrary notwithstanding. All the state officers are also bound by oath to support this constitution. These provisions cannot be understood otherwise than as binding the state judges and other officers, to execute the continental laws in their own proper departments within the state. For all questions, other than those between citizens of the same state, are at once put within the jurisdiction of the continental courts. As no authority remains to the state judges, but to decide questions between citizens of the same state, and those judges are to be bound by the laws of Congress, it clearly follows, that all questions between citizens of the same state are to be decided by the general laws and not by the local ones.

Authority is also given to the continental courts, to try all causes between a state and its own citizens. A question of property between these parties rarely occurs. . . . The only case of the kind in which the state would probably be sued, would be upon the state notes. The endless confusion that would arise from making the estates of individuals answerable, must be obvious to every one.

There is another sense in which the clause relating to causes between the state and individuals is to be understood . . . . This is the whole branch of the law relating to criminal prosecutions. In all such cases, the state is plaintiff, and the person accused is defendant. The process, therefore, will be, for the attorney-general of the state to commence his suit before a continental court. Considering the state as a party, the cause must be tried in another, and all the expense of transporting witnesses incurred. The individual is to take his trial among strangers, friendless and unsupported, without its being known whether he is habitually a good or a bad man; and consequently with one essential circumstance wanting by which to determine whether the action was performed maliciously or accidentally. All these inconveniences are avoided by the present important restriction, that the cause shall be tried by a jury of the vicinity, and tried in the county where the offence was committed. But by the proposed *derangement,* I can call it by no softer name, a man must be ruined to prove his innocence. . . . [We] shall be subject to all the horrors of a divided sovereignty, not knowing whether to obey the Congress or the State. We shall find it impossible to please two masters. . . . Advantage will be taken of a popular commotion, and even the venerable forms of the state be done away, while the new system will be enforced in its utmost rigour by an army.—I am the more apprehensive of a standing army, on account of a clause in the new constitution which empowers Congress to keep one at all times; but this constitution is evidently such that it cannot stand any considerable time without an army. Upon this principle one is very wisely provided. Our present government knows of no such thing.

AGRIPPA

AGRIPPA, VIII

25 DECEMBER 1787

To the People.

It has been proved, by indisputable evidence, that power is not the grand principle of union among the parts of a very extensive empire; and that when this principle is pushed beyond the degree necessary for rendering justice between man and man, it debases the character of individuals, and renders them less secure in their persons and property. Civil liberty consists in the consciousness of that security, and is best guarded by political liberty, which is the share that every citizen has in the government. Accordingly all our accounts agree, that in those empires which are commonly called despotick, and which comprehend by far the greatest part of the world, the government is most fluctuating, and property least secure. In those countries insults are borne by the sovereign, which, if offered to one of our governours, would fill us with horrour, and we should think the government dissolving.

The common conclusion from this reasoning is an exceedingly unfair one, that we must then separate, and form distinct confederacies. This would be true if there was no principle to substitute in the room of power. Fortunately there is one. This is commerce. All the states have local advantages, and in a considerable degree separate interests. They are, therefore, in a situation to supply each other's wants. Carolina, for instance, is inhabited by planters, while the Massachusetts is more engaged in commerce and manufactures. Congress has the power of deciding their differences. The most friendly intercourse may therefore be established between them. A diversity of produce, wants and interests, produces commerce; and commerce, where there is a common, equal and moderate authority to preside, produces friendship.

The same principles apply to the connection with the new settlers in the west. Many supplies they want for which they must look to the older settlements, and the greatness of their crops enables them to make payments. Here, then, we have a bond of union which applies to all parts of the empire, and would continue to operate if the empire comprehended all America.

We are now, in the strictest sense of the terms, a federal republick. Each part has within its own limits the sovereignty over its citizens, while some of the general concerns are committed to Congress. The complaints of the deficiency of the Congressional powers are confined to two articles. They are not able to raise a revenue by taxation, and they have not a complete regulation of the intercourse between us and foreigners. For each of these complaints there is some foundation, but not enough to justify the clamour which has been raised. Congress, it is true, owes a debt which ought to be paid. A considerable part of it has been paid. . . . We can, without difficulty, pay as much annually as shall clear the interest of our state debt, and our share of the interest on the continental one. But if we surrender the impost, we shall still, by this new constitution, be held to pay our full proportion of the remaining debt, as if nothing had been done. The impost will not be considered as being paid by this state, but by the continent. The federalists, indeed, tell us that the state debts will all be incorporated with the continental debt, and all paid out of one fund. In this as in all other instances, they endeavour to support their scheme of consolidation by delusion. Not one word is said in the book in favour of such a scheme, and there is no reason to think it true. . . .

AGRIPPA

AGRIPPA, XII

11 JANUARY 1788

To THE MASSACHUSETTS CONVENTION.
Gentlemen,

✿   ✿   ✿   ✿

It is universally agreed that the object of every just government is to render the people happy, by securing their persons and possessions from wrong. To this end it is necessary that there should be local laws and institutions; for a people inhabiting various climates will unavoidably have local habits and different modes of life, and these must be consulted in making the laws. It is much easier to adapt the laws to the manners of the people, than to make manners conform to laws. The idle and dissolute inhabitants of the south require a different regimen from the sober and active people of the north. Hence, among other reasons, is derived the necessity of local governments, who may enact, repeal, or alter regulations as the circumstances of each part of the empire may require. . . . Many circumstances render us an essentially different people from the inhabitants of the southern states. The unequal distribution of property, the toleration of slavery, the ignorance and poverty of the lower classes, the softness of the climate and dissoluteness of manners, mark their character. Among us, the care that is taken of education, small and nearly equal estates, equality of rights, and the severity of the climate, renders the people active, industrious and sober. Attention to religion and good morals is a distinguishing trait in our character. It is plain, therefore, that we require for our regulation laws which will not suit the circumstances of our southern brethren, and that laws made for them would not apply to us. Unhappiness would be the uniform product of such laws; for no state can be happy when the laws contradict the general habits of the people, nor can any state retain its freedom while there is a power to make and enforce such laws. We may go further, and say, that it is impossible for any single legislature so fully to comprehend the circumstances of the different parts of a very extensive dominion as to make laws adapted to those circumstances.

Hence arises in most nations of extensive territory, the necessity of armies, to cure the defect of the laws. . . .

AGRIPPA

AGRIPPA, XIII

14 JANUARY 1788

TO THE MASSACHUSETTS CONVENTION.

Gentlemen,

The question then arises, what is the kind of government best adapted to the object of securing our persons and possessions from violence? I answer, a *Federal Republick*. By this kind of government each state reserves to itself the right of making and altering its laws for internal regulation, and the right of executing those laws without any external restraint, while the general concerns of the empire are committed to an assembly of delegates, each accountable to his own constituents. This is the happy form under which we live, and which seems to mark us out as a people chosen of God. No instance can be produced of any other kind of government so stable and energetick as the republican.

The objection drawn from the Greek and Roman states does not apply to the question. Republicanism appears there in its most disadvantageous form. Arts and domestic employments were generally committed to slaves, while war was almost the only business worthy of a citizen. Hence arose their internal dissensions. Still they exhibited proofs of legislative wisdom and judicial integrity hardly to be found among their monarchick neighbors. On the other hand we find Carthage cultivating commerce, and extending her dominions for the long space of seven centuries, during which term the internal tranquillity was never disturbed by her citizens. Her national power was so respectable, that for a long time it was doubtful whether Carthage or Rome should rule. . . . The present state of Europe, and the vigour and tranquillity of our own governments, after experiencing this form for a century and an half, are decided proofs in favour of those governments which encourage commerce. A comparison of our own country, first with Europe and then with the other parts of the world, will prove, beyond a doubt, that the greatest share of freedom is enjoyed by the citizens, so much more does commerce flourish. The reason is, that every citizen has an influence in making the laws, and thus they are conformed to the general interests of the state; but in every other kind of government they are frequently made in favour of a part of the community at the expense of the rest.

. . . There cannot, from the history of mankind, be produced an instance of rapid growth in extent, in numbers, in arts, and in trade, that will bear any comparison with our country. This is owing to what the friends of the new system, and the enemies of the revolution, for I take them to be nearly the same, would term *our extreme liberty*. Already, have our ships visited every part of the world, and brought us their commodities in greater perfection, and at a more moderate price, than we ever before experienced. The ships of other nations crowd to our ports, seeking an intercourse with us. All the estimates of every party make the balance of trade for the present year to be largely in our favour. Already have some very useful, and some elegant manufactures got established among us, so that our country every day is becoming independent in her resources. Two-thirds of the continental debt has been paid since the war, and we are in alliance with some of the most respectable powers of Europe. The western lands, won from Britain by the sword, are an ample fund for the principal of all our public debts; and every new sale excites that manly pride which is essential to national virtue. All this happiness arises from the freedom of our institutions and the limited nature of our government; a government that is respected from principles of affection, and obeyed with alacrity. . . .

❧　❧　❧　❧

AGRIPPA

AGRIPPA, XVII

20 JANUARY 1788

To the Massachusetts Convention.
　Gentlemen,

❧　❧　❧　❧

It has been shown in the course of this paper, that when people institute government, they of course delegate all rights not expressly reserved. . . .

Bills of rights, reserved by authority of the people, are, I believe, peculiar to America. A careful observance of the abuse practised in other countries has had its just effect by inducing our people to guard against them. We find the happiest consequences to flow from it. The separate governments know their powers, their objects, and operations. We are therefore not perpetually tormented with new experiments. For a single instance of abuse among us there are thousands in other countries. On the other hand, the people know their rights, and feel happy in the possession of their freedom, both civil and political. Active industry is the consequence of their security, and within one year the circumstances of the state and of individuals have improved to a degree never before known in this commonwealth. Though our bill of rights does not, perhaps, contain all the cases in which power might be safely reserved, yet it affords a protection to the persons and possessions of individuals not known in any foreign country. In some respects the power of government is a little too confined. In many other countries we find the people resisting their governours for exercising their power in an unaccustomed mode. But for want of a bill of rights the resistance is always, by the principles of their government, a rebellion which nothing but success can justify. In our constitution we have aimed at delegating the necessary powers of government and confining their operation to beneficial purposes. At present we appear to have come very near the truth. Let us therefore have wisdom and virtue enough to preserve it inviolate. . . . Let us not flatter ourselves that we shall always have good men to govern us. If we endeavour to be like other nations we shall have more bad men than good ones to exercise extensive powers. That circumstance alone will corrupt them. While they fancy themselves the viceregents of God, they will resemble him only in power, but will always depart from his wisdom and goodness.

AGRIPPA

AGRIPPA, XVIII

5 FEBRUARY 1788

TO THE MASSACHUSETTS CONVENTION.
Gentlemen,

    ✿   ✿   ✿   ✿

It is now generally understood that it is for the security of the people that the powers of the government should be lodged in different branches. By this means publick business will go on when they all agree, and stop when they disagree. The advantage of checks in government is thus manifested where the concurrence of different branches is necessary to the same act, but the advantage of a division of business is advantageous in other respects. As in every extensive empire, local laws are necessary to suit the different interests, no single legislature is adequate to the business. All human capacities are limited to a narrow space, and as no individual is capable of practising a great variety of trades, no single legislature is capable of managing all the variety of national and state concerns. Even if a legislature was capable of it, the business of the judicial department must, from the same cause, be slovenly done. Hence arises the necessity of a division of the business into national and local. Each department ought to have all the powers necessary for executing its own business, under such limitations as tend to secure us from any inequality in the operations of government. I know it is often asked against whom in a government by representation is a bill of rights to secure us? I answer, that such a government is indeed a government by ourselves; but as a just government protects all alike, it is necessary that the sober and industrious part of the community should be defended from the rapacity and violence of the vicious and idle. A bill of rights, therefore, ought to set forth the purposes for which the compact is made, and serves to secure the minority against the usurpation and tyranny of the majority. It is a just observation of his excellency, doctor Adams, in his learned defence of the American constitutions that unbridled passions produce the same effect, whether in a king, nobility, or a mob. The experience of all mankind has proved the prevalence of a disposition to use power wantonly. It is therefore as necessary to defend an individual against the majority in a republick as against the king in a monarchy. Our state constitution has wisely guarded this point. The present confederation has also done it.

I confess that I have yet seen no sufficient reason for not

amending the confederation, though I have weighed the argument with candour; I think it would be much easier to amend it than the new constitution. . . . Here the question is not so much what the amendments ought to be, as in what manner they shall be made; whether they shall be made as conditions of our accepting the constitution, or whether we shall first accept it, and then try to amend it. I can hardly conceive that it should seriously be made a question. If the first question, whether we will receive it as it stands, be negatived, as it undoubtedly ought to be, while the conviction remains that amendments are necessary; the next question will be, what amendments shall be made? Here permit an individual . . . to propose such articles as appear to him necessary for preserving the rights of the state. . . . If the new constitution means no more than the friends of it acknowledge, they certainly can have no objection to affixing a declaration in favor of the rights of states and of citizens, especially as a majority of the states have not yet voted upon it.

"Resolved, that the constitution lately proposed for the United States be received only upon the following conditions:

"1. Congress shall have no power to alter the time, place or manner of elections, nor any authority over elections, otherwise than by fining such state as shall neglect to send its representatives or senators, a sum not exceeding the expense of supporting its representatives or senators one year.

"2. Congress shall not have the power of regulating the intercourse between the states, nor to levy any direct tax on polls or estates, or any excise.

"3. Congress shall not have power to try causes between a state and citizens of another state, nor between citizens of different states; nor to make any laws relative to the transfer of property between those parties, nor any other matter which shall originate in the body of any state.

"4. It shall be left to every state to make and execute its own laws, except laws impairing contracts, which shall not be made at all.

"5. Congress shall not incorporate any trading companies, nor alienate the territory of any state. And no treaty, ordinance or law of the United States shall be valid for these purposes.

"6. Each state shall have the command of its own militia.

"7. No continental army shall come within the limits of any state, other than garrison to guard the publick stores, without the consent of such states in time of peace.

"8. The president shall be chosen annually and shall serve but one year, and shall be chosen successively from the different states, changing every year.

"9. The judicial department shall be confined to cases in which ambassadours are concerned, to cases depending upon treaties, to offences committed upon the high seas, to the capture of prizes, and to cases in which a foreigner residing in some foreign country shall be a party, and an American state or citizen shall be the other party, provided no suit shall be brought upon a state note.

"10. Every state may emit bills of credit without making them a tender, and may coin money, of silver, gold or copper, according to the continental standard.

"11. No powers shall be exercised by Congress or the president but such as are expressly given by this constitution and not excepted against by this declaration. And any officer of the United States offending against an individual state shall be held accountable to such state, as any other citizen would be.

"12. No officer of Congress shall be free from arrest for debt [but] by authority of the state in which the debt shall be due.

"13. Nothing in this constitution shall deprive a citizen of any state of the benefit of the bill of rights established by the constitution of the state in which he shall reside, and such bill of rights shall be considered as valid in any court of the United States where they shall be pleaded.

"14. In all those causes which are triable before the continental courts, the trial by jury shall be held sacred."

These at present appear to me the most important points to be guarded. I have mentioned a reservation of excise to the separate states, because it is necessary, that they should have some way to discharge their own debts, and because it is placing them in an humiliating & disgraceful situation to depute them to transact the business of international government without the means to carry it on. It is necessary also, as a check on the national government, for it has hardly been known that any government having the powers of war, peace, and revenue, has failed to engage in needless and wanton expense. A reservation of this kind is therefore necessary to preserve the importance of the state governments: without this the extremes of the empire will in a very short time sink into the same degradation and contempt with respect to the middle state as Ireland, Scotland, & Wales, are in with regard to England. All the men of genius and wealth will resort to the seat of government, that will be center of revenue, and of business, which the extremes will be drained to supply.

. . . For my own part, I am fully of opinion that it would be best to reject this plan, and pass an explicit resolve, defining the powers of Congress to regulate the intercourse between us and foreign nations, under such restrictions as shall render their regulations equal in all parts of the empire. . . .

❊   ❊   ❊   ❊

. . . In point of convenience, the confederation amended would be infinitely preferable to the proposed constitution. In amending the former, we know the powers granted, and are subject to no perplexity; but in reforming the latter, the business is excessively intricate, and great part of the checks on Congress are lost. . . .

AGRIPPA

ELBRIDGE GERRY(?)

☆☆

Observations by a Columbian Patriot

☆☆

1788

❋　　❋　　❋　　❋

All writers on government agree, and the feelings of the human mind witness the truth of these political axioms, that man is born free and possessed of certain unalienable rights—that government is instituted for the protection, safety and happiness of the people . . . . That the origin of all power is in the people, and that they have an incontestible right to check the creatures of their own creation, vested with certain powers to guard the life, liberty and property of the community: And if certain selected bodies of men, deputed on these principles, determine contrary to the wishes and expectations of their constituents, the people have an undoubted right to reject their decisions, to call

---

From Ford, Pamphlets, *pp. 6–17. Ford's indication of the pagination in the original pamphlet has been omitted. 1630 copies of this pamphlet were distributed to local anti-Federalist committees in New York. Rufus King in 1788 attributed authorship of the pamphlet to Gerry. This authorship was accepted by Ford and other historians, including S. E. Morison in his article on Gerry in the* Dictionary of American Biography. *However, Charles Warren, "Elbridge Gerry, James Warren, Mercy Warren and the Ratification of the Federal Constitution in Massachusetts,"* Proceedings, Massachusetts Historical Society, *LXIV (March 1931), 143–164, has presented evidence that Mercy Warren claimed the authorship. Cecelia M. Kenyon, ed.,* The Anti-Federalists *(1966), p. xlix, accepts Warren's claim.*

181

for a revision of their conduct, to depute others in their room, or if they think proper, to demand further time for deliberation on matters of the greatest moment . . . . [Some] are endeavouring by all the arts of insinuation, and influence, to betray the people of the United States, into an acceptance of a most complicated system of government; marked on the one side with the *dark, secret* and *profound intrigues,* of the statesman, long practised in the purlieus of despotism and on the other, with the ideal projects of *young ambition,* with its wings just expanded to soar to a summit, which imagination has painted in such gawdy colours as to intoxicate the *inexperienced votary,* and to send *him* rambling from State to State, to collect materials to construct the ladder of preferment.

. . . Some gentlemen, with laboured zeal, have spent much time in urging the necessity of government, from the embarrassments of trade—the want of respectability abroad and confidence of the public engagements at home:—These are obvious truths which no one denies; and there are few who do not unite in the general wish for the restoration of public faith, the revival of commerce, arts, agriculture, and industry, under a lenient, peaceable and energetick government: But the most sagacious advocates for the party have not by fair discusion, and rational argumentation, evinced the necessity of adopting this many headed monster; of such motley mixture, that its enemies cannot trace a feature of Democratick or Republican extract; nor have its friends the courage to denominate a Monarchy, an Aristocracy, or an Oligarchy, and the favoured bantling must have passed through the short period of its existence without a name, had not Mr. *Wilson,* in the fertility of his genius, suggested the happy epithet of a *Federal Republic.* . . . [The] fundamental principle of a free government is the equal representation of a free people——And I will *first* observe with a justly celebrated writer, "That the principal aim of society is to protect individuals in the absolute rights which were vested in them by the immediate laws of nature, but which could not be preserved in peace, without the mutual intercourse which is gained by the institution of friendly and social communities." . . .

2. There is no security in the profered system, either for the rights of conscience or the liberty of the Press: Despotism usually while it is gaining ground, will suffer men to think, say, or write what they please; but when once established, if it is thought necessary to subserve the purposes, of arbitrary power, the most unjust restrictions may take place in the first instance, and an *imprimator* on the Press in the next, may silence the complaints, and forbid the most decent remonstrances of an injured and oppressed people.

3. There are no well defined limits of the Judiciary Powers, they seem to be left as a boundless ocean, that has broken over the chart of the Supreme Lawgiver, *"thus far shalt thou go and no further"* . . . .

4. The Executive and the Legislative are so dangerously blended as to give just cause of alarm, and everything relative thereto, is couched in such ambiguous terms—in such vague and indefinite expression, as is a sufficient ground without any objection, for the reprobation of a system, that the authors dare not hazard to a clear investigation.

5. The abolition of trial by jury in civil causes.—This mode of trial the learned Judge Blackstone observes, "has been coeval with the first rudiments of civil government, that property, liberty and life, depend on maintaining in its legal force the constitutional trial by jury." . . .

6. Though it has been said by Mr. *Wilson* and many others, that a Standing-Army is necessary for the dignity and safety of America, yet freedom revolts at the idea, when the Divan, or the Despot, may draw out his dragoons to suppress the murmurs of a few, who may yet cherish those sublime principles which call forth the exertions, and lead to the best improvements of the human mind. . . .

7. Notwithstanding the delusory promise to guarantee a Republican form of government to every State in the Union—If the most discerning eye could discover any meaning at all in the engagement, there are no resources left for the support

of internal government, or the liquidation of the debts of the State. . . .

8. As the new Congress are empowered to determine their own salaries, the requisitions for this purpose may not be very moderate, and the drain for public moneys will probably rise past all calculation . . . .

9. There is no provision for a rotation, nor anything to prevent the perpetuity of office in the same hands for life; which by a little well timed bribery, will probably be done, to the exclusion of men of the best abilities from their share in the offices of government. . . .

10. The inhabitants of the United States, are liable to be draged from the vicinity of their own country, or state, to answer the litigious or unjust suit of an adversary, on the most distant borders of the Continent: in short the appelate jurisdiction of the Supreme Federal Court, includes an unwarrantable stretch of power over the liberty, life, and property of the subject, through the wide Continent of America.

11. One Representative to thirty thousand inhabitants is a very inadequate representation; and every man who is not lost to all sense of freedom to his country, must reprobate the idea of Congress altering by law, or on any pretence whatever, interfering with any regulations for time, places, and manner of choosing our own Representatives.

12. If the sovereignty of America is designed to be elective, the surcumscribing the votes to only ten electors in this State, and the same proportion in all the others, is nearly tantamount to the exclusion of the voice of the people in the choice of their first magistrate. . . .

13. A Senate chosen for six years will, in most instances, be an appointment for life, as the influence of such a body over the minds of the people will be coequal to the extensive powers with which they are vested, and they will not only forget, but be forgotten by their constituents—a branch of the Supreme Legislature thus set beyond all responsibility is totally repugnant to every principle of a free government.

14. There is no provision by a bill of rights to guard against the dangerous encroachments of power in too many instances to be named . . . . The rights of individuals ought to be the primary object of all government, and cannot be too securely guarded by the most explicit declarations in their favor. This has been the opinion of the Hampdens, the Pyms, and many other illustrious names, that have stood forth in defence of English liberties; and even the Italian master in politicks, the subtle and renouned Machiavel acknowledges, that no republic ever yet stood on a stable foundation without satisfying the common people.

15. The difficulty, if not impracticability, of exercising the equal and equitable powers of government by a single legislature over an extent of territory that reaches from the Mississippi to the Western lakes, and from them to the Atlantic Ocean, is an insuperable objection to the adoption of the new system. . . .

16. . . . [Not] one legislature in the United States had the most distant idea when they first appointed members for a convention, entirely commercial, or when they afterwards authorized them to consider on some amendments of the Federal union, that they would without any warrant from their constituents, presume on so bold and daring a stride, as ultimately to destroy the state governments, and offer a *consolidated system* . . . .

17. The first appearance of the article which declares the ratification of nine states sufficient for the establishment of the new system, wears the face of dissension, is a subversion of the union of Confederated States, and tends to the introduction of anarchy and civil convulsions, and may be a means of involving the whole country in blood.

18. The mode in which this constitution is recommended to the people to judge without either the advice of Congress, or the legislatures of the several states is very reprehensible—it is an attempt to force it upon them before it could be thoroughly understood . . . .

. . . [When] we contemplate the nature of men and consider them originally on an equal footing, subject to the same feelings, stimulated by the same passions, and recollecting the struggles they have recently made, for the security of their civil rights; it cannot be expected that the inhabitants of the Massachusetts, can be easily lulled into a fatal security, by the declamatory effusions of gentlemen, who, contrary to the experience of all ages would perswade them there is no danger to be apprehended, from vesting discretionary powers in the hands of man, which he may, or may not abuse. The very suggestion, that we ought to trust to the precarious hope of amendments and redress, after we have voluntarily fixed the shackles on our own necks should have awakened to a double degree of caution. . . .

. . . And the people at large are already sensible, that the liberties which America has claimed, which reason has justified, and which have been so gloriously defended by the swords of the brave; are not about to fall before the tyranny of foreign conquest: it is native usurpation that is shaking the foundations of peace, and spreading the sable curtain of despotism over the United States. . . .

Passion, prejudice, and error, are characteristics of human nature; and as it cannot be accounted for on any principles of philosophy, religion, or good policy; to these shades in the human character must be attributed the mad zeal of some, to precipitate to a blind adoption of the measures of the late federal convention, without giving opportunity for better information to those who are misled by influence or ignorance into erroneous opinions.——Litterary talents may be prostituted, and the powers of genius debased to subserve the purposes of ambition or avarice; but the feelings of the heart will dictate the language of truth, and the simplicity of her accents will proclaim the infamy of those, who betray the rights of the people, under the specious, and popular pretence of *justice, consolidation,* and *dignity.*

❋   ❋   ❋   ❋

GEORGE CLINTON

****

Letters of Cato

****

CATO, II

11 OCTOBER 1787

To the Citizens of the State of New York:

❋   ❋   ❋   ❋

. . . The states in Congress suggested, that the articles of confederation had provided for making alterations in the confederation—that there were defects therein, and as a means to remedy which, a Convention of delegates, appointed by the different states, was resolved expedient to be held for the sole and express purpose of revising it, and reporting to Congress and the different legislatures such alterations and provisions therein as should (when agreed to in Congress and confirmed by the several states) render the federal constitution adequate to the exigencies of government. . . . For the sole and express purpose aforesaid a Convention of delegates is formed at Philadelphia: what have they done? Have they revised the confederation, and has Congress agreed to their report?—neither is the

---

From Ford, Essays: *Cato, II, pp. 250, 252–254 (footnote omitted); Cato, III, pp. 255–258; Cato, IV, pp. 260, 261–264; Cato, V, pp. 265, 267–269; Cato, VI, pp. 270–274.*

187

fact. This Convention have exceeded the authority given to them, and have transmitted to Congress a new political fabric, essentially and fundamentally distinct and different from it, in which the different states do not retain separately their sovereignty and independency, united by a confederate league— but one entire sovereignty, a consolidation of them into one government—in which new provisions and powers are not made and vested in Congress, but in an assembly, senate, and president, who are not known in the articles of confederation. Congress, without agreeing to, or approving of, this system *proffered* by the Convention, have sent it to the different legislatures, not for their confirmation, but to submit it to the people; not in conformity to their own resolution, but in conformity to the resolution of the Convention made and provided in that case. Was it, then, from the face of the foregoing facts, the intention of Congress, and of this and the other states, that the essence of our present national government should be annihilated, or that it should be retained and only have an increase of substantial necessary powers? Congress, sensible of this latter principle, and that the Convention had taken on themselves a power which neither they nor the other states had a right to delegate to them, and that they could not agree to and approve of this consolidated system, nor the states confirm it—have been silent on its character; and although many have dwelt on their unanimity, it is no less than the unanimity of opinion that it originated in an assumption of power, which your voice alone can sanctify. This new government, therefore, founded in usurpation, is referred to your opinion as the origin of power not heretofore delegated, and, to this end, the exercise of the prerogative of free examination is essentially necessary; and yet you are unhesitatingly to acquiesce, and if you do not, the American Fabius, if we may believe Cæsar is to command an army to impose it. . . .

CATO

CATO, III

25 OCTOBER 1787

To the Citizens of the State of New York:

❋ ❋ ❋ ❋

The freedom, equality and independence which you enjoyed by nature, induced you to consent to a political power. The same principles led you to examine the errors and vices of a British superintendence, to divest yourselves of it, and to reassume a new political shape. It is acknowledged that there are defects in this, and another is tendered to you for acceptance; the great question then, that arises on this new political principle, is, whether it will answer the ends for which it is said to be offered to you, and for which all men engage in political society, to wit, the preservation of their lives, liberties, and estates.

The recital, or premises on which the new form of government is erected, declares a consolidation or union of all the thirteen parts, or states, into one great whole, under the firm of the United States, for all the various and important purposes therein set forth. But whoever seriously considers the immense extent of territory comprehended within the limits of the United States, together with the variety of its climates, productions, and commerce, the difference of extent, and number of inhabitants in all; the dissimilitude of interest, morals, and politics, in almost every one, will receive it as an intuitive truth, that a consolidated republican form of government therein, can never *form a perfect union, establish justice, insure domestic tranquility, promote the general welfare, and secure the blessings of liberty to you and your posterity,* for to these objects it must be directed: this unkindred legislature therefore, composed of interests opposite and dissimilar in their nature, will in its exercise, emphatically be like a house divided against itself.

The governments of Europe have taken their limits and form from adventitious circumstances, and nothing can be argued on the motive of agreement from them; but these adventitious political principles, have nevertheless produced effects that have attracted the attention of philosophy, which have established axioms in the science of politics therefrom, as irrefragable as any in Euclid. It is natural, says Montesquieu, *to a republic to have only a small territory, otherwise it cannot long subsist: in a large one, there are men of large fortunes, and consequently of less moderation; there are too great deposits to trust in the hands of a single subject; an ambitious person soon becomes sensible that he may be happy, great, and glorious by oppressing his fellow citizens, and that he might raise himself to grandeur, on the ruins of his country. In large republics, the public good is sacrificed to a thousand views; in a small one, the interest of the public is easily perceived, better understood, and more within the reach of every citizen; abuses have a less extent, and of course are less protected*—he also shows you, that the duration of the republic of Sparta was owing to its having continued with the same extent of territory after all its wars; and that the ambition of Athens and Lacedemon to command and direct the union, lost them their liberties, and gave them a monarchy.

From this picture, what can you promise yourselves, on the score of consolidation of the United States into one government? Impracticability in the just exercise of it, your freedom insecure, even this form of government limited in its continuance, the employments of your country disposed of to the opulent, . . . you must risk much, by indispensably placing trusts of the greatest magnitude, into the hands of individuals whose ambition for power, and aggrandizement, will oppress and grind you—where from the vast extent of your territory, and the complication of interests, the science of government will become intricate and perplexed, and too mysterious for you to understand and observe; and by which you are to be conducted into a monarchy, either limited or despotic; the latter, Mr. Locke remarks, *is a government derived from neither nature nor compact.*

Political liberty, the great Montesquieu again observes, *consists in security, or at least in the opinion we have of security;* and this *security,* therefore, or the *opinion,* is best obtained in moderate governments, where the mildness of the laws, and the equality of the manners, beget a confidence in the people, which produces this security, or the opinion. This moderation in governments depends in a great measure on their limits, connected with their political distribution.

The extent of many of the states of the Union, is at this time almost too great for the superintendence of a republican form of government, and must one day or other revolve into more vigorous ones, or by separation be reduced into smaller and more useful, as well as moderate ones. You have already observed the feeble efforts of Massachusetts against their insurgents; with what difficulty did they quell that insurrection; and is not the province of Maine at this moment on the eve of separation from her? The reason of these things is, that for the security of the *property* of the community, in which expressive term Mr. Locke makes life, liberty, and estate, to consist—the wheels of a republic are necessarily slow in their operation; hence in large free republics, the evil sometimes is not only begun, but almost completed, before they are in a situation to turn the current into a contrary progression: the extremes are also too remote from the usual seat of government, and the laws, therefore, too feeble to afford protection to all its parts, and insure *domestic tranquility* without the aid of another principle. If, therefore, this state, and that of North Carolina, had an army under their control, they never would have lost Vermont, and Frankland, nor the state of Massachusetts suffer an insurrection, or the dismemberment of her fairest district, but the exercise of a principle which would have prevented these things, if we may believe the experience of ages, would have ended in the destruction of their liberties.

Will this consolidated republic, if established, in its exercise beget such confidence and compliance, among the citizens of these states, as to do without the aid of a standing army? I deny that it will. The malcontents in each state, who will not be a few, nor the least important, will be exciting factions against it—the fear of a dismemberment of some of its parts, and the necessity to enforce the execution of revenue laws (a fruitful source of oppression) on the extremes and in the other districts of the government, will incidentally and necessarily require a permanent force, to be kept on foot: will not political security, and even the opinion of it, be extinguished? Can mildness and moderation exist in a government where the primary incident in its exercise must be force? Will not violence destroy confidence, and can equality subsist where the extent, policy, and practice of it will naturally lead to make odious distinctions among citizens?

The people who may compose this national legislature from the southern states, in which, from the mildness of the climate, the fertility of the soil, and the value of its productions, wealth is rapidly acquired, and where the same causes naturally lead to luxury, dissipation, and a passion for aristocratic distinction; where slavery is encouraged, and liberty of course less respected and protected; who know not what it is to acquire property by their own toil, nor to economize with the savings of industry— will these men, therefore, be as tenacious of the liberties and interests of the more northern states, where freedom, independence, industry, equality and frugality are natural to the climate and soil, as men who are your own citizens, legislating in your own state, under your inspection, and whose manners and fortunes bear a more equal resemblance to your own?

❖   ❖   ❖   ❖

CATO

CATO, IV

8 NOVEMBER 1787

To the Citizens of the State of New York:

❊   ❊   ❊   ❊

It is remarked by Montesquieu, in treating of republics, that *in all magistracies, the greatness of the power must be compensated by the brevity of the duration, and that a longer time than a year would be dangerous.* It is, therefore, obvious to the least intelligent mind to account why great power in the hands of a magistrate, and that power connected with considerable duration, may be dangerous to the liberties of a republic, the deposit of vast trusts in the hands of a single magistrate, enables him in their exercise to create a numerous train of dependents; this tempts his *ambition,* which in a republican magistrate is also remarked, *to be pernicious,* and the duration of his office for any considerable time favors his views, gives him the means and time to perfect and execute his designs, *he therefore fancies that he may be great and glorious by oppressing his fellow-citizens, and raising himself to permanent grandeur on the ruins of his country.* And here it may be necessary to compare the vast and important powers of the president, together with his continuance in office, with the foregoing doctrine—his eminent magisterial situation will attach many adherents to him, and he will be surrounded by expectants and courtiers, his power of nomination and influence on all appointments, the strong posts in each state comprised within his superintendence, and garrisoned by troops under his direction, his control over the army, militia, and navy, the unrestrained power of granting pardons for treason, which may be used to screen from punishment those whom he had secretly instigated to commit the crime, and thereby prevent a discovery of his own guilt, his duration in office for four years: these, and various other principles evidently prove the truth of the position, that if the president is possessed of ambition, he has power and time sufficient to ruin his country.

Though the president, during the sitting of the legislature, is assisted by the senate, yet he is without a constitutional council in their recess; he will therefore be unsupported by proper information and advice, and will generally be directed by minions and favorites, or a council of state will grow out of the principal officers of the great departments, the most dangerous council in a free country.

The ten miles square, which is to become the seat of government, will of course be the place of residence for the president and the great officers of state; the same observations of a great man will apply to the court of a president possessing the powers of a monarch, that is observed of that of a monarch—*ambition with idleness—baseness with pride—the thirst of riches without labor—aversion to truth—flattery—treason—perfidy—violation of engagements—contempt of civil duties—hope from the magistrate's weakness; but above all, the perpetual ridicule of virtue—* these, he remarks, are the characteristics by which the courts in all ages have been distinguished.

*　　*　　*　　*

The establishment of a vice-president is as unnecessary as it is dangerous. This officer, for want of other employment, is made president of the senate, thereby blending the executive and legislative powers, besides always giving to some one state, from which he is to come, an unjust pre-eminence.

It is a maxim in republics that the representative of the people should be of their immediate choice; but by the manner in which the president is chosen, he arrives to this office at the fourth or fifth hand, nor does the highest vote, in the way he is elected, determine the choice, for it is only necessary that he should be taken from the highest of five, who may have a plurality of votes.

. . . Every American Whig, not long since, bore his emphatic testimony against a monarchical government, though limited, because of the dangerous inequality that it created among citizens as relative to their rights and property; and wherein does this president invested with his powers and prerogatives, essentially differ from the king of Great Britain (save as to name, the creation of nobility, and some immaterial incidents, the offspring of absurdity and locality). The direct prerogatives of the president, as springing from his political character, are among the following: It is necessary, in order to distinguish him from the rest of the community, and enable him to keep, and maintain his court, that . . . his revenue, should be such as to enable him to appear with the splendor of a prince; he has the power of receiving ambassadors from, and a great influence on their appointments to foreign courts; as also to make treaties, leagues, and alliances with foreign states, assisted by the Senate, which when made become the supreme law of land: he is a constituent part of the legislative power, for every bill which shall pass the House of Representatives and Senate is to be presented to him for approbation . . . ; he will have a great share in the power of making peace, coining money, etc., and all the various objects of legislation, expressed or implied in this Constitution: for though it may be asserted that the king of Great Britain has the express power of making peace or war, yet he never thinks it prudent to do so without the advice of his Parliament, from whom he is to derive his support, and therefore these powers, in both president and king, are substantially the same: he is the generalissimo of the nation, and of course has the command and control of the army, navy and militia; he is the general conservator of the peace of the union—he may pardon all offences, except in cases of impeachment, and the principal fountain of all offices and employments. Will not the exercise of these powers therefore tend either to the establishment of a vile and arbitrary aristocracy or monarchy? The safety of the people in a republic depends on the share or proportion they have in the government;

but experience ought to teach you, that when a man is at the head of an elective government invested with great powers, and interested in his re-election, in what circle appointments will be made; by which means an *imperfect aristocracy* bordering on monarchy may be established.

You must, however, my countrymen, beware that the advocates of this new system do not deceive you by a fallacious resemblance between it and your own state government which you so much prize; and, if you examine, you will perceive that the chief magistrate of this state is your immediate choice, controlled and checked by a just and full representation of the people, divested of the prerogative of influencing war and peace, making treaties, receiving and sending embassies, and commanding standing armies and navies, which belong to the power of the confederation, and will be convinced that this government is no more like a true picture of your own than an Angel of Darkness resembles an Angel of Light.

CATO

CATO, V

22 NOVEMBER 1787

To the Citizens of the State of New York.

❖   ❖   ❖   ❖

. . . [The] next thing to be considered . . . is the first article of this new government, which comprises the erection of the house of representatives and the senate, and prescribes their various powers and objects of legislation. The most general objections to the first article, that biennial elections for representatives are a departure from the safe democratic principles of annual ones—that the number of representatives are too few; that the apportionment and principles of increase are unjust; that no attention has been paid to either the numbers or property in each state in forming the senate; that the mode in which they are appointed and their duration will lead to the establishment of an aristocracy; that the senate and president are improperly connected, both as to appointments and the making of treaties, which are to become the supreme law of the land; that the judicial, in some measure, to wit, as to the trial of impeachments, is placed in the senate, a branch of the legislative, and sometimes a branch of the executive; that Congress have the improper power of making or altering the regulations prescribed by the different legislatures, respecting the time, place and manner of holding elections for representatives, and the time and manner of chosing senators; that standing armies may be established, and appropriation of money made for their support for two years; that the militia of the most remote state may be marched into those states situated at the opposite extreme of this continent; that the slave trade is, to all intents and purposes, permanently established, and a slavish capitation or poll-tax may at any time be levied; these are some of the many evils that will attend the adoption of this government.

But, with respect to the first objection, it may be remarked that a well-digested democracy has this advantage over all others, to wit: that it affords to many the opportunity to be advanced to the supreme command, and the honors they thereby enjoy fill them with a desire of rendering themselves worthy of them; hence this desire becomes part of their education, is matured in manhood, and produces an ardent affection for their country, and it is the opinion of the great Sidney and Montesquieu that this is, in a great measure, produced by annual election of magistrates.

If annual elections were to exist in this government, and learning and information to become more prevalent, you never would want men to execute whatever you could design. . . . [Sidney] remarks . . . that *it was also thought that free cities, by frequent election of magistrates, became nurseries of great and able men, every man endeavoring to excel others, that he might be advanced to the honor he had no other title to, than what might arise from his merit or reputation;* but the framers of this *perfect government,* as it is called, have departed from this democratical principle, and established biennial elections for the house of representatives, who are to be chosen by the people, and sextennial for the senate, who are to be chosen by the legislatures of the different states, and have given to the executive the unprecedented power of making temporary senators, in case of vacancies by resignation or otherwise, and so far forth establishing a precedent for virtual representation (though, in fact, their original appointment is virtual), thereby influencing the choice of the legislatures . . . ; this temporary member, during his time of appointment, will of course act by a power derived from the executive, and for, and under his immediate influence.

It is a very important objection to this government, that the representation consists of so few; too few to resist the influence of corruption, and the temptation to treachery, against which all governments ought to take precautions—how guarded you have been on this head, in your own state constitution, and yet the number of senators and representatives proposed for this vast continent does not equal those of your own state; how great the disparity, if you compare them with the aggregate numbers in the United States. . . . Another thing that may be suggested against the small number of representatives is, that but few of you will have a chance of sharing even in this branch of the legislature; and that the choice will be confined to a very few. The more complete it is, the better will your interests be preserved, and the greater the opportunity you will have to participate in government, one of the principal securities of a free people . . . .

CATO

CATO, VI

16 DECEMBER 1787

To the People of the State of New York.

The next objection that arises against this proffered constitution is, that the apportionment of representatives and direct taxes are unjust. The words, as expressed in this article, are "representatives and direct taxes shall be apportioned among the several states . . . according to their respective numbers, which shall be determined by adding to the whole number of free persons . . . three-fifths of all other persons." . . . [The] mode of legislation in the infancy of free communities was by the collective body, and this consisted of free persons, or those whose age admitted them to the right of mankind and citizenship, whose sex made them capable of protecting the state, and whose birth may be denominated Free Born . . . ; hence is derived this maxim in free governments, that representation ought to bear a proportion to the number of free inhabitants in a community; this principle your own state constitution, and others, have observed in the establishment of a future census, in order to apportion the representatives . . . . But, what aid can the community derive from the assistance of women, infants and slaves, in their deliberation, or in their defence? and what motives, therefore, could the convention have in departing from the just and rational principle of representation, which is the governing principle of this state and of all America?

The doctrine of taxation is a very important one, and nothing requires more wisdom and prudence than the regulation of that portion, which is taken from, and of that which is left to the subject—and if you anticipate what will be the enormous expense of this new government added also to your own, little will that portion be which will be left to you. I know there are politicians who believe that you should be loaded with taxes, in order to make you industrious, and, perhaps, there are some of this opinion in the convention, but it is an erroneous principle. For, what can inspire you with industry, if the greatest measure of your labors are to be swallowed up in taxes? . . . [For] this government to discharge all its incidental expenses, besides paying the interest on the home and foreign debts, will require more money than its commerce can afford; and . . . you will find, that if heavy duties are laid on merchandise, . . . the price of the commodities . . . must be increased; the consumers will be fewer; the merchants must import less; trade will languish, and this source of revenue in a great measure be dried up; but if you examine this a little further you will find that this revenue, managed in this way, will come out of you, and be a very heavy and ruinous one, at least. . . . Thus the laborer, mechanic, and farmer must feel it in the purchase of their utensils and clothing— wages, etc., must rise with the price of things or they must be ruined; and that must be the case with the farmer, whose produce will not increase, in the ratio, with labor, utensils and clothing; for that he must sell at the usual price or lower perhaps, caused by the decrease of trade; the consequence will be that he must mortgage his farm, and then comes inevitable bankruptcy.

*   *   *   *

In every civilized community, even in those of the most democratic kind, there are principles which lead to an aristocracy— these are superior talents, fortunes and public employments. But in free governments the influence of the two former is resisted by the equality of the laws, and the latter by the frequency of elections, and the chance that every one has in sharing in public business; but when this natural and artificial eminence is assisted by principles interwoven in this government; when the senate, so important a branch of the legislature, is so far removed from the people as to have little or no connection with them; when their duration in office is such as to have the resemblance to perpetuity; when they are connected with the executive, by the appointment of all officers, and also to become a judiciary for the trial of officers of their own appointments; added to all this, when none but men of opulence will hold a seat, what is there left to resist and repel this host of influence and power? Will the feeble efforts of the house of representatives, in whom your security ought to subsist, consisting of about seventy-three, be able to hold the balance against them, when, from the fewness of members in this house, the senate will have in their power to poison even a majority of that body by douceurs of office for themselves or friends? From causes like this both Montesquieu and Hume have predicted the decline of the British government into that of an absolute one; but the liberties of this country, it is probable, if this system is adopted, will be strangled in their birth; for whenever the executive and senate can destroy the independence of the majority in the house of representatives, then where is your security? . . . But you are told to adopt this government first, and you will always be able to alter it afterwards; this would first be submitting to be slaves and then taking care of your liberty; and when your chains are on, then to act like freemen.

✽　　✿　　✿　　✿

CATO

RICHARD HENRY LEE

Letters of the Federal Farmer

LETTER II

9 OCTOBER 1787

Dear Sir,

The essential parts of a free and good government are a full and equal representation of the people in the legislature, and the jury trial of the vicinage in the administration of justice—a full and equal representation, is that which possesses the same interests, feelings, opinions, and views the people themselves would were they all assembled—a fair representation, therefore, should be so regulated, that every order of men in the community, according to the common course of elections, can have a share in it—in order to allow professional men, merchants, traders, farmers, mechanics, &c. to bring a just proportion of their best informed men respectively into the legislature, the representation must be considerably numerous—We have about 200 state senators in the United States, and a less number than that of federal representatives cannot, clearly, be a full representation of this people, in the affairs of internal taxation and police, were there but one legislature for the whole union. The representation

---

From Ford, Pamphlets: *Letter II, pp. 288–293; Letter III, pp. 294, 295–299. Ford's indication of the pagination in the original pamphlet has been omitted.*

cannot be equal, or the situation of the people proper for one government only—if the extreme parts of the society cannot be represented as fully as the central—It is apparently impracticable that this should be the case in this extensive country——it would be impossible to collect a representation of the parts of the country five, six, and seven hundred miles from the seat of government.

Under one general government alone, there could be but one judiciary, one supreme and a proper number of inferior courts. I think it would be totally impracticable in this case to preserve a due administration of justice, and the real benefits of the jury trial of the vicinage——there are now supreme courts in each state in the union, and a great number of county and other courts subordinate to each supreme court——most of these supreme and inferior courts are itinerant, and hold their sessions in different parts every year of their respective states, counties and districts —with all these moving courts, our citizens, from the vast extent of the country, must travel very considerable distances from home to find the place where justice is administered. . . .

If it were possible to consolidate the states, and preserve the features of a free government, still it is evident that the middle states, the parts of the union, about the seat of government, would enjoy great advantages, while the remote states would experience the many inconveniences of remote provinces. Wealth, offices, and the benefits of government would collect in the centre: and the extreme states; and their principal towns, become much less important.

There are other considerations which tend to prove that the idea of one consolidated whole, on free principles, is ill-founded ——the laws of a free government rest on the confidence of the people, and operate gently—and never can extend the influence very far——if they are executed on free principles, about the centre, where the benefits of the government induce the people to support it voluntarily; yet they must be executed on the principles of fear and force in the extremes——This has been the case with every extensive republic of which we have any accurate account.

There are certain unalienable and fundamental rights, which in forming the social compact, ought to be explicitly ascertained and fixed—a free and enlightened people, in forming this compact, will not resign all their rights to those who govern, and they will fix limits to their legislators and rulers . . . . These rights should be made the basis of every constitution; and if a people be so situated, or have such different opinions that they cannot agree in ascertaining and fixing them, it is a very strong argument against their attempting to form one entire society, to live under one system of laws only.——I confess, I never thought the people of these states differed essentially in these respects; they having derived all these rights from one common source, the British systems; and having in the formation of their state constitutions, discovered that their ideas relative to these rights are very similar. However, it is now said that the states differ so essentially in these respects, and even in the important article of the trial by jury, that when assembled in convention, they can agree to no words by which to establish that trial . . . . If so, we proceed to consolidate the states on no solid basis whatever.

But I do not pay much regard to the reasons given for not bottoming the new constitution on a better bill of rights. I still believe a complete federal bill of rights to be very practicable. . . .

In examining the proposed constitution carefully, we must clearly perceive an unnatural separation of these powers from the substantial representation of the people. The state governments will exist, with all their governors, senators, representatives, officers and expences; in these will be nineteen twentieths of the representatives of the people; they will have a near connection, and their members an immediate intercourse with the people; and the probability is, that the state governments will possess the confidence of the people, and be considered generally as their immediate guardians.

The general government will consist of a new species of executive, a small senate, and a very small house of representatives. As many citizens will be more than three hundred miles from the seat of this government as will be nearer to it, its judges and officers cannot be very numerous, without making our governments very expensive. Thus will stand the state and the general governments, should the constitution be adopted without any alterations in their organization; but as to powers, the general government will possess all essential ones, at least on paper, and those of the states a mere shadow of power. And therefore, unless the people shall make some great exertions to restore to the state governments their powers in matters of internal police; as the powers to lay and collect, exclusively, internal taxes, to govern the militia, and to hold the decisions of their own judicial courts upon their own laws final, the balance cannot possibly continue long; but the state governments must be annihilated, or continue to exist for no purpose.

. . . The powers lodged in the general government, if exercised by it, must intimately effect the internal police of the states, as well as external concerns; and there is no reason to expect the numerous state governments, and their connections, will be very friendly to the execution of federal laws in those internal affairs, which hitherto have been under their own immediate management. There is more reason to believe, that the general government, far removed from the people, and none of its members elected oftener than once in two years, will be forgot or neglected, and its laws in many cases disregarded, unless a multitude of officers and military force be continually kept in view, and employed to enforce the execution of the laws, and to make the government feared and respected. . . . Neglected laws must first lead to anarchy and confusion; and a military execution of laws is only a shorter way to the same point— despotic government.

Your's, &c.

THE FEDERAL FARMER

LETTER III

10 OCTOBER 1787

Dear Sir,

*   *   *   *

First. As to the organization——the house of representatives, the democrative branch, as it is called, is to consist of 65 members: that is, about one representative for fifty thousand inhabitants, to be chosen biennially . . . . I have no idea that the interests, feelings, and opinions of three or four millions of people, especially touching internal taxation, can be collected in such a house.——In the nature of things, nine times in ten, men of the elevated classes in the community only can be chosen—— Connecticut, for instance, will have five representatives——not one man in a hundred of those who form the democrative branch in the state legislature, will, on a fair computation, be one of the five.—The people of this country, in one sense, may all be democratic; but if we make the proper distinction between the few men of wealth and abilities, and consider them, as we ought, as the natural aristocracy of the country, and the great body of the people, the middle and lower classes, as the democracy, this federal representative branch will have but very little democracy in it . . . .

In considering the practicability of having a full and equal representation of the people from all parts of the union, not only distances and different opinions, customs and views, common in extensive tracts of country, are to be taken into view, but many differences peculiar to Eastern, Middle, and Southern States. . . . The Eastern states are very democratic, and composed chiefly of moderate freeholders; they have but few rich men and no slaves; the Southern states are composed chiefly of rich planters and slaves; they have but few moderate freeholders, and the prevailing influence, in them is generally a dissipated aristocracy: The Middle states partake partly of the Eastern and partly of the Southern character.

＊ ＊ ＊ ＊

The house of representatives is on the plan of consolidation, but the senate is entirely on the federal plan; and Delaware will have as much constitutional influence in the senate, as the largest state in the union . . . . I suppose it was impracticable for the three large states, as they were called, to get the senate formed on any other principles: But this only proves, that we cannot form one general government on equal and just principles—and proves, that we ought not to lodge in it such extensive powers before we are convinced of the practicability of organizing it on just and equal principles. . . .

. . . [When] we examine the powers of the president, and the forms of the executive, we shall perceive that the general government, in this part, will have a strong tendency to aristocracy, or the government of the few. . . .

. . . The plan does not present a well balanced government: The senatorial branch of the legislative and the executive are substantially united, and the president, or the state executive magistrate, may aid the senatorial interest when weakest, but never can effectually support the democratic, however it may be opposed . . . .

＊ ＊ ＊ ＊

Your's, &c.

THE FEDERAL FARMER

GEORGE MASON, PATRICK HENRY,

AND

JAMES MONROE

☆☆

In the Ratifying Convention of Virginia

☆☆

4–12 JUNE 1788

Mr. GEORGE MASON. Mr. Chairman, whether the Constitution be good or bad, the present clause clearly discovers that it is a national government, and no longer a Confederation. I mean that clause which gives the first hint of the general government laying direct taxes. The assumption of this power of laying direct taxes does, of itself, entirely change the confederation of the states into one consolidated government. This power, being at discretion, unconfined, and without any kind of control, must carry every thing before it. The very idea of converting what was formerly a confederation to a consolidated government, is totally subversive of every principle which has hitherto governed us. This power is calculated to annihilate totally the state governments. Will the people of this great community submit to be individually taxed by two different and distinct powers? Will they suffer themselves to be doubly harassed? These two concurrent powers cannot exist long together; the one will destroy the other: the general government being paramount to, and in every respect more powerful than

---

From Elliot, III: Mason's remarks, pp. 29–34; Henry's remarks, pp. 44–54, 56–61, 63, 315–318, 324–327; Monroe's remarks, pp. 207–209, 211–212, 214, 216–222.

the state governments, the latter must give way to the former. Is it to be supposed that one national government will suit so extensive a country, embracing so many climates, and containing inhabitants so very different in manners, habits, and customs? It is ascertained, by history, that there never was a government over a very extensive country without destroying the liberties of the people: history also, supported by the opinions of the best writers, shows us that monarchy may suit a large territory, and despotic governments ever so extensive a country, but that popular governments can only exist in small territories. Is there a single example, on the face of the earth, to support a contrary opinion? Where is there one exception to this general rule? Was there ever an instance of a general national government extending over so extensive a country, abounding in such a variety of climates, &c., where the people retained their liberty? I solemnly declare that no man is a greater friend to a firm union of the American states than I am; but, sir, if this great end can be obtained without hazarding the rights of the people, why should we recur to such dangerous principles? . . . It is not well known that what would be a proper tax in one state would be grievous in another? . . . Sixty-five members cannot possibly know the situation and circumstances of all the inhabitants of this immense continent. When a certain sum comes to be taxed, and the mode of levying to be fixed, they will lay the tax on that article which will be most productive and easiest in the collection, without consulting the real circumstances or convenience of a country, with which, in fact, they cannot be sufficiently acquainted.

The mode of levying taxes is of the utmost consequence; and yet here it is to be determined by those who have neither knowledge of our situation, nor a common interest with us, nor a fellow-feeling for us. The subject of taxation differs in three fourths, nay, I might say with truth, in four fifths of the states. If we trust the national government with an effectual way of raising the necessary sums, it is sufficient: every thing we do further is trusting the happiness and rights of the people. Why, then, should we give up this dangerous power of individual taxation? . . . If, instead of giving this oppressive power, we give them such an effectual alternative as will answer the purpose, without encountering the evil and danger that might arise from it, then I would cheerfully acquiesce . . . . I candidly acknowledge the inefficacy of the Confederation; but requisitions have been made which were impossible to be complied with— requisitions for more gold and silver than were in the United States. If we give the general government the power of demanding their quotas of the states, with an alternative of laying direct taxes in case of non-compliance, then the mischief would be avoided; and the certainty of this conditional power would, in all human probability, prevent the application, and the sums necessary for the Union would be then laid by the states, by those who know how it can best be raised, by those who have a fellow-feeling for us. . . . Why, then, not leave this power to be exercised by those who know the mode most convenient for the inhabitants, and not by those who must necessarily apportion it in such manner as shall be oppressive? With respect to the representation so much applauded, I cannot think it such a full and free one as it is represented; but I must candidly acknowledge that this defect results from the very nature of the government. It would be impossible to have a full and adequate representation in the general government; it would be too expensive and too unwieldy. We are, then, under the necessity of having this a very inadequate representation. Is this general representation to be compared with the real, actual, substantial representation of the state legislatures? It cannot bear a comparison. To make representation real and actual, the number of representatives ought to be adequate; they ought to mix with the people, think as they think, feel as they feel,—ought to be perfectly amenable to them, and thoroughly acquainted with their interest and condition. Now, these great ingredients are either not at all, or in a small degree, to be found in our federal representatives; so that we have no real, actual, substantial representation: but I acknowledge it results from the nature of the government. . . . To a government which, in the nature of things, cannot but be defective, no powers ought to be given but such as are absolutely necessary. There is one thing in it which I conceive to be extremely dangerous. Gentlemen may talk of public virtue and confidence; we shall be told that the House of Representatives will consist of the most virtuous men on the continent, and that in their hands we may trust our dearest rights. This, like all other assemblies, will be composed of some bad and some good men; and, considering the natural lust of power so inherent in man, I fear the thirst of power will prevail to oppress the people. What I conceive to be so dangerous, is the provision with respect to the number of representatives: it does not expressly provide that we shall have one for every thirty thousand, but that the number shall not exceed that proportion. The utmost that we can expect . . . is, that the present number shall be continued to us . . . . Now, will not this be complied with, although it should be decreased? Suppose Congress should say that we should have one for every forty thousand; will not the Constitution be complied with? . . . The worthy gentleman tells us that we have no reason to fear; but I always fear for the rights of the people. I do not pretend to inspiration; but I think it is apparent as the day, that the members will attend to local, partial interests, to prevent an augmentation of their number. I know not how they will be chosen, but, whatever be the mode of choosing, our present number will be ten; and suppose our state is laid off in ten districts,—those gentlemen who shall be sent from those districts will lessen their own power and influence in their respective districts if they increase their number; for the greater the number of men among whom any given quantum of power is divided, the less the power of each individual. Thus they will have a local interest to prevent the increase of, and perhaps they will lessen their own number. . . . Nay, they may reduce the number from sixty-five to one from each state, without violating the Constitution; and thus the number, which is now too small, would then be infinitely too much so. But my principal objection is, that the Confederation is converted to one general consolidated government, which . . . is one of the worst curses that can possibly befall a nation. Does any man suppose that one general national government can exist in so extensive a country as this? I hope that a government may be framed which may suit us, by drawing a line between the general and state governments, and prevent that dangerous clashing of interest and power, which must, as it now stands, terminate in the destruction of one or the other. When we come to the judiciary, we shall be more convinced that this government will terminate in the annihilation of the state governments: the question then will be, whether a consolidated government can preserve the freedom and secure the rights of the people.

If such amendments be introduced as shall exclude danger, I shall most gladly put my hand to it. When such amendments as shall, from the best information, secure the great essential rights of the people, shall be agreed to by gentlemen, I shall most heartily make the greatest concessions, and concur in any reasonable measure to obtain the desirable end of conciliation and unanimity. An indispensable amendment in this case is, that Congress shall not exercise the power of raising direct taxes till the states shall have refused to comply with the requisitions of Congress. . . . Should this power be restrained, I shall withdraw my objections to this part of the Constitution; but as it stands, it is an objection so strong in my mind, that its amendment is with me a *sine qua non* of its adoption. . . .

Mr. HENRY. . . . Have they said, We, the states? Have they made a proposal of a compact between states? If they had, this would be a confederation. It is otherwise most clearly a consolidated government. The question turns, sir, on that poor little thing—the expression, We, the *people,* instead of the *states,* of

America. I need not take much pains to show that the principles of this system are extremely pernicious, impolitic, and dangerous. Is this a monarchy, like England—a compact between prince and people, with checks on the former to secure the liberty of the latter? Is this a confederacy, like Holland—an association of a number of independent states, each of which retains its individual sovereignty? It is not a democracy, wherein the people retain all their rights securely. Had these principles been adhered to, we should not have been brought to this alarming transition, from a confederacy to a consolidated government. We have no detail of these great considerations, which, in my opinion, ought to have abounded before we should recur to a government of this kind. Here is a resolution as radical as that which separated us from Great Britain. It is radical in this transition; our rights and privileges are endangered, and the sovereignty of the states will be relinquished . . . . The rights of conscience, trial by jury, liberty of the press, all your immunities and franchises, all pretensions to human rights and privileges, are rendered insecure, if not lost, by this change . . . . Is this tame relinquishment of rights worthy of freemen? Is it worthy of that manly fortitude that ought to characterize republicans? It is said eight states have adopted this plan. I declare that if twelve states and a half had adopted it, I would, with manly firmness, and in spite of an erring world, reject it. You are not to inquire how your trade may be increased, nor how you are to become a great and powerful people, but how your liberties can be secured; for liberty ought to be the direct end of your government.

. . . Is it necessary for your liberty that you should abandon those great rights by the adoption of this system? Is the relinquishment of the trial by jury and the liberty of the press necessary for your liberty? Will the abandonment of your most sacred rights tend to the security of your liberty? Liberty, the greatest of all earthly blessings—give us that precious jewel, and you may take every thing else! . . . Guard with jealous attention the public liberty. Suspect every one who approaches that jewel.

Unfortunately nothing will preserve it but downright force. Whenever you give up that force, you are inevitably ruined. . . . We are come hither to preserve the poor commonwealth of Virginia, if it can be possibly done: something must be done to preserve your liberty and mine. The Confederation, this same despised government, merits, in my opinion, the highest encomium: it carried us through a long and dangerous war; it rendered us victorious in that bloody conflict with a powerful nation; it has secured us a territory greater than any European monarch possesses: and shall a government which has been thus strong and vigorous, be accused of imbecility, and abandoned for want of energy? Consider what you are about to do before you part with the government. . . .

. . . In the clause under consideration, there is the strangest language that I can conceive. I mean, when it says that there shall not be more representatives than one for every thirty thousand. . . . This may be satisfied by one representative from each state. Let our numbers be ever so great, this immense continent may, by this artful expression, be reduced to have but thirteen representatives. I confess this construction is not natural; but the ambiguity of the expression lays a good ground for a quarrel. Why was it not clearly and unequivocally expressed, that they should be entitled to have one for every thirty thousand? This would have obviated all disputes . . . . How does your trial by jury stand? In civil cases gone—not sufficiently secured in criminal—this best privilege is gone. But we are told that we need not fear; because those in power, being our representatives, will not abuse the powers we put in their hands. I am not well versed in history, but I will submit to your recollection, whether liberty has been destroyed most often by the licentiousness of the people, or by the tyranny of rulers. I imagine, sir, you will find the balance on the side of tyranny. . . . Most of the human race are now in this deplorable condition; and those nations who have gone in search of grandeur, power, and splendor, have also fallen a sacrifice, and been the victims of their own folly. While they acquired those visionary blessings, they lost their freedom. My great objection to this government is, that it does not leave us the means of defending our rights, or of waging war against tyrants. . . . Have we the means of resisting desciplined armies, when our only defence, the militia, is put into the hands of Congress? . . . Is there a disposition in the people of this country to revolt against the dominion of laws? Has there been a single tumult in Virginia? Have not the people of Virginia, when laboring under the severest pressure of accumulated distresses, manifested the most cordial acquiescence in the execution of the laws? What could be more awful than their unanimous acquiescence under general distresses? . . . Whither is the spirit of America gone? Whither is the genius of America fled? It was but yesterday, when our enemies marched in triumph through our country. Yet the people of this country could not be appalled by their pompous armaments: they stopped their career, and victoriously captured them. Where is the peril, now, compared to that? . . .

. . . [It] appears that three fourths of the states must ultimately agree to any amendments that may be necessary. Let us consider the consequence of this. . . . Two thirds of the Congress, or of the state legislatures, are necessary even to propose amendments. If one third of these be unworthy men, they may prevent the application for amendments; but what is destructive and mischievous, is, that three fourths of the state legislatures, or of the state conventions, must concur in the amendments when proposed! In such numerous bodies, there must necessarily be some designing, bad men. To suppose that so large a number as three fourths of the states will concur, is to suppose that they will possess genius, intelligence, and integrity, approaching to miraculous. . . . A trifling minority may reject the most salutary amendments. Is this an easy mode of securing the public liberty? It is, sir, a most fearful situation, when the most contemptible minority can prevent the alteration of the most oppressive government; for it may, in many respects, prove to be such. Is this the spirit of republicanism?

        ❖   ❖   ❖   ❖

This, sir, is the language of democracy—that a majority of the community have a right to alter government when found to be oppressive. But how different is the genius of your new Constitution from this! How different from the sentiments of freemen, that a contemptible minority can prevent the good of the majority! . . .

A standing army we shall have, also, to execute the execrable commands of tyranny; and how are you to punish them? Will you order them to be punished? Who shall obey these orders? Will your mace-bearer be a match for a disciplined regiment? . . . What resistance could be made? The attempt would be madness. You will find all the strength of this country in the hands of your enemies; their garrisons will naturally be the strongest places in the country. Your militia is given up to Congress, also, in another part of this plan: they will therefore act as they think proper: all power will be in their own possession. . . .

        ❖   ❖   ❖   ❖

. . . The distinction between a national government and a confederacy is not sufficiently discerned. Had the delegates, who were sent to Philadelphia, a power to propose a consolidated government instead of a confederacy? Were they not deputed by states, and not by the people? The assent of the people, in their collective capacity, is not necessary to the formation of a federal government. The people have no right to enter into leagues, alliances, or confederations; they are not the proper agents for this purpose. States and foreign powers are the only proper agents for this kind of government. Show me an instance where the people have exercised this business. Has it not always gone through the legislatures? I refer you to the treaties with France, Holland, and other nations. How were they made? Were they not made by the states? Are the people, therefore, in their aggregate capacity, the proper persons to form a confederacy? This, therefore, ought to depend on the consent of the legislatures, the people having never sent delegates to make any proposition for changing the government. . . .

Consider our situation, sir: go to the poor man, and ask him what he does. He will inform you that he enjoys the fruits of his labor, under his own fig-tree, with his wife and children around him, in peace and security. Go to every other member of society, —you will find the same tranquil ease and content; you will find no alarms or disturbances. Why, then, tell us of danger, to terrify us into an adoption of this new form of government? And yet who knows the dangers that this new system may produce? They are out of the sight of the common people: they cannot foresee latent consequences. I dread the operation of it on the middling and lower classes of people: it is for them I fear the adoption of this system. . . .

❉   ❉   ❉   ❉

. . . Besides the expenses of maintaining the Senate and other house in as much splendor as they please, there is to be a great and mighty President, with very extensive powers—the powers of a king. He is to be supported in extravagant magnificence; so that the whole of our property may be taken by this American government, by laying what taxes they please, giving themselves what salaries they please, and suspending our laws at their pleasure. . . . I believe I should take up very little of your time in enumerating the little power that is left to the government of Virginia; for this power is reduced to little or nothing: their garrisons, magazines, arsenals, and forts, which will be situated in the strongest places within the states; their ten miles square, with all the fine ornaments of human life, added to their powers, and taken from the states, will reduce the power of the latter to nothing.

*   *   *   *

In this scheme of energetic government, the people will find two sets of tax-gatherers—the state and the federal sheriffs. This, it seems to me, will produce such dreadful oppression as the people cannot possibly bear. The federal sheriff may commit what oppression, make what distresses, he pleases, and ruin you with impunity; for how are you to tie his hands? Have you any sufficiently decided means of preventing him from sucking your blood by speculations, commissions, and fees? Thus thousands of your people will be most shamefully robbed . . . .

*   *   *   *

Your President may easily become king. Your Senate is so imperfectly constructed that your dearest rights may be sacrificed by what may be a small minority; and a very small minority may continue forever unchangeably this government, although horridly defective. Where are your checks in this government? Your strongholds will be in the hands of your enemies. It is on a supposition that your American governors shall be honest, that all the good qualities of this government are founded; but its defective and imperfect construction puts it in their power to perpetrate the worst of mischiefs, should they be bad men; and, sir, would not all the world, from the eastern to the western hemisphere, blame our distracted folly in resting our rights upon the contingency of our rulers being good or bad? Show me that age and country where the rights and liberties of the people were placed on the sole chance of their rulers being good men, without a consequent loss of liberty! . . .

*   *   *   *

What can be more defective than the clause concerning the elections? The control given to Congress over the time, place, and manner of holding elections, will totally destroy the end of suffrage. The elections may be held at one place, and the most inconvenient in the state; or they may be at remote distances from those who have a right of suffrage: hence nine out of ten must either not vote at all, or vote for strangers; for the most influential characters will be applied to, to know who are the most proper to be chosen. I repeat, that the control of Congress over the *manner,* &c., of electing, well warrants this idea. The natural consequence will be, that this democratic branch will possess none of the public confidence; the people will be prejudiced against representatives chosen in such an injudicious manner. . . .

. . . Where is the responsibility—that leading principle in the British government? In that government, a punishment certain and inevitable is provided; but in this, there is no real, actual punishment for the grossest mal-administration. They may go without punishment, though they commit the most outrageous violation on our immunities. . . .

This, sir, is my great objection to the Constitution, that there is no true responsibility—and that the preservation of our liberty depends on the single chance of men being virtuous enough to make laws to punish themselves.

. . . The Senate, by making treaties, may destroy your liberty and laws for want of responsibility. Two thirds of those that shall happen to be present, can, with the President, make treaties that shall be the supreme law of the land; they may make the most ruinous treaties; and yet there is no punishment for them. . . .

＊　　＊　　＊　　＊

Permit me, sir, to say, that a great majority of the people, even in the adopting states, are averse to this government. I believe I would be right to say, that they have been egregiously misled. Pennsylvania has, *perhaps,* been tricked into it. If the other states who have adopted it have not been tricked, still they were too much hurried into its adoption. There were very respectable minorities in several of them; and if reports be true, a clear majority of the people are averse to it. If we also accede, and it should prove grievous, the peace and prosperity of our country, which we all love, will be destroyed. This government has not the affection of the people at present. Should it be oppressive, their affections will be totally estranged from it; and, sir, you know that a government, without their affections, can neither be durable nor happy. . . .

✻   ✻   ✻   ✻

The necessity of amendments is universally admitted. . . . Reason, self-preservation, and every idea of propriety, powerfully urge us to secure the dearest rights of human nature. Shall we, in direct violation of these principles, rest this security upon the uncertainty of its being obtained by a few states, more weak and less respectable than ourselves, and whose virtue and magnanimity may be overborne by the example of so many adopting states? *Poor* Rhode Island, and North Carolina, and even New York, surrounded with federal walls on every side, may not be magnanimous enough to reject; and if they do reject it, they will have but little influence to obtain amendments. I ask, if amendments be necessary, from whence can they be so properly proposed as from this state? The example of Virginia is a powerful thing, particularly with respect to North Carolina, whose supplies must come *through* Virginia. Every possible opportunity of procuring amendments is gone, our power and political salvation are gone, if we ratify unconditionally. . . .

We are told that all powers not given are reserved. . . . The English history is frequently recurred to by gentlemen. Let us advert to the conduct of the people of that country. The people of England lived without a declaration of rights till the war in the time of Charles I. That king made usurpations upon the rights of the people. Those rights were, in a great measure, before that time undefined. Power and privilege then depended on implication and logical discussion. Though the declaration of rights was obtained from that king, his usurpations cost him his life. The limits between the liberty of the people, and the prerogative of the king, were still not clearly defined.

The rights of the people continued to be violated till the Stuart family was banished, in the year 1688. The people of England magnanimously defended their rights, banished the tyrant, and prescribed to William, Prince of Orange, by the bill of rights, on what terms he should reign; and this bill of rights put an end to all construction and implication. Before this, sir, the situation of the public liberty of England was dreadful. For upwards of a century, the nation was involved in every kind of calamity, till the bill of rights put an end to all, by defining the rights of the people, and limiting the king's prerogative. . . . It is alleged that several states, in the formation of their government, omitted a bill of rights. To this I answer, that they had the substance of a bill of rights contained in their constitutions, which is the same thing. . . .

Of what advantage is it to the American Congress to take away this great and general security? . . . Why is the trial by jury taken away? All the learned arguments that have been used on this occasion do not prove that it is secured. Even the advocates for the plan do not all concur in the certainty of its security. Wherefore is religious liberty not secured? . . . This sacred right ought not to depend on constructive, logical reasoning.

When we see men of such talents and learning compelled to use their utmost abilities to convince themselves that there is no danger, is it not sufficient to make us tremble? . . . If gentlemen believe that the apprehensions of men will be quieted, they are mistaken, since our best-informed men are in doubt with respect to the security of our rights. Those who are not so well informed will spurn at the government. When our common citizens, who are not possessed with such extensive knowledge and abilities, are called upon to change their bill of rights . . .

for construction and implication, will they implicitly acquiesce? Our declaration of rights tells us that "all men are by nature free and independent," &c. [Here Mr. Henry read the declaration of rights.] Will they exchange these rights for logical reasons? . . . The present opinions of individuals will be buried in entire oblivion when those rights will be thought of. . . .

          ✿   ✿   ✿   ✿

The honorable gentleman was pleased to say that the representation of the people was the vital principle of this government. I will readily agree that it ought to be so. But I contend that this principle is only nominally, and not substantially, to be found there. We contended with the British about representation. They offered us such a representation as Congress now does. They called it a virtual representation. . . . Is there but a virtual representation in the upper house? The states are represented, *as states,* by two senators each. This is virtual, not actual. They encounter you with Rhode Island and Delaware. This is not an actual representation. What does the term *representation* signify? It means that a certain district—a certain association of men—should be represented in the government, for certain ends. . . . Here, sir, this populous state has not an adequate share of legislative influence. The two petty states of Rhode Island and Delaware, which, together, are infinitely inferior to this state in extent and population, have double her weight, and can counteract her interest. I say that the representation in the Senate, as applicable to states, is not actual. Representation is not, therefore, the vital principle of this government. . . .

          ✿   ✿   ✿   ✿

The honorable gentleman did our judiciary honor in saying that they had firmness to counteract the legislature in some cases. Yes, sir, our judges opposed the acts of the legislature. We have this landmark to guide us. They had fortitude to declare that they were the judiciary, and would oppose unconstitutional acts. Are you sure that your federal judiciary will act thus? Is that judiciary as well constructed, and as independent of the other branches, as our state judiciary? . . . I take it as the highest encomium on this country, that the acts of the legislature, if unconstitutional, are liable to be opposed by the judiciary.

        ❖   ❖   ❖   ❖

As to the western country, notwithstanding our representation in Congress, and notwithstanding any regulation that may be made by Congress, it may be lost. The seven Northern States are determined to give up the Mississippi. We are told that, in order to secure the navigation of that river, it was necessary to give it up, for twenty-five years, to the Spaniards, and that thereafter we should enjoy it forever, without any interruption from them. . . . Did we not know of the fallibility of human nature, we might rely on the present structure of this government. We might depend that the rules of propriety, and the general interest of the Union, would be observed. But the depraved nature of man is well known. He has a natural bias towards his own interest, which will prevail over every consideration, unless it be checked. It is the interest and inclination of the seven Northern States to relinquish this river. If you enable them to do so, will the mere propriety of consulting the interest of the other six states refrain them from it? . . .

. . . The efforts of our ten men will avail very little when opposed by the northern majority. If our ten men be disposed to sacrifice our interest, we cannot detect them. Under the color of being outnumbered by the northern representatives, they can always screen themselves. When they go to the general government, they may make a bargain with the northern delegates. They may agree to tax our citizens in any manner which may be proposed by the northern members; in consideration of which, the latter may make them some favorite concessions. The Northern States will never assent to regulations promotive of southern aggrandizement. Notwithstanding what gentlemen say of the probable virtue of our representatives, I dread the depravity of human nature. I wish to guard against it by proper checks, and trust nothing to accident or chance. I will never depend on so slender a protection as the possibility of being represented by virtuous men.

✿   ✿   ✿   ✿

Mr. MONROE. Mr. Chairman, I cannot avoid expressing the great anxiety which I feel upon the present occasion—an anxiety that proceeds not only from a high sense of the importance of the subject, but from a profound respect for this august and venerable assembly. When we contemplate the fate that has befallen other nations . . . and observe how prone all human institutions have been to decay; how subject the best-formed and most wisely organized governments have been to lose their checks and totally dissolve; how difficult it has been for mankind, in all ages and countries, to preserve their dearest rights and best privileges, impelled as it were by an irresistible fate of despotism; . . . some gloomy apprehensions must necessarily crowd upon it. This consideration is sufficient to teach us the limited capacity of the human mind—how subject the wisest men have been to error. . . .

The American states exhibit at present a new and interesting spectacle to the eyes of mankind. Modern Europe, for more than twelve centuries past, has presented to view one of a very different kind. In all the nations of that quarter of the globe, there hath been a constant effort, on the part of the people, to extricate themselves from the oppression of their rulers; but with us the object is of a very different nature—to establish the dominion of law over licentiousness—to increase the powers of the national government to such extent, and organize it in such manner, as to enable it to discharge its duties, and manage the affairs of the states, to the best advantage. There are two circumstances remarkable in our colonial settlement:—1st, the exclusive monopoly of our trade; 2nd, that it was settled by the commons of England only. The revolution, in having emancipated us from the shackles of Great Britain, has put the entire government in the hands of one order of people only—freemen; not of nobles and freemen. This is a peculiar trait in the character of this revolution. That this sacred deposit may be always retained there, is my most earnest wish and fervent prayer. That union is the first object for the security of our political happiness . . . . From New Hampshire to Georgia, (Rhode Island excepted,) the people have uniformly manifested a strong attachment to the Union. This attachment has resulted from a persuasion of its utility and necessity. . . . [Permit] me to speak of what must influence the happiness and duration of leagues. These principally depend on the following circumstances: 1st, the happy construction of the government of the members of the union; 2d, the security from foreign danger. For instance, monarchies united would separate soon; aristocracies would preserve their union longer; but democracies, unless separated by some extraordinary circumstance, would last forever. The causes of half the wars that have thinned the ranks of mankind, and depopulated nations, are caprice, folly, and ambition: these belong to the higher orders of governments, where the passions of one, or of a few individuals, direct the fate of the rest of the community. But it is otherwise with democracies, where there is an equality among the citizens, and a foreign and powerful enemy, especially a monarch, may crush weaker neighbors. . . .

     ❊   ❊   ❊   ❊

. . . The causes which, with other nations, rendered leagues ineffectual and inadequate to the security and happiness of the people, do not exist here. What is the form of our state governments? They are all similar in their structure—perfectly democratic. The freedom of mankind has found an asylum here which it could find nowhere else. Freedom of conscience is enjoyed here in the fullest degree. Our states are not disturbed by a contrariety of religious opinions, and other causes of quarrels which other nations have. They have no causes of internal variance. Causes of war between the states have been represented in all those terrors which splendid genius and brilliant imagination can so well depict. But, sir, I conceive they are imaginary—mere creatures of fancy. I will admit that there was a contrariety of sentiments—a contest in which I was a witness in some respects —a contest respecting the western unsettled lands. . . . The progress of this dispute gave uneasiness to the true friends of America; but territorial claims may now be said to be adjusted. Have not Virginia, North Carolina, and other states, ceded their claims to Congress? The disputes between Virginia and Maryland are also settled; nor is there an existing controversy between any of the states at present. Thus, sir, this great source of public calamity has been terminated without the adoption of this government.

Have we any danger to fear from the European countries? . . . Our situation is relatively the same to all foreign powers. View the distance between us and them: the wide Atlantic—an ocean three thousand miles across—lies between us. If there be any danger to these states to be apprehended from any of those countries, it must be Great Britain and Spain, whose colonies are contiguous to our country. . . .

＊　　＊　　＊　　＊

What are the powers which the federal government ought to have? I will draw the line between the powers necessary to be given to the federal, and those which ought to be left to the state governments. To the former I would give control over the national affairs; to the latter I would leave the care of local interests. Neither the Confederation, nor this Constitution, answers this discrimination. To make the first a proper federal government, I would add to it one great power—I would give it an absolute control over commerce. To render the system under consideration safe and proper I would take from it one power only—I mean that of direct taxation. I conceive its other powers are sufficient without this. My objections to this power are, that I conceive it not necessary, impracticable under a democracy, (if exercised,) as tending to anarchy, or the subversion of liberty, and probably the latter. In the first place, it is unnecessary, because exigencies will not require it. The demands and necessities of government are now greater than they will be hereafter, because of the expenses of the war in which we were engaged, which cost us the blood of our best citizens, and which ended so gloriously.

* * * *

. . . Is it possible to make a law that shall operate alike in all the states? Is it possible that there should be sufficient intelligence for the men of Georgia to know the situation of the men of New Hampshire? Is there a precise similitude of situation in each state? Compare the situation of the citizens in different states.

Are there not a thousand circumstances showing clearly that there can be no law that can be uniform in its operation throughout the United States? . . . What is the extent of the power of laying and collecting direct taxes? Does it not give to the United States all the resources of the individual states? Does it not give an absolute control over the resources of all the states? If you give the resources of the several states to the general government, in what situation are the states left? I therefore think the general government will preponderate.

Besides its possession of all the resources of the country, there are other circumstances that will enable it to triumph in the conflict with the states. Gentlemen of influence and character, men of distinguished talents, of eminent virtue, and great endowments, will compose the general government. In what situation will the different states be, when all the talents and abilities of the country will be against them?

* * * *

. . . The Confederation has been deservedly reprobated for its inadequacy to promote the public welfare. But this change is, in my opinion, very dangerous. It contemplates objects with which a federal government ought never to interfere. The concurrent interfering power of laying taxes on the people will occasion a perpetual conflict between the general and individual governments; which, for the reasons I have already mentioned, must terminate to the disadvantage, if not in the annihilation, of the latter. Can it be presumed that the people of America can patiently bear such a double oppression? Is it not to be presumed that they will endeavor to get rid of one of the oppressors? I fear, sir, that it will ultimately end in the establishment of a monarchical government. The people, in order to be delivered from one species of tyranny, may submit to another. . . . My attachment to the Union and an energetic government is such, that I would consent to give the general government every power contained in that plan, except that of taxation.

* * * *

. . . There is a distinction between this government and ancient and modern ones. The division of power in ancient governments, or in any government at present in the world, was founded on different principles from those of this government. What was the object of the distribution of power in Rome? It will not be controverted, that there was a composition or mixture of aristocracy, democracy, and monarchy, each of which had a repellent quality which enabled it to preserve itself from being destroyed by the other two; so that the balance was continually maintained. This is the case in the English government, which has the most similitude to our own. There they have distinct orders in the government, which possess real, efficient repellent qualities. . . . The wisdom of the English constitution has given a share of legislation to each of the three branches, which enables it effectually to defend itself, and which preserves the liberty of the people of that country.

What is the object of the division of power in America? Why is the government divided into different branches? For a more faithful and regular administration. Where is there a check? We have more to apprehend from the union of these branches than from the subversion of any; and this union will destroy the rights of the people. There is nothing to prevent this coalition; but the contest which will probably subsist between the general government and the individual governments will tend to produce it. There is a division of sovereignty between the national and state governments. How far, then, will they coalesce together? Is it not to be supposed that there will be a conflict between them? If so, will not the members of the former combine together? Where, then, will be the check to prevent encroachments on the rights of the people? There is not a third essentially distinct branch, to preserve a just equilibrium, or to prevent such encroachments. In developing this plan of government, we ought to attend to the necessity of having checks. I can see no real checks in it.

❖   ❖   ❖   ❖

I have never yet heard or read, in the history of mankind, of a concurrent exercise of power by two parties, without producing a struggle between them. . . . Now, sir, as to the responsibility. Let us begin with the House of Representatives, which is the most democratic part. The representatives are elected by the people; but what is the responsibility? At the expiration of the time for which they are elected, the people may discontinue them: but if they commit high crimes, how are they to be punished? I apprehend the general government cannot punish them, because it would be a subversion of the rights of the people. The state legislatures cannot punish them, because they have no control over them in any one instance. In the next, consider the responsibility of the senators. To whom are they amenable? I apprehend, to none. They are punishable neither by the general government nor by the state legislatures. The latter may call them to an account, but they have no power to punish them.

Let us now consider the responsibility of the President. He is elected for four years, and not excluded from reëlection. Suppose he violates the laws and Constitution, or commits high crimes. By whom is he to be tried?—By his own council—by those who advise him to commit such violations and crimes? This subverts the principles of justice, as it secures him from punishment. He commands the army of the United States till he is condemned. Will not this be an inducement to foreign nations to use their arts and intrigues to corrupt his counsellors? If he and his counsellors can escape punishment with so much facility, what a delightful prospect must it be for a foreign nation, which may be desirous of gaining territorial or commercial advantages over us, to practise on them! . . . The variety of the offices at his disposal will acquire him the favor and attachment of those who aspire after them, and of the officers and their friends. . . . I presume that when once he is elected, he may be elected forever. . . . Powerful men in different states will form a friendship with him. For these reasons, I conceive, the same President may always be continued, and be in fact elected by Congress, instead of independent and intelligent electors. It is a misfortune, more than once experienced, that the representatives of the states do not pursue the particular interest of their own state. When we take a more accurate view of the principles of the Senate, we shall have grounds to fear that the interest of our state may be totally neglected; nay, that our legislative influence will be as if we were actually expelled or banished out of Congress. . . . Consider the connection of the Senate with the executive. Has it not an authority over all the acts of the executive? What are the acts which the President can do without them? What number is requisite to make treaties? A very small number. Two thirds of those who may *happen* to be present, may, with the President, make treaties that shall sacrifice the dearest interests of the Southern States—which may relinquish part of our territories—which may dismember the United States. There is no check to prevent this; there is no responsibility, or power to punish it. He is to nominate, and, by and with the advice and consent of the Senate, to appoint, ambassadors, other public ministers and consuls, judges of the Supreme Court, and all other officers of the United States. The concurrence of a bare majority of those who may be present will enable him to do these important acts. It does not require the consent of two thirds even of those who may be present. Thus I conceive the government is put entirely into the hands of seven states; indeed, into the hands of two thirds of a majority. . . .

Upon reviewing this government, I must say, under my present impression, I think it a dangerous government, and calculated to secure neither the interests nor the rights of our countrymen. Under such a one, I shall be averse to embark the best hopes and prospects of a free people. We have struggled long to bring about this revolution, by which we enjoy our present freedom and security. Why, then, this haste—this wild precipitation?

❖   ❖   ❖   ❖

JOHN LANSING

AND

MELANCTON SMITH

In the Ratifying Convention of New York

20–23 JUNE 1788

Mr. LANSING.

❋ ❋ ❋ ❋

. . . We ought . . . to be extremely cautious how we establish a government which may give distinct interests to the rulers and governed, so as to induce the former to pursuits adverse to the happiness of the United States.

It has been observed, that, as the people must, of necessity, delegate essential powers either to the individual or general sovereignties, it is perfectly immaterial where they are lodged; but, as the state governments will always possess a better representation of the feelings and interests of the people at large, it is obvious that those powers can be deposited with much greater safety with the state than the general government.

I am equally averse to cherishing, on this occasion, the idea of obtaining a perfection which never existed, and to despairing of making important amendments to the system now offered for consideration; for, sir, however much I may be disposed to perpetuate union, however sensible of the defects of the existing

From Elliot, II: Lansing's remarks, pp. 217–219; Smith's remarks, pp. 245–249, 280–281.

232

Confederation, I cannot help differing from those gentlemen who are of opinion it is incapable of amelioration.

I would ask, What are the objections which have been so ably urged against it? They are comprised under two heads. First, it affords no defence against foreign assault; second, no security to domestic tranquillity. Both these objects might be compassed if Congress could be vested with a power to raise men and money.

Requisitions made under the existing Confederation by Congress, it is allowed, are insufficient; but this defect might, in a great measure, have been remedied by permitting the United States to legislate on individuals after the requisitions had been made, and not been complied with. If the requisition could be thus enforced, loans of money might be negotiated when necessary, and Congress be authorized to raise money to replace them.

The languishing situation of our commerce has also been attributed to the impotence of Congress; but I think their journals will justify me in the assertion that all the states, excepting two, had passed laws to enable Congress to regulate commerce, and that those two were not indisposed to vest that power.

*   *   *   *

. . . I know not that history furnishes an example of a confederated republic coercing the states composing it by the mild influence of laws operating on the individuals of those states. This, therefore, I suppose to be a new experiment in politics; and, as we cannot always accurately ascertain the results of political measures, and as reasoning on them has been frequently found fallacious, we should not too confidently predict those to be produced by the new system.

The dangers to which we shall be exposed by a dissolution of the Union, have been represented; but, however much I may wish to preserve the Union, apprehensions of its dissolution ought not to induce us to submit to any measure which may involve in its consequences the loss of civil liberty. Conquest can do no more, in the state of civilization, than to subject us to be ruled by persons in whose appointment we have no agency. This, sir, is the worst we can apprehend at all events; and, as I suppose a government so organized, and possessing the powers mentioned in the proposed Constitution, will unavoidably terminate in the depriving us of that invaluable privilege, I am content to risk a probable, but, on this occasion, a mere possible evil, to avoid a certain one. But if a dissolution of the Union should unfortunately ensue, what have we to apprehend? We are connected, both by interest and affection, with the New England States; we harbor no animosities against each other; we have no interfering territorial claims; our manners are nearly similar, and they are daily assimilating, and mutual advantages will probably prompt to mutual concessions, to enable us to form a union with them. I, however, contemplate the idea of a possible dissolution with pain, and I make these remarks with the most sincere reluctance, only in answer to those which were offered by the honorable gentleman from New York.

Mr. SMITH.

* * * *

To determine whether the number of representatives proposed by this Constitution is sufficient, it is proper to examine the qualifications which this house ought to possess, in order to exercise their power discreetly for the happiness of the people. The idea that naturally suggests itself to our minds, when we speak of representatives, is, that they resemble those they represent. They should be a true picture of the people, possess a knowledge of their circumstances and their wants, sympathize in all their distresses, and be disposed to seek their true interests. The knowledge necessary for the representative of a free people not only comprehends extensive political and commercial information, such as is acquired by men of refined education, who have leisure to attain to high degrees of improvement, but it should also comprehend that kind of acquaintance with the common concerns and occupations of the people, which men of the middling class of life are, in general, more competent to than those of a superior class. To understand the true commercial interests of a country, not only requires just ideas of the general commerce of the world, but also, and principally, a knowledge of the productions of your own country, and their value, what your soil is capable of producing, the nature of your manufactures, and the capacity of the country to increase both. To exercise the power of laying taxes, duties, and excises, with discretion, requires something more than an acquaintance with the abstruse parts of the system of finance. It calls for a knowledge of the circumstances and ability of the people in general— a discernment how the burdens imposed will bear upon the different classes.

From these observations results this conclusion—that the number of representatives should be so large, as that, while it embraces the men of the first class, it should admit those of the middling class of life. I am convinced that this government is so constituted that the representatives will generally be composed of the first class in the community, which I shall distinguish by the name of the *natural aristocracy* of the country. I do not mean to give offence by using this term. I am sensible this idea is treated by many gentlemen as chimerical. I shall be asked what is meant by the *natural aristocracy*, and told that no such distinction of classes of men exists among us. It is true, it is our singular felicity that we have no legal or hereditary distinctions of this kind; but still there are real differences. Every society naturally divides itself into classes. The Author of nature has bestowed on some greater capacities than others; birth, education, talents, and wealth, create distinctions among men as visible, and of as much influence, as titles, stars, and garters. In every society, men of this class will command a superior degree of respect; and if the government is so constituted as to admit but few to exercise the powers of it, it will, according to the natural course of things, be in their hands. Men in the middling class, who are qualified as representatives, will not be so anxious to be chosen as those of the first. When the number is so small, the office will be highly elevated and distinguished; the style in which the members live will probably be high; circumstances of this kind will render the place of a representative not a desirable one to sensible, substantial men, who have been used to walk in the plain and frugal paths of life.

Besides, the influence of the great will generally enable them to succeed in elections. It will be difficult to combine a district of country containing thirty or forty thousand inhabitants,—frame your election laws as you please,—in any other character, unless it be in one of conspicuous military, popular, civil, or legal talents. The great easily form associations; the poor and middling class form them with difficulty. If the elections be by plurality,—as probably will be the case in this state,—it is almost certain none but the great will be chosen, for they easily unite their interests: the common people will divide, and their divisions will be promoted by the others. There will be scarcely a chance of their uniting in any other but some great man, unless in some popular demagogue, who will probably be destitute of principle. A substantial yeoman, of sense and discernment, will hardly ever be chosen. From these remarks, it appears that the government will fall into the hands of the few and the great. This will be a government of oppression. I do not mean to declaim against the great, and charge them indiscriminately with want of principle and honesty. The same passions and prejudices govern all men. The circumstances in which men are placed in a great measure give a cast to the human character. Those in middling circumstances have less temptation; they are inclined by habit, and the company with whom they associate, to set bounds to their passions and appetites. If this is not sufficient, the want of means to gratify them will be a restraint: they are obliged to employ their time in their respective callings;

hence the substantial yeomanry of the country are more temperate, of better morals, and less ambition, than the great. The latter do not feel for the poor and middling class; the reasons are obvious—they are not obliged to use the same pains and labor to procure property as the other. They feel not the inconveniences arising from the payment of small sums. The great consider themselves above the common people, entitled to more respect, do not associate with them; they fancy themselves to have a right of preëminence in every thing. In short, they possess the same feelings, and are under the influence of the same motives, as an hereditary nobility. I know the idea that such a distinction exists in this country is ridiculed by some; but I am not the less apprehensive of danger from their influence on this account. Such distinctions exist all the world over, have been taken notice of by all writers on free government, and are founded in the nature of things. It has been the principal care of free governments to guard against the encroachments of the great. Common observation and experience prove the existence of such distinctions. Will any one say that there does not exist in this country the pride of family, of wealth, of talents, and that they do not command influence and respect among the common people? Congress, in their address to the inhabitants of the province of Quebec, in 1775, state this distinction in the following forcible words, quoted from the Marquis Beccaria: "In every human society there is an essay continually tending to confer on one part the height of power and happiness, and to reduce the other to the extreme of weakness and misery. The intent of good laws is to oppose this effort, and to diffuse their influence universally and equally." We ought to guard against the government being placed in the hands of this class. They cannot have that sympathy with their constituents which is necessary to connect them closely to their interests. Being in the habit of profuse living, they will be profuse in the public expenses. They find no difficulty in paying their taxes, and therefore do not feel public burdens. Besides, if they govern, they will enjoy the emoluments of the government. The middling class, from their frugal habits, and feeling themselves the public burdens, will be careful how they increase them.

But I may be asked, Would you exclude the first class in the community from any share in legislation? I answer, By no means. They would be factious, discontented, and constantly disturbing the government. It would also be unjust. They have their liberties to protect, as well as others, and the largest share of property. But my idea is, that the Constitution should be so framed as to admit this class, together with a sufficient number of the middling class to control them. You will then combine the abilities and honesty of the community, a proper degree of information, and a disposition to pursue the public good. A representative body, composed principally of respectable yeomanry, is the best possible security to liberty. When the interest of this part of the community is pursued, the public good is pursued, because the body of every nation consists of this class, and because the interest of both the rich and the poor are involved in that of the middling class. No burden can be laid on the poor but what will sensibly affect the middling class. Any law rendering property insecure would be injurious to them. When, therefore, this class in society pursue their own interest, they promote that of the public, for it is involved in it.

In so small a number of representatives, there is great danger from corruption and combination. A great politician has said that every man has his price. I hope this is not true in all its extent; but I ask the gentleman to inform me what government there is in which it has not been practised. Notwithstanding all that has been said of the defects in the constitution of the ancient confederacies in the Grecian republics, their destruction is to be imputed more to this cause than to any imperfection in their forms of government. This was the deadly poison that effected their dissolution. This is an extensive country, increasing in population and growing in consequence. Very many lucrative offices will be in the grant of the government, which will be objects of avarice and ambition. How easy will it be to gain over a sufficient number, in the bestowment of offices, to promote the views and the purposes of those who grant them! Foreign corruption is also to be guarded against. A system of corruption is known to be the system of government in Europe. It is practised without blushing; and we may lay it to our account, it will be attempted amongst us. The most effectual as well as natural security against this is a strong democratic branch in the legislature, frequently chosen, including in it a number of the substantial, sensible yeomanry of the country. Does the House of Representatives answer this description? I confess, to me they hardly wear the complexion of a democratic branch; they appear the mere shadow of representation. . . .

     ❀   ❀   ❀   ❀

. . . The gentleman wishes me to describe what I meant by representing the feelings of the people. If I recollect right, I said the representative ought to understand and govern his conduct by the true interest of the people. . . . All I said was, that mankind were influenced, in a great degree, by interests and prejudices; that men, in different ranks of life, were exposed to different temptations, and that ambition was more peculiarly the passion of the rich and great. The gentleman supposes the poor have less sympathy with the sufferings of their fellow-creatures, for that those who feel most distress themselves, have the least regard to the misfortunes of others. Whether this be reasoning or declamation, let all who hear us determine. I observed, that the rich were more exposed to those temptations which rank and power hold out to view; that they were more luxurious and intemperate, because they had more fully the means of enjoyment; that they were more ambitious, because more in the hope of success. The gentleman says my principle is not true, for that a poor man will be as ambitious to be a constable as a rich man to be a governor; but he will not injure his country so much by the party he creates to support his ambition.

. . . My idea of aristocracy is not new; it is embraced by many writers on government. I would refer the gentleman for a definition of it to the Hon. JOHN ADAMS, one of our natural aristocrats. This writer will give him a description the most ample and satisfactory. . . . My argument was, that, in order to have a true and genuine representation, you must receive the middling class of people into your government, such as compose the body of this assembly. I observed that a representation from the United States could not be so constituted as to represent completely the feelings and interests of the people; but that we ought to come as near this object as possible. . . .

✻　　✻　　✻　　✻

PART IV

Defense of the Constitution by
The Federalist

1 [ALEXANDER HAMILTON]

***

Introduction

***

To the People of the State of New York:

After an unequivocal experience of the inefficiency of the subsisting federal government, you are called upon to deliberate on a new Constitution for the United States of America. The subject speaks its own importance; comprehending in its consequences nothing less than the existence of the UNION, the safety and welfare of the parts of which it is composed, the fate of an empire in many respects the most interesting in the world. It has been frequently remarked that it seems to have been reserved to the people of this country, by their conduct and example, to decide the important question, whether societies of men are really capable or not of establishing good government from reflection and choice, or whether they are forever destined to depend for their political constitutions on accident and force. If there be any truth in the remark, the crisis at which we are arrived may with propriety be regarded as the era in which that decision is to be made; and a wrong election of the part we shall act may, in this view, deserve to be considered as the general misfortune of mankind.

This idea will add the inducements of philanthropy to those of patriotism, to heighten the solicitude which all considerate and good men must feel for the event. Happy will it be if our choice should be directed by a judicious estimate of our true interests, unperplexed and unbiased by considerations not connected with the public good. But this is a thing more ardently to be wished than seriously to be expected. The plan offered to our deliberations affects too many particular interests, innovates upon too many local institutions, not to involve in its discussion a variety of objects foreign to its merits, and of views, passions and prejudices little favorable to the discovery of truth.

Among the most formidable of the obstacles which the new Constitution will have to encounter may readily be distinguished the obvious interest of a certain class of men in every State to resist all changes which may hazard a diminution of the power, emolument, and consequence of the offices they hold under the State establishments; and the perverted ambition of another class of men, who will either hope to aggrandize themselves by the confusions of their country, or will flatter themselves with fairer prospects of elevation from the subdivision of the empire into several partial confederacies than from its union under one government.

It is not, however, my design to dwell upon observations of this nature. I am well aware that it would be disingenuous to resolve indiscriminately the opposition of any set of men (merely because their situations might subject them to suspicion) into interested or ambitious views. Candor will oblige us to admit that even such men may be actuated by upright intentions; and it cannot be doubted that much of the opposition which has made its appearance, or may hereafter make its appearance, will spring from sources, blameless at least, if not respectable— the honest errors of minds led astray by preconceived jealousies and fears. So numerous indeed and so powerful are the causes which serve to give a false bias to the judgment, that we, upon many occasions, see wise and good men on the wrong as well as on the right side of questions of the first magnitude to society. This circumstance, if duly attended to, would furnish a lesson of moderation to those who are ever so much persuaded of their being in the right in any controversy. And a further reason for caution, in this respect, might be drawn from the reflection that we are not always sure that those who advocate the truth are influenced by purer principles than their antagonists. Ambition, avarice, personal animosity, party opposition, and many other motives not more laudable than these, are apt to operate as well upon those who support as those who oppose the right side of a question. Were there not even inducements to moderation, nothing could be more ill-judged than that intolerant spirit which has, at all times, characterized political parties. For in politics, as in religion, it is equally absurd to aim at making proselytes by fire and sword. Heresies in either can rarely be cured by persecution.

And yet, however just these sentiments will be allowed to be, we have already sufficient indications that it will happen in this as in all former cases of great national discussion. A torrent of angry and malignant passions will be let loose. To judge from the conduct of the opposite parties, we shall be led to conclude that they will mutually hope to evince the justness of their opinions, and to increase the number of their converts by the loudness of their declamations and the bitterness of their invectives. An enlightened zeal for the energy and efficiency of government will be stigmatized as the offspring of a temper fond of despotic power and hostile to the principles of liberty. An over-scrupulous jealousy of danger to the rights of the people, which is more commonly the fault of the head than of the heart, will be represented as mere pretence and artifice, the stale bait for popularity at the expense of the public good. It will be forgotten, on the one hand, that jealousy is the usual concomitant of love, and that the noble enthusiasm of liberty is apt to be infected with a spirit of narrow and illiberal distrust. On the other hand, it will be equally forgotten that the vigor of government is essential to the security of liberty; that, in the contemplation of a sound and well-informed judgment, their interest can never be separated; and that a dangerous ambition more often lurks behind the specious mask of zeal for the rights of the people than under the forbidding appearance of zeal for the firmness and efficiency of government. History will teach us that the former has been found a much more certain road to the introduction of despotism than the latter, and that of those men who have overturned the liberties of republics, the greatest number have begun their career by paying an obsequious court to the people; commencing demagogues, and ending tyrants.

In the course of the preceding observations, I have had an eye, my fellow-citizens, to putting you upon your guard against all attempts, from whatever quarter, to influence your decision in a matter of the utmost moment to your welfare, by any impressions other than those which may result from the evidence of truth. You will, no doubt, at the same time, have collected from the general scope of them, that they proceed from a source not unfriendly to the new Constitution. Yes, my countrymen, I own to you that, after having given it an attentive consideration, I am clearly of opinion it is your interest to adopt it. I am convinced that this is the safest course for your liberty, your dignity, and your happiness. I affect not reserves which I do not feel. I will not amuse you with an appearance of deliberation when I have decided. I frankly acknowledge to you my convictions, and I will freely lay before you the reasons on which they are founded. The consciousness of good intentions disdains ambiguity. I shall not, however, multiply professions on this head. My motives must remain in the depository of my own breast. My arguments will be open to all, and may be judged of by all. They shall at least be offered in a spirit which will not disgrace the cause of truth.

I propose, in a series of papers, to discuss the following interesting particulars:—*The utility of the UNION to your political prosperity—The insufficiency of the present Confederation to preserve that Union—The necessity of a government at least equally energetic with the one proposed, to the attainment of this object—The conformity of the proposed Constitution to the true principles of republican government—Its analogy to your own State constitution*—and lastly, *The additional security which its adoption will afford to the preservation of that species of government, to liberty, and to property.*

In the progress of this discussion I shall endeavor to give a satisfactory answer to all the objections which shall have made their appearance, that may seem to have any claim to your attention.

It may perhaps be thought superfluous to offer arguments to prove the utility of the UNION, a point, no doubt, deeply engraved on the hearts of the great body of the people in every State, and one, which it may be imagined, has no adversaries. But the fact is, that we already hear it whispered in the private circles of those who oppose the new Constitution, that the thirteen States are of too great extent for any general system, and that we must of necessity resort to separate confederacies of distinct portions of the whole.[1] This doctrine will, in all probability, be gradually propagated, till it has votaries enough to countenance an open avowal of it. For nothing can be more evident, to those who are able to take an enlarged view of the subject, than the alternative of an adoption of the new Constitution or a dismemberment of the Union. It will therefore be of use to begin by examining the advantages of that Union, the certain evils, and the probable dangers, to which every State will be exposed from its dissolution. This shall accordingly constitute the subject of my next address.

PUBLIUS

---

[1] The same idea, tracing the arguments to their consequences is held out in several of the late publications against the new Constitution.—PUBLIUS

6 [ALEXANDER HAMILTON]

****

Disunion and Dissension among the States

****

To the People of the State of New York:

The three last numbers of this paper have been dedicated to an enumeration of the dangers to which we should be exposed, in a state of disunion, from the arms and arts of foreign nations. I shall now proceed to delineate dangers of a different and, perhaps, still more alarming kind—those which will in all probability flow from dissensions between the States themselves, and from domestic factions and convulsions. These have been already in some instances slightly anticipated; but they deserve a more particular and more full investigation.

A man must be far gone in Utopian speculations who can seriously doubt that, if these States should either be wholly disunited, or only united in partial confederacies, the subdivisions into which they might be thrown would have frequent and violent contests with each other. To presume a want of motives for such contests as an argument against their existence, would be to forget that men are ambitious, vindictive, and rapacious. To look for a continuation of harmony between a number of independent, unconnected sovereignties in the same neighborhood, would be to disregard the uniform course of human events, and to set at defiance the accumulated experience of ages.

The causes of hostility among nations are innumerable. There are some which have a general and almost constant operation upon the collective bodies of society. Of this description are the

248

love of power or the desire of pre-eminence and dominion—the jealousy of power, or the desire of equality and safety. There are others which have a more circumscribed though an equally operative influence within their spheres. Such are the rivalships and competitions of commerce between commercial nations. And there are others, not less numerous than either of the former, which take their origin entirely in private passions; in the attachments, enmities, interests, hopes, and fears of leading individuals in the communities of which they are members. Men of this class, whether the favorites of a king or of a people, have in too many instances abused the confidence they possessed; and assuming the pretext of some public motive, have not scrupled to sacrifice the national tranquillity to personal advantage or personal gratification.

*   *   *   *

Is it not . . . the true interest of all nations to cultivate the same benevolent and philosophic spirit? If this be their true interest, have they in fact pursued it? Has it not, on the contrary, invariably been found that momentary passions, and immediate interests, have a more active and imperious control over human conduct than general or remote considerations of policy, utility, or justice? Have republics in practice been less addicted to war than monarchies? Are not the former administered by *men* as well as the latter? Are there not aversions, predilections, rivalships, and desires of unjust acquisitions, that affect nations as well as kings? Are not popular assemblies frequently subject to the impulses of rage, resentment, jealousy, avarice, and of other irregular and violent propensities? Is it not well known that their determinations are often governed by a few individuals in whom they place confidence, and are, of course, liable to be tinctured by the passions and views of those individuals? Has commerce hitherto done any thing more than change the objects of war? Is not the love of wealth as domineering and enterprising a passion as that of power or glory? Have there not been as many wars founded upon commercial motives since that has become the prevailing system of nations, as were before occasioned by the cupidity of territory or dominion? Has not the spirit of commerce, in many instances, administered new incentives to the appetite, both for the one and for the other? Let experience, the least fallible guide of human opinions, be appealed to for an answer to these inquiries.

Sparta, Athens, Rome, and Carthage were all republics; two of them, Athens and Carthage, of the commercial kind. Yet were they as often engaged in wars, offensive and defensive, as the neighboring monarchies of the same times. Sparta was little better than a well-regulated camp; and Rome was never sated of carnage and conquest.

         ❀   ❀   ❀   ❀

The provinces of Holland . . . took a leading and conspicuous part in the wars of Europe. They had furious contests with England for the dominion of the seas, and were among the most persevering . . . opponents of Louis XIV.

In the government of Britain the representatives of the people compose one branch of the national legislature. Commerce has been for ages the predominant pursuit of that country. Few nations, nevertheless, have been more frequently engaged in war; and the wars in which that kingdom has been engaged have, in numerous instances, proceeded from the people.

There have been, if I may so express it, almost as many popular as royal wars. The cries of the nation and the importunities of their representatives have, upon various occasions, dragged their monarchs into war, or continued them in it, contrary to their inclinations, and sometimes contrary to the real interests of the state. In that memorable struggle for superiority between the rival houses of *Austria* and *Bourbon,* which so long kept Europe in a flame, it is well known that the antipathies of the English against the French, seconding the ambition, or rather the avarice, of a favorite leader,[1] protracted the war beyond the

---

[1] The Duke of Marlborough.—PUBLIUS

limits marked out by sound policy, and for a considerable time in opposition to the views of the court.

The wars of these two last-mentioned nations have in a great measure grown out of commercial considerations,—the desire of supplanting and the fear of being supplanted, either in particular branches of traffic or in the general advantages of trade and navigation.

From this summary of what has taken place in other countries, whose situations have borne the nearest resemblance to our own, what reason can we have to confide in those reveries which would seduce us into an expectation of peace and cordiality between the members of the present confederacy, in the state of separation? Have we not already seen enough of the fallacy and extravagance of those idle theories which have amused us with promises of an exemption from the imperfections, weaknesses, and evils incident to society in every shape? Is it not time to awake from the deceitful dream of a golden age, and to adopt as a practical maxim for the direction of our political conduct that we, as well as the other inhabitants of the globe, are yet remote from the happy empire of perfect wisdom and perfect virtue?

Let the point of extreme depression to which our national dignity and credit have sunk, let the inconveniences felt everywhere from a lax and ill administration of government, let the revolt of a part of the State of North Carolina, the late menacing disturbances in Pennsylvania, and the actual insurrections and rebellions in Massachusetts, declare——!

So far is the general sense of mankind from corresponding with the tenets of those who endeavor to lull asleep our apprehensions of discord and hostility between the States, in the event of disunion, that it has from long observation of the progress of society become a sort of axiom in politics, that vicinity, or nearness of situation, constitutes nations natural enemies. An intelligent writer expresses himself on this subject to this effect: "NEIGHBORING NATIONS [says he] are naturally enemies of each other, unless their common weakness forces them to league in a CONFEDERATIVE REPUBLIC, and their constitution prevents the differences that neighborhood occasions, extinguishing that secret jealousy which disposes all states to aggrandize themselves at the expense of their neighbors." [2] This passage, at the same time, points out the EVIL and suggests the REMEDY.

PUBLIUS

---

[2] Vide "Principes des Négociations" par l'Abbé de Mably.—PUBLIUS

7 [ALEXANDER HAMILTON]

Causes of Wars among the States If Disunited

To the People of the State of New York:

It is sometimes asked, with an air of seeming triumph, what inducements could the States have, if disunited, to make war upon each other? It would be a full answer to this question to say—precisely the same inducements which have, at different times, deluged in blood all the nations in the world. But, unfortunately for us, the question admits of a more particular answer. There are causes of differences within our immediate contemplation, of the tendency of which, even under the restraints of a federal constitution, we have had sufficient experience to enable us to form a judgment of what might be expected if those restraints were removed.

Territorial disputes have at all times been found one of the most fertile sources of hostility among nations. Perhaps the greatest proportion of wars that have desolated the earth have sprung from this origin. This cause would exist among us in full force. We have a vast tract of unsettled territory within the boundaries of the United States. There still are discordant and undecided claims between several of them, and the dissolution of the Union would lay a foundation for similar claims between them all. It is well known that they have heretofore had serious and animated discussion concerning the rights to the lands which were ungranted at the time of the Revolution, and which usually went under the name of crown lands. The States within

253

the limits of whose colonial governments they were comprised have claimed them as their property, the others have contended that the rights of the crown in this article devolved upon the Union; especially as to all that part of the Western territory which, either by actual possession, or through the submission of the Indian proprietors, was subjected to the jurisdiction of the king of Great Britain, till it was relinquished in the treaty of peace. This, it has been said, was at all events an acquisition to the Confederacy by compact with a foreign power. It has been the prudent policy of Congress to appease this controversy, by prevailing upon the States to make cessions to the United States for the benefit of the whole. This has been so far accomplished as, under a continuation of the Union, to afford a decided prospect of an amicable termination of the dispute. A dismemberment of the Confederacy, however, would revive this dispute, and would create others on the same subject. At present, a large part of the vacant Western territory is, by cession at least, if not by any anterior right, the common property of the Union. If that were at an end, the States which made the cession, on a principle of federal compromise, would be apt, when the motive of the grant had ceased, to reclaim the lands as a reversion. The other States would no doubt insist on a proportion, by right of representation. Their argument would be, that a grant, once made, could not be revoked; and that the justice of participating in territory acquired or secured by the joint efforts of the Confederacy, remained undiminished. If, contrary to probability, it should be admitted by all the States, that each had a right to a share of this common stock, there would still be a difficulty to be surmounted, as to a proper rule of apportionment. Different principles would be set up by different States for this purpose; and as they would affect the opposite interests of the parties, they might not easily be susceptible of a pacific adjustment.

In the wide field of Western territory, therefore, we perceive an ample theatre for hostile pretensions, without any umpire or common judge to interpose between the contending parties. To reason from the past to the future, we shall have good ground to apprehend, that the sword would sometimes be appealed to as the arbiter of their differences. The circumstances of the dispute between Connecticut and Pennsylvania, respecting the land at Wyoming, admonish us not to be sanguine in expecting an easy accommodation of such differences. The articles of confederation obliged the parties to submit the matter to the decision of a federal court. The submission was made, and the court decided in favor of Pennsylvania. But Connecticut gave strong indications of dissatisfaction with that determination; nor did she appear to be entirely resigned to it, till, by negotiation and management, something like an equivalent was found for the loss she supposed herself to have sustained. Nothing here said is intended to convey the slightest censure on the conduct of that State. She no doubt sincerely believed herself to have been injured by the decision; and States, like individuals, acquiesce with great reluctance in determinations to their disadvantage.

Those who had an opportunity of seeing the inside of the transactions which attended the progress of the controversy between this State and the district of Vermont, can vouch the opposition we experienced, as well from States not interested as from those which were interested in the claim; and can attest the danger to which the peace of the Confederacy might have been exposed, had this State attempted to assert its rights by force. Two motives preponderated in that opposition: one, a jealousy entertained of our future power; and the other, the interest of certain individuals of influence in the neighboring States, who had obtained grants of land under the actual government of that district. Even the States which brought forward claims, in contradiction to ours, seemed more solicitous to dismember this State, than to establish their own pretensions. These were New Hampshire, Massachusetts, and Connecticut. New Jersey and Rhode Island, upon all occasions, discovered a warm zeal for the independence of Vermont; and Maryland, till alarmed by the appearance of a connection between Canada and that State, entered deeply into the same views. These being small States, saw with an unfriendly eye the perspective of our growing greatness. In a review of these transactions we may trace some of the causes which would be likely to embroil the States with each other, if it should be their unpropitious destiny to become disunited.

The competitions of commerce would be another fruitful source of contention. The States less favorably circumstanced would be desirous of escaping from the disadvantages of local situation, and of sharing in the advantages of their more fortunate neighbors. Each State, or separate confederacy, would pursue a system of commercial policy peculiar to itself. This would occasion distinctions, preferences, and exclusions, which would beget discontent. The habits of intercourse, on the basis of equal privileges, to which we have been accustomed since the earliest settlement of the country, would give a keener edge to those causes of discontent than they would naturally have independent of this circumstance. *We should be ready to denominate injuries those things which were in reality the justifiable acts of independent sovereignties consulting a distinct interest.* The spirit of enterprise, which characterizes the commercial part of America, has left no occasion of displaying itself unimproved. It is not at all probable that this unbridled spirit would pay much respect to those regulations of trade by which particular States might endeavor to secure exclusive benefits to their own citizens. The infractions of these regulations, on one side, the efforts to prevent and repel them, on the other, would naturally lead to outrages, and these to reprisals and wars.

The opportunities which some States would have of rendering others tributary to them by commercial regulations would be impatiently submitted to by the tributary States. The relative situation of New York, Connecticut, and New Jersey, would afford an example of this kind. New York, from the necessities of revenue, must lay duties on her importations. A great part of these duties must be paid by the inhabitants of the two other States in the capacity of consumers of what we import. New York would neither be willing nor able to forego this advantage. Her citizens would not consent that a duty paid by them should be remitted in favor of the citizens of her neighbors; nor would it be practicable, if there were not this impediment in the way, to distinguish the customers in our own markets. Would Connecticut and New Jersey long submit to be taxed by New York for her exclusive benefit? Should we be long permitted to remain in the quiet and undisturbed enjoyment of a metropolis, from the possession of which we derived an advantage so odious to our neighbors, and, in their opinion, so oppressive? Should we be able to preserve it against the incumbent weight of Connecticut on the one side, and the co-operating pressure of New Jersey on the other? These are questions that temerity alone will answer in the affirmative.

The public debt of the Union would be a further cause of collision between the separate States or confederacies. The apportionment, in the first instance, and the progressive extinguishment afterwards, would be alike productive of ill-humor and animosity. How would it be possible to agree upon a rule of apportionment satisfactory to all? There is scarcely any that can be proposed which is entirely free from real objections. These, as usual, would be exaggerated by the adverse interest of the parties. There are even dissimilar views among the States as to the general principle of discharging the public debt. Some of them, either less impressed with the importance of national credit, or because their citizens have little, if any, immediate interest in the question, feel an indifference, if not a repugnance, to the payment of the domestic debt at any rate. These would be inclined to magnify the difficulties of a distribution. Others of them, a numerous body of whose citizens are creditors to the public beyond the proportion of the State in the total amount of the national debt, would be strenuous for some equitable and effective provision. The procrastinations of the former would excite the resentments of the latter. The settlement of a rule would, in the meantime, be postponed by real differences of opinion and affected delays. The citizens of the States interested would clamor; foreign powers would urge for the satisfaction of their just demands, and the peace of the States would be hazarded to the double contingency of external invasion and internal contention.

Suppose the difficulties of agreeing upon a rule surmounted, and the apportionment made. Still there is great room to suppose that the rule agreed upon would, upon experiment, be found to bear harder upon some States than upon others. Those which were sufferers by it would naturally seek for a mitigation of the burden. The others would as naturally be disinclined to a revision, which was likely to end in an increase of their own incumbrances. Their refusal would be too plausible a pretext to the complaining States to withhold their contributions, not to be embraced with avidity; and the non-compliance of these States with their engagements would be a ground of bitter discussion and altercation. If even the rule adopted should in practice justify the equality of its principle, still delinquencies in payments on the part of some of the States would result from a diversity of other causes—the real deficiency of resources; the mismanagement of their finances; accidental disorders in the management of the government; and, in addition to the rest, the reluctance with which men commonly part with money for purposes that have outlived the exigencies which produced them, and interfere with the supply of immediate wants. Delinquencies, from whatever causes, would be productive of complaints, recriminations, and quarrels. There is, perhaps, nothing more likely to disturb the tranquillity of nations than their being bound to mutual contributions for any common object that does not yield an equal and coincident benefit. For it is an observation, as true as it is trite, that there is nothing men differ so readily about as the payment of money.

Laws in violation of private contracts, as they amount to aggressions on the rights of those States whose citizens are injured by them, may be considered as another probable source of hostility. We are not authorized to expect that a more liberal or more equitable spirit would preside over the legislations of the individual States hereafter, if unrestrained by any additional checks, than we have heretofore seen in too many instances disgracing their several codes. We have observed the disposition to retaliation excited in Connecticut, in consequence of the enormities perpetrated by the Legislature of Rhode Island; and we may reasonably infer that, in similar cases under other circumstances, a war, not of *parchment,* but of the sword, would chastise such atrocious breaches of moral obligation and social justice.

The probability of incompatible alliances between the different States or confederacies and different foreign nations, and the effects of this situation upon the peace of the whole, have been sufficiently unfolded in some preceding papers. From the view they have exhibited of this part of the subject, this conclusion is to be drawn, that America, if not connected at all, or only by the feeble tie of a simple league, offensive and defensive, would, by the operation of such jarring alliances, be gradually entangled in all the pernicious labyrinths of European politics and wars; and by the destructive contentions of the parts into which she was divided, would be likely to become a prey to the artifices and machinations of powers equally the enemies of them all. *Divide et impera* [1] must be the motto of every nation that either hates or fears us. . . .

PUBLIUS

---

[1] Divide and command.—PUBLIUS

9 [ALEXANDER HAMILTON]

****

Union as a Barrier to Faction and Insurrection

****

To the People of the State of New York:

A Firm Union will be of the utmost moment to the peace and liberty of the States, as a barrier against domestic faction and insurrection. It is impossible to read the history of the petty republics of Greece and Italy without feeling sensations of horror and disgust at the distractions with which they were continually agitated, and at the rapid succession of revolutions by which they were kept in a state of perpetual vibration between the extremes of tyranny and anarchy. If they exhibit occasional calms, these only serve as short-lived contrasts to the furious storms that are to succeed. If now and then intervals of felicity open to view, we behold them with a mixture of regret, arising from the reflection that the pleasing scenes before us are soon to be overwhelmed by the tempestuous waves of sedition and party rage. If momentary rays of glory break forth from the gloom, while they dazzle us with a transient and fleeting brilliancy, they at the same time admonish us to lament that the vices of government should pervert the direction and tarnish the lustre of those bright talents and exalted endowments for which the favored soils that produced them have been so justly celebrated.

From the disorders that disfigure the annals of those republics the advocates of despotism have drawn arguments, not only against the forms of republican government, but against the very principles of civil liberty. They have decried all free government as inconsistent with the order of society, and have indulged themselves in malicious exultation over its friends and partisans. Happily for mankind, stupendous fabrics reared on the basis of liberty, which have flourished for ages, have, in a few glorious instances, refuted their gloomy sophisms. And, I trust, America will be the broad and solid foundation of other edifices, not less magnificent, which will be equally permanent monuments of their errors.

But it is not to be denied that the portraits they have sketched of republican government were too just copies of the originals from which they were taken. If it had been found impracticable to have devised models of a more perfect structure, the enlightened friends to liberty would have been obliged to abandon the cause of that species of government as indefensible. The science of politics, however, like most other sciences, has received great improvement. The efficacy of various principles is now well understood, which were either not known at all, or imperfectly known to the ancients. The regular distribution of power into distinct departments; the introduction of legislative balances and checks; the institution of courts composed of judges holding their offices during good behavior; the representation of the people in the legislature by deputies of their own election: these are wholly new discoveries, or have made their principal progress towards perfection in modern times. They are means, and powerful means, by which the excellences of republican government may be retained and its imperfections lessened or avoided. To this catalogue of circumstances that tend to the amelioration of popular systems of civil government, I shall venture, however novel it may appear to some, to add one more, on a principle which has been made the foundation of an objection to the new Constitution; I mean the ENLARGEMENT of the ORBIT within which such systems are to revolve, either in respect to the dimensions of a single State, or to the consolidation of several smaller States into one great Confederacy. The latter is that which immediately concerns the object under consideration. It will, however, be of use to examine the principle in its application to a single State, which shall be attended to in another place.

The utility of a Confederacy, as well to suppress faction and to guard the internal tranquillity of States, as to increase their external force and security, is in reality not a new idea. It has been practised upon in different countries and ages, and has received the sanction of the most approved writers on the subjects of politics. The opponents of the plan proposed have, with great assiduity, cited and circulated the observations of Montesquieu on the necessity of a contracted territory for a republican government. But they seem not to have been apprised of the sentiments of that great man expressed in another part of his work, nor to have adverted to the consequences of the principle to which they subscribe with such ready acquiescence.

When Montesquieu recommends a small extent for republics, the standards he had in view were of dimensions far short of the limits of almost every one of these States. Neither Virginia, Massachusetts, Pennsylvania, New York, North Carolina, nor Georgia can by any means be compared with the models from which he reasoned and to which the terms of his description apply. If we therefore take his ideas on this point as the criterion of truth, we shall be driven to the alternative either of taking refuge at once in the arms of monarchy, or of splitting ourselves into an infinity of little, jealous, clashing, tumultuous commonwealths, the wretched nurseries of unceasing discord, and the miserable objects of universal pity or contempt. Some of the writers who have come forward on the other side of the question seem to have been aware of the dilemma; and have even been bold enough to hint at the division of the larger States as a desirable thing. Such an infatuated policy, such a desperate expedient, might, by the multiplication of petty offices, answer the views of men who possess not qualifications to extend their influence beyond the narrow circles of personal intrigue, but it could never promote the greatness or happiness of the people of America.

Referring the examination of the principle itself to another place, as has been already mentioned, it will be sufficient to remark here that, in the sense of the author who has been most emphatically quoted upon the occasion, it would only dictate a reduction of the SIZE of the most considerable MEMBERS of the Union, but would not militate against their being all comprehended in one confederate government. And this is the true question, in the discussion of which we are at present interested.

So far are the suggestions of Montesquieu from standing in opposition to a general Union of the States, that he explicitly treats of a CONFEDERATE REPUBLIC as the expedient for extending the sphere of popular government, and reconciling the advantages of monarchy with those of republicanism.

"It is very probable" (says he [1]) that mankind would have been obliged at length to live constantly under the government of a single person, had they not contrived a kind of constitution that has all the internal advantages of a republican, together with the external force of a monarchical, government. I mean a CONFEDERATE REPUBLIC.

"This form of government is a convention by which several smaller *states* agree to become members of a larger *one*, which they intend to form. It is a kind of assemblage of societies that constitute a new one, capable of increasing, by means of new associations, till they arrive to such a degree of power as to be able to provide for the security of the united body.

"A republic of this kind, able to withstand an external force, may support itself without any internal corruption. The form of this society prevents all manner of inconveniences.

"If a single member should attempt to usurp the supreme authority, he could not be supposed to have an equal authority and credit in all the confederate states. Were he to have too great influence over one, this would alarm the rest. Were he to subdue a part, that which would still remain free might oppose him with forces independent of those which he had usurped,

---

[1] "Spirit of Laws," vol. i., book ix., chap. i.—PUBLIUS

and overpower him before he could be settled in his usurpation.

"Should a popular insurrection happen in one of the confederate states, the others are able to quell it. Should abuses creep into one part, they are reformed by those that remain sound. The state may be destroyed on one side, and not on the other; the confederacy may be dissolved, and the confederates preserve their sovereignty.

"As this government is composed of small republics, it enjoys the internal happiness of each; and with respect to its external situation, it is possessed, by means of the association, of all the advantages of large monarchies."

I have thought it proper to quote at length these interesting passages, because they contain a luminous abridgment of the principal arguments in favor of the Union, and must effectually remove the false impressions which a misapplication of other parts of the work was calculated to make. They have, at the same time, an intimate connection with the more immediate design of this paper; which is, to illustrate the tendency of the Union to repress domestic faction and insurrection.

A distinction, more subtle than accurate, has been raised between a *confederacy* and a *consolidation* of the States. The essential characteristic of the first is said to be, the restriction of its authority to the members in their collective capacities, without reaching to the individuals of whom they are composed. It is contended that the national council ought to have no concern with any object of internal administration. An exact equality of suffrage between the members has also been insisted upon as a leading feature of a confederate government. These positions are, in the main, arbitrary; they are supported neither by principle nor precedent. It had indeed happened, that governments of this kind have generally operated in the manner which the distinction, taken notice of, supposes to be inherent in their nature; but there have been in most of them extensive exceptions to the practice, which serve to prove, as far as example will go, that there is no absolute rule on the subject. And it will be clearly shown, in the course of this investigation, that as far as the principle contended for has prevailed, it has been the cause of incurable disorder and imbecility in the government.

The definition of a *confederate republic* seems simply to be "an assemblage of societies," or an association of two or more states into one state. The extent, modifications, and objects of the federal authority are mere matters of discretion. So long as the separate organization of the members be not abolished; so long as it exists, by a constitutional necessity, for local purposes; though it should be in perfect subordination to the general authority of the union, it would still be, in fact and in theory, an association of states, or a confederacy. The proposed Constitution, so far from implying an abolition of the State governments, makes them constituent parts of the national sovereignty, by allowing them a direct representation in the Senate, and leaves in their possession certain exclusive and very important portions of sovereign power. This fully corresponds, in every rational import of the terms, with the idea of a federal government.

✸ ✸ ✸ ✸

PUBLIUS

10 [JAMES MADISON]

The Size and Variety of the Union as a Check on Faction

To the People of the State of New York:

Among the numerous advantages promised by a well-constructed Union, none deserves to be more accurately developed than its tendency to break and control the violence of faction. The friend of popular governments never finds himself so much alarmed for their character and fate, as when he contemplates their propensity to this dangerous vice. He will not fail, therefore, to set a due value on any plan which, without violating the principles to which he is attached, provides a proper cure for it. The instability, injustice, and confusion introduced into the public councils, have, in truth, been the mortal diseases under which popular governments have everywhere perished; as they continue to be the favorite and fruitful topics from which the adversaries to liberty derive their most specious declamations. The valuable improvements made by the American constitutions on the popular models, both ancient and modern, cannot certainly be too much admired; but it would be an unwarrantable partiality, to contend that they have as effectually obviated the danger on this side, as was wished and expected. Complaints are everywhere heard from our most considerate and virtuous citizens, equally the friends of public and private faith, and of public and personal liberty, that our governments are too un-

266

stable, that the public good is disregarded in the conflicts of rival parties, and that measures are too often decided, not according to the rules of justice and the rights of the minor party, but by the superior force of an interested and overbearing majority. However anxiously we may wish that these complaints had no foundation, the evidence of known facts will not permit us to deny that they are in some degree true. It will be found, indeed, on a candid review of our situation, that some of the distresses under which we labor have been erroneously charged on the operation of our governments; but it will be found, at the same time, that other causes will not alone account for many of our heaviest misfortunes; and, particularly, for that prevailing and increasing distrust of public engagements, and alarm for private rights, which are echoed from one end of the continent to the other. These must be chiefly, if not wholly, effects of the unsteadiness and injustice with which a factious spirit has tainted our public administrations.

By a faction, I understand a number of citizens, whether amounting to a majority or minority of the whole, who are united and actuated by some common impulse of passion, or of interest, adverse to the rights of other citizens, or to the permanent and aggregate interests of the community.

There are two methods of curing the mischiefs of faction: the one, by removing its causes; the other, by controlling its effects.

There are again two methods of removing the causes of faction: the one, by destroying the liberty which is essential to its existence; the other, by giving to every citizen the same opinions, the same passions, and the same interests.

It could never be more truly said than of the first remedy, that it was worse than the disease. Liberty is to faction what air is to fire, an aliment without which it instantly expires. But it could not be less folly to abolish liberty, which is essential to political life, because it nourishes faction, than it would be to wish the annihilation of air, which is essential to animal life, because it imparts to fire its destructive agency.

The second expedient is as impracticable as the first would be unwise. As long as the reason of man continues fallible, and he is at liberty to exercise it, different opinions will be formed. As long as the connection subsists between his reason and his self-love, his opinions and his passions will have a reciprocal influence on each other: and the former will be objects to which the latter will attach themselves. The diversity in the faculties of men, from which the rights of property originate, is not less an insuperable obstacle to a uniformity of interests. The protection of these faculties is the first object of government. From the protection of different and unequal faculties of acquiring property, the possession of different degrees and kinds of property immediately results; and from the influence of these on the sentiments and views of the respective proprietors, ensues a division of the society into different interests and parties.

The latent causes of faction are thus sown in the nature of man; and we see them everywhere brought into different degrees of activity, according to the different circumstances of civil society. A zeal for different opinions concerning religion, concerning government, and many other points, as well of speculation as of practice; an attachment to different leaders ambitiously contending for pre-eminence and power; or to persons of other descriptions whose fortunes have been interesting to the human passions, have, in turn, divided mankind into parties, inflamed them with mutual animosity, and rendered them much more disposed to vex and oppress each other than to co-operate for their common good. So strong is this propensity of mankind to fall into mutual animosities, that where no substantial occasion presents itself, the most frivolous and fanciful distinctions have been sufficient to kindle their unfriendly passions and excite their most violent conflicts. But the most common and durable source of factions has been the various and unequal distribution of property. Those who hold and those who are without property have ever formed distinct interests in society. Those who are creditors, and those who are debtors, fall under a like discrimination. A landed interest, a manufacturing interest, a mercantile interest, a moneyed interest, with many lesser interests, grow up of necessity in civilized nations, and divide them into different classes, actuated by different sentiments and views. The regulation of these various and interfering interests forms the principal task of modern legislation, and involves the spirit of party and faction in the necessary and ordinary operations of the government.

No man is allowed to be a judge in his own cause, because his interest would certainly bias his judgment, and, not improbably, corrupt his integrity. With equal, nay with greater reason, a body of men are unfit to be both judges and parties at the same time; yet what are many of the most important acts of legislation, but so many judicial determinations, not indeed concerning the rights of single persons, but concerning the rights of large bodies of citizens? And what are the different classes of legislators but advocates and parties to the causes which they determine? Is a law proposed concerning private debts? It is a question to which the creditors are parties on one side and the debtors on the other. Justice ought to hold the balance between them. Yet the parties are, and must be, themselves the judges; and the most numerous party, or, in other words, the most powerful faction must be expected to prevail. Shall domestic manufactures be encouraged, and in what degree, by restrictions on foreign manufactures? are questions which would be differently decided by the landed and the manufacturing classes, and probably by neither with a sole regard to justice and the public good. The apportionment of taxes on the various descriptions of property is an act which seems to require the most exact impartiality; yet there is, perhaps, no legislative act in which greater opportunity and temptation are given to a predominant party to trample on the rules of justice. Every shilling with which they overburden the inferior number, is a shilling saved to their own pockets.

It is in vain to say that enlightened statesmen will be able to adjust these clashing interests, and render them all subservient to the public good. Enlightened statesmen will not always be at the helm. Nor, in many cases, can such an adjustment be made at all without taking into view indirect and remote considerations, which will rarely prevail over the immediate interest which one party may find in disregarding the rights of another or the good of the whole.

The inference to which we are brought is, that the *causes* of faction cannot be removed, and that relief is only to be sought in the means of controlling its *effects*.

If a faction consists of less than a majority, relief is supplied by the republican principle, which enables the majority to defeat its sinister views by regular vote. It may clog the administration, it may convulse the society; but it will be unable to execute and mask its violence under the forms of the Constitution. When a majority is included in a faction, the form of popular government, on the other hand, enables it to sacrifice to its ruling passion or interest both the public good and the rights of other citizens. To secure the public good and private rights against the danger of such a faction, and at the same time to preserve the spirit and the form of popular government, is then the great object to which our inquiries are directed. Let me add that it is the great desideratum by which this form of government can be rescued from the opprobrium under which it has so long labored, and be recommended to the esteem and adoption of mankind.

By what means is this object attainable? Evidently by one of two only. Either the existence of the same passion or interest in a majority at the same time must be prevented, or the majority, having such coexistent passion or interest, must be rendered, by their number and local situation, unable to concert and carry into effect schemes of oppression. If the impulse and the opportunity be suffered to coincide, we well know that neither moral nor religious motives can be relied on as an adequate control. They are not found to be such on the injustice and violence of individuals, and lose their efficacy in proportion to the number combined together, that is, in proportion as their efficacy becomes needful.

From this view of the subject it may be concluded that a pure democracy, by which I mean a society consisting of a small number of citizens, who assemble and administer the government in person, can admit of no cure for the mischiefs of faction. A common passion or interest will, in almost every case, be felt by a majority of the whole; a communication and concert result from the form of government itself; and there is nothing to check the inducements to sacrifice the weaker party or an obnoxious individual. Hence it is that such democracies have ever been spectacles of turbulence and contention; have ever been found incompatible with personal security or the rights of property; and have in general been as short in their lives as they have been violent in their deaths. Theoretic politicians, who have patronized this species of government, have erroneously supposed that by reducing mankind to a perfect equality in their political rights, they would, at the same time, be perfectly equalized and assimilated in their possessions, their opinions, and their passions.

A republic, by which I mean a government in which the scheme of representation takes place, opens a different prospect, and promises the cure for which we are seeking. Let us examine the points in which it varies from pure democracy, and we shall comprehend both the nature of the cure and the efficacy which it must derive from the Union.

The two great points of difference between a democracy and a republic are: first, the delegation of the government, in the latter, to a small number of citizens elected by the rest; secondly, the greater number of citizens, and greater sphere of country, over which the latter may be extended.

The effect of the first difference is, on the one hand, to refine and enlarge the public views, by passing them through the medium of a chosen body of citizens, whose wisdom may best discern the true interest of their country, and whose patriotism and love of justice will be least likely to sacrifice it to temporary or partial considerations. Under such a regulation, it may well happen that the public voice, pronounced by the representatives of the people, will be more consonant to the public good than if pronounced by the people themselves, convened for the purpose. On the other hand, the effect may be inverted. Men of factious tempers, of local prejudices, or of sinister designs, may, by intrigue, by corruption, or by other means, first obtain the suffrages, and then betray the interests, of the people. The question resulting is, whether small or extensive republics are more favorable to the election of proper guardians of the public weal; and it is clearly decided in favor of the latter by two obvious considerations:

In the first place, it is to be remarked that, however small the republic may be, the representatives must be raised to a certain number, in order to guard against the cabals of a few; and that, however large it may be, they must be limited to a certain number, in order to guard against the confusion of a multitude. Hence, the number of representatives in the two cases not being in proportion to that of the two constituents, and being proportionally greater in the small republic, it follows that, if the proportion of fit characters be not less in the large than in the small republic, the former will present a greater option, and consequently a greater probability of a fit choice.

In the next place, as each representative will be chosen by a greater number of citizens in the large than in the small republic, it will be more difficult for unworthy candidates to practise with success the vicious arts by which elections are too often carried; and the suffrages of the people being more free, will be more likely to centre in men who possess the most attractive merit and the most diffusive and established characters.

It must be confessed that in this, as in most other cases, there is a mean, on both sides of which inconveniences will be found to lie. By enlarging too much the number of electors, you render the representative too little acquainted with all their local circumstances and lesser interests; as by reducing it too much, you render him unduly attached to these, and too little fit to comprehend and pursue great and national objects. The federal Constitution forms a happy combination in this respect; the great and aggregate interests being referred to the national, the local and particular to the State legislatures.

The other point of difference is, the greater number of citizens and extent of territory which may be brought within the compass of republican than of democratic government; and it is this circumstance principally which renders factious combinations less to be dreaded in the former than in the latter. The smaller the society, the fewer probably will be the distinct parties and interests composing it; the fewer the distinct parties and interests, the more frequently will a majority be found of the same party; and the smaller the number of individuals composing a majority, and the smaller the compass within which they are placed, the most easily will they concert and execute their plans of oppression. Extend the sphere, and you take in a greater variety of parties and interests; you make it less probable that a majority of the whole will have a common motive to invade the rights of other citizens; or if such a common motive exists, it will be more difficult for all who feel it to discover their own strength, and to act in unison with each other. Besides other impediments, it may be remarked that, where there is a consciousness of unjust or dishonorable purposes, communication is always checked by distrust in proportion to the number whose concurrence is necessary.

Hence, it clearly appears, that the same advantage which a republic has over a democracy, in controlling the effects of faction, is enjoyed by a large over a small republic,—is enjoyed by the Union over the States composing it. Does the advantage consist in the substitution of representatives whose enlightened views and virtuous sentiments render them superior to local prejudices and to schemes of injustice? It will not be denied that the representation of the Union will be most likely to possess these requisite endowments. Does it consist in the greater security afforded by a greater variety of parties, against the event of any one party being able to outnumber and oppress the rest?

In an equal degree does the increased variety of parties comprised within the Union, increase this security. Does it, in fine, consist in the greater obstacles opposed to the concert and accomplishment of the secret wishes of an unjust and interested majority? Here, again, the extent of the Union gives it the most palpable advantage.

The influence of factious leaders may kindle a flame within their particular States, but will be unable to spread a general conflagration through the other States. A religious sect may degenerate into a political faction in a part of the Confederacy; but the variety of sects dispersed over the entire face of it must secure the national councils against any danger from that source. A rage for paper money, for an abolition of debts, for an equal division of property, or for any other improper or wicked project, will be less apt to pervade the whole body of the Union than a particular member of it; in the same proportion as such a malady is more likely to taint a particular county or district, than an entire State.

In the extent and proper structure of the Union, therefore, we behold a republican remedy for the diseases most incident to republican government. And according to the degree of pleasure and pride we feel in being republicans, ought to be our zeal in cherishing the spirit and supporting the character of Federalists.

PUBLIUS

15 [ALEXANDER HAMILTON]

Defects of the Confederation

To the People of the State of New York:

✳   ✳   ✳   ✳

In pursuance of the plan which I have laid down for the discussion of the subject, the point next in order to be examined is the "insufficiency of the present Confederation to the preservation of the Union." It may perhaps be asked what need there is of reasoning or proof to illustrate a position which is not either controverted or doubted, to which the understandings and feelings of all classes of men assent, and which in substance is admitted by the opponents as well as by the friends of the new Constitution. It must in truth be acknowledged that, however these may differ in other respects, they in general appear to harmonize in this sentiment, at least, that there are material imperfections in our national system, and that something is necessary to be done to rescue us from impending anarchy. The facts that support this opinion are no longer objects of speculation. . . .

We may indeed with propriety be said to have reached almost the last stage of national humiliation. There is scarcely any thing that can wound the pride or degrade the character of an independent nation which we do not experience. Are there engagements to the performance of which we are held by every tie respectable among men? These are the subjects of constant and unblushing violation. Do we owe debts to foreigners and to our own citizens contracted in a time of imminent peril for the preservation of our political existence? These remain without any proper or satisfactory provision for their discharge. Have we valuable territories and important posts in the possession of a foreign power which, by express stipulations, ought long since to have been surrendered? These are still retained, to the prejudice of our interests, not less than of our rights. Are we in a condition to resent or to repel the aggression? We have neither troops, nor treasury, nor government.[1] Are we even in a condition to remonstrate with dignity? The just imputations on our own faith, in respect to the same treaty, ought first to be removed. Are we entitled by nature and compact to a free participation in the navigation of the Mississippi? Spain excludes us from it. Is public credit an indispensable resource in time of public danger? We seem to have abandoned its cause as desperate and irretrievable. Is commerce of importance to national wealth? Ours is at the lowest point of declension. Is respectability in the eyes of foreign powers a safeguard against foreign encroachments? The imbecility of our government even forbids them to treat with us. Our ambassadors abroad are the mere pageants of mimic sovereignty. Is a violent and unnatural decrease in the value of land a symptom of national distress? The price of improved land in most parts of the country is much lower than can be accounted for by the quantity of waste land at market, and can only be fully explained by that want of private and public confidence, which are so alarmingly prevalent among all ranks, and which have a direct tendency to depreciate property of every kind. Is private credit the friend and patron of industry? That most useful kind which relates to borrowing and lending is reduced within the narrowest limits, and this still more from an opinion of insecurity than from the scarcity of money. To shorten

---

[1] "I mean for the Union."—PUBLIUS

an enumeration of particulars which can afford neither pleasure nor instruction, it may in general be demanded, what indication is there of national disorder, poverty, and insignificance that could befall a community so peculiarly blessed with natural advantages as we are, which does not form a part of the dark catalogue of our public misfortunes.

This is the melancholy situation to which we have been brought by those very maxims and councils which would now deter us from adopting the proposed Constitution; and which, not content with having conducted us to the brink of a precipice, seem resolved to plunge us into the abyss that awaits us below. Here, my countrymen, impelled by every motive that ought to influence an enlightened people, let us make a firm stand for our safety, our tranquillity, our dignity, our reputation. Let us at last break the fatal charm which has too long seduced us from the paths of felicity and prosperity.

It is true, as has been before observed, that facts, too stubborn to be resisted, have produced a species of general assent to the abstract proposition that there exist material defects in our national system; but the usefulness of the concession, on the part of the old adversaries of federal measures, is destroyed by a strenuous opposition to a remedy, upon the only principles that can give it a chance of success. While they admit that the government of the United States is destitute of energy, they contend against conferring upon it those powers which are requisite to supply that energy. They seem still to aim at things repugnant and irreconcilable; at an augmentation of federal authority, without a diminution of State authority; at sovereignty in the Union, and complete independence in the members. They still, in fine, seem to cherish with blind devotion the political monster of an *imperium in imperio*. This renders a full display of the principal defects of the Confederation necessary, in order to show that the evils we experience do not proceed from minute or partial imperfections, but from fundamental errors in the structure of the building, which cannot be amended otherwise than by an alteration in the first principles and main pillars of the fabric.

The great and radical vice in the construction of the existing Confederation is in the principle of LEGISLATION for STATES or GOVERNMENTS, in their CORPORATE or COLLECTIVE CAPACITIES, and as contradistinguished from the INDIVIDU-ALS of which they consist. Though this principle does not run through all the powers delegated to the Union, yet it pervades and governs those on which the efficacy of the rest depends. Except as to the rule of apportionment, the United States has an indefinite discretion to make requisitions for men and money; but they have no authority to raise either, by regulations extending to the individual citizens of America. The consequence of this is, that though in theory their resolutions concerning those objects are laws, constitutionally binding on the members of the Union, yet in practice they are mere recommendations which the States observe or disregard at their option.

It is a singular instance of the capriciousness of the human mind, that after all the admonitions we have had from experience on this head, there should still be found men who object to the new Constitution, for deviating from a principle which has been found the bane of the old, and which is in itself evidently incompatible with the idea of GOVERNMENT; a principle, in short, which, if it is to be executed at all, must substitute the violent and sanguinary agency of the sword to the mild influence of the magistracy.

There is nothing absurd or impracticable in the idea of a league or alliance between independent nations for certain defined purposes precisely stated in a treaty regulating all the details of time, place, circumstance, and quantity; leaving nothing to future discretion; and depending for its execution on the good faith of the parties. . . . In the early part of the present century there was an epidemical rage in Europe for this species of compacts, from which the politicians of the times fondly hoped for benefits which were never realized. With a view to establishing the equilibrium of power and the peace of that part of the world, all the resources of negotiations were exhausted, and triple and quadruple alliances were formed; but they were scarcely formed before they were broken, giving an instructive but afflicting lesson to mankind, how little dependence is to be placed on treaties which have no other sanction than the obligations of good faith, and which oppose general considerations of peace and justice to the impulse of any immediate interest or passion.

If the particular States in this country are disposed to stand in a similar relation to each other, and to drop the project of a general DISCRETIONARY SUPERINTENDENCE, the scheme would indeed be pernicious, and would entail upon us all the mischiefs which have been enumerated under the first head; but it would have the merit of being, at least, consistent and practicable. Abandoning all views towards a confederate government, this would bring us to a simple alliance offensive and defensive; and would place us in a situation to be alternate friends and enemies of each other, as our mutual jealousies and rivalships, nourished by the intrigues of foreign nations, should prescribe to us.

But if we are unwilling to be placed in this perilous situation; if we still will adhere to the design of a national government, or, which is the same thing, of a superintending power, under the direction of a common council, we must resolve to incorporate into our plan those ingredients which may be considered as forming the characteristic difference between a league and a government; we must extend the authority of the Union to the persons of the citizens,—the only proper objects of government.

Government implies the power of making laws. It is essential to the idea of a law, that it be attended with a sanction; or, in other words, a penalty or punishment for disobedience. If there be no penalty annexed to disobedience, the resolutions or commands which pretend to be laws will, in fact, amount to nothing more than advice or recommendation. This penalty, whatever it may be, can only be inflicted in two ways: by the agency of the courts and ministers of justice, or by military force; by the COERCION of the magistracy, or by the COERCION of arms. The first kind can evidently apply only to men; the last kind must of necessity, be employed against bodies politic, or communities, or States. It is evident that there is no process of a court by which the observance of the laws can, in the last resort, be enforced. Sentences may be denounced against them for violations of their duty; but these sentences can only be carried into execution by the sword. In an association where the general authority is confined to the collective bodies of the communities that compose it, every breach of the laws must involve a state of war; and military execution must become the only instrument of civil obedience. Such a state of things can certainly not deserve the name of government, nor would any prudent man choose to commit his happiness to it.

There was a time when we were told that breaches, by the States, of the regulations of the federal authority were not to be expected; that a sense of common interest would preside over the conduct of the respective members, and would beget a full compliance with all the constitutional requisitions of the Union. This language, at the present day, would appear as wild as a great part of what we now hear from the same quarter will be thought, when we shall have received further lessons from that best oracle of wisdom, experience. It at all times betrayed an ignorance of the true springs by which human conduct is actuated and belied the original inducements to the establishment of civil power. Why has government been instituted at all? Because the passions of men will not conform to the dictates of reason and justice, without constraint. Has it been found that bodies of men act with more rectitude or greater disinterestedness than individuals? The contrary of this has been inferred by all accurate observers of the conduct of mankind; and the inference is founded upon obvious reasons. Regard to reputation has a less active influence, when the infamy of a bad action is to be divided among a number, than when it is to fall singly upon one. A spirit of faction, which is apt to mingle its poison in the deliberations of all bodies of men, will often hurry the persons of whom they are composed into improprieties and excesses, for which they would blush in a private capacity.

In addition to all this, there is, in the nature of sovereign power, an impatience of control, that disposes those who are invested with the exercise of it, to look with an evil eye upon all external attempts to restrain or direct its operations. From this spirit it happens, that in every political association which is formed upon the principle of uniting in a common interest a number of lesser sovereignties, there will be found a kind of eccentric tendency in the subordinate or inferior orbs, by the operation of which there will be a perpetual effort in each to fly off from the common centre. This tendency is not difficult to be accounted for. It has its origin in the love of power. Power controlled or abridged is almost always the rival and enemy of that power by which it is controlled or abridged. This simple proposition will teach us, how little reason there is to expect, that the persons intrusted with the administration of the affairs of the particular members of a confederacy will at all times be ready, with perfect good-humor, and an unbiased regard to the public weal, to execute the resolutions or decrees of the general authority. The reverse of this results from the constitution of human nature.

If, therefore, the measures of the Confederacy cannot be executed without the intervention of the particular administrations, there will be little prospect of their being executed at all. The rulers of the respective members, whether they have a constitutional right to do it or not, will undertake to judge of the propriety of the measures themselves. They will consider the conformity of the thing proposed or required to their immediate interests or aims; the momentary conveniences or inconveniences that would attend its adoption. All this will be done; and in a spirit of interested and suspicious scrutiny, without that knowledge of national circumstances and reasons of state, which is essential to a right judgment, and with that strong predilection in favor of local objects, which can hardly fail to mislead the decision. The same process must be repeated in every member of which the body is constituted; and the execution of the plans, framed by the councils of the whole, will always fluctuate on the discretion of the ill-formed and prejudiced opinion of every part. Those who have been conversant in the proceedings of popular assemblies; who have seen how difficult it often is, where there is no exterior pressure of circumstances, to bring them to harmonious resolutions on important points, will readily conceive how impossible it must be to induce a number of such assemblies, deliberating at a distance from each other, at different times, and under different impressions, long to cooperate in the same views and pursuits.

In our case, the concurrence of thirteen distinct sovereign wills is requisite, under the Confederation, to the complete execution of every important measure that proceeds from the Union. It has happened as was to have been foreseen. The measures of the Union have not been executed; the delinquencies of the State have, step by step, matured themselves to an extreme, which has, at length, arrested all the wheels of the national government, and brought them to an awful stand. Congress at this time scarcely possess the means of keeping up the forms of administration, till the States can have time to agree upon a more substantial substitute for the present shadow of a federal government. Things did not come to this desperate extremity at once. The causes which have been specified produced at first only unequal and disproportionate degrees of compliance with the requisitions of the Union. The greater deficiencies of some States furnished the pretext of example and the temptation of interest to the complying, or to the least delinquent States. Why should we do more in proportion than those who are embarked with us in the same political voyage? Why should we consent to bear more than our proper share of the common burden? These were suggestions which human selfishness could not withstand, and which even speculative men, who looked forward to remote consequences, could not, without hesitation, combat. Each State, yielding to the persuasive voice of immediate interest or convenience, has successively withdrawn its support, till the frail and tottering edifice seems ready to fall upon our heads, and to crush us beneath its ruins.

PUBLIUS

The Confederation:
Lack of Powers and of Proper Ratification

To the People of the State of New York:

❋   ❋   ❋   ❋

The right of equal suffrage among the States is another exceptionable part of the Confederation. Every idea of proportion and every rule of fair representation conspire to condemn a principle, which gives to Rhode Island an equal weight in the scale of power with Massachusetts, or Connecticut, or New York; and to Delaware an equal voice in the national deliberations with Pennsylvania, or Virginia, or North Carolina. Its operation contradicts the fundamental maxim of republican government, which requires that the sense of the majority should prevail. Sophistry may reply, that sovereigns are equal, and that a majority of the votes of the States will be a majority of confederated America. But this kind of logical legerdemain will never counteract the plain suggestions of justice and common-sense. It may happen that this majority of States is a small minority of the people of America[1]; and two thirds of the people of America could not long be persuaded, upon the credit of artificial distinction and syl-

---

[1] New Hampshire, Rhode Island, New Jersey, Delaware, Georgia, South Carolina, and Maryland are a majority of the whole number of the States, but they do not contain one third of the people.—PUBLIUS

logistic subtleties, to submit their interests to the management and disposal of one third. The larger States would after a while revolt from the idea of receiving the law from the smaller. To acquiesce in such a privation of their due importance in the political scale, would be not merely to be insensible to the love of power, but even to sacrifice the desire of equality. It is neither rational to expect the first, nor just to require the last. The smaller States, considering how peculiarly their safety and welfare depend on union, ought readily to renounce a pretension which, if not relinquished, would prove fatal to its duration.

It may be objected to this, that not seven but nine States, or two thirds of the whole number, must consent to the most important resolutions; and it may be thence inferred, that nine States would always comprehend a majority of the Union. But this does not obviate the impropriety of an equal vote between States of the most unequal dimensions and populousness; nor is the inference accurate in point of fact; for we can enumerate nine States which contain less than a majority of the people [2]; and it is constitutionally possible that these nine may give the vote. Besides, there are matters of considerable moment determinable by a bare majority; and there are others, concerning which doubts have been entertained, which, if interpreted in favor of the sufficiency of a vote of seven States, would extend its operation to interests of the first magnitude. In addition to this, it is to be observed that there is a probability of an increase in the number of States, and no provision for a proportional augmentation of the ratio of votes.

But this is not all: what at first sight may seem a remedy, is, in reality, a poison. To give a minority a negative upon the majority (which is always the case where more than a majority is requisite to a decision), is, in its tendency, to subject the sense of the greater number to that of the lesser. Congress, from the non-attendance of a few States, have been frequently in the

---

[2] Add New York and Connecticut to the foregoing seven, and they will be less than a majority.—PUBLIUS

situation of a Polish diet, where a single VOTE has been sufficient to put a stop to all their movements. A sixtieth part of the Union, which is about the proportion of Delaware and Rhode Island, has several times been able to oppose an entire bar to its operations. This is one of those refinements which, in practice, has an effect the reverse of what is expected from it in theory. The necessity of unanimity in public bodies, or of something approaching towards it, has been founded upon a supposition that it would contribute to security. But its real operation is to embarrass the administration, to destroy the energy of the government, and to substitute the pleasure, caprice, or artifices of an insignificant, turbulent, or corrupt junto, to the regular deliberations and decisions of a respectable majority. In those emergencies of a nation, in which the goodness or badness, the weakness or strength of its government, is of the greatest importance, there is commonly a necessity for action. The public business must, in some way or other, go forward. If a pertinacious minority can control the opinion of a majority, respecting the best mode of conducting it, the majority, in order that something may be done, must conform to the views of the minority; and thus the sense of the smaller number will overrule that of the greater, and give a tone to the national proceedings. Hence, tedious delays; continual negotiation and intrigue; contemptible compromises of the public good. And yet, in such a system, it is even happy when such compromises can take place: for upon some occasions things will not admit of accommodation; and then the measures of government must be injuriously suspended, or fatally defeated. It is often, by the impracticability of obtaining the concurrence of the necessary number of votes, kept in a state of inaction. Its situation must always savor of weakness, sometimes border upon anarchy.

It is not difficult to discover, that a principle of this kind gives greater scope to foreign corruption, as well as to domestic faction, than that which permits the sense of the majority to decide; though the contrary of this has been presumed. The mistake has proceeded from not attending with due care to the mischiefs that may be occasioned by obstructing the progress of government at certain critical seasons. When the concurrence of a large number is required by the Constitution to the doing of any national act, we are apt to rest satisfied that all is safe, because nothing improper will be likely *to be done;* but we forget how much good may be prevented, and how much ill may be produced, by the power of hindering the doing what may be necessary, and of keeping affairs in the same unfavorable posture in which they may happen to stand at particular periods.

Suppose, for instance, we were engaged in a war, in conjunction with one foreign nation, against another. Suppose the necessity of our situation demanded peace, and the interest or ambition of our ally led him to seek the prosecution of war, with views that might justify us in making separate terms. In such a state of things, this ally of ours would evidently find it much easier, by his bribes and intrigues, to tie up the hands of government from making peace, where two thirds of all the votes were requisite to that object, than where a simple majority would suffice. In the first case, he would have to corrupt a smaller number; in the last, a greater number. Upon the same principle, it would be much easier for a foreign power with which we were at war to perplex our councils and embarrass our exertions. And, in a commercial view, we may be subjected to similar inconveniences. A nation, with which we might have a treaty of commerce, could with much greater facility prevent our forming a connection with her competitor in trade, though such a connection should be ever so beneficial to ourselves.

Evils of this description ought not to be regarded as imaginary. One of the weak sides of republics, among their numerous advantages, is that they afford too easy an inlet to foreign corruption. An hereditary monarch, though often disposed to sacrifice his subjects to his ambition, has so great a personal interest in the government and in the external glory of the nation, that it is not easy for a foreign power to give him the equivalent for what he would sacrifice by treachery to the state. The world has accordingly been witness to few examples of this species of royal prostitution, though there have been abundant specimens of every other kind.

In republics, persons elevated from the mass of the community, by the suffrages of their fellow-citizens, to stations of great pre-eminence and power, may find compensations for betraying their trust, which, to any but minds animated and guided by superior virtue, may appear to exceed the proportion of interest they have in the common stock, and to overbalance the obligations of duty. Hence it is that history furnishes us with so many mortifying examples of the prevalency of foreign corruption in republican governments. How much this contributed to the ruin of the ancient commonwealths has been already delineated. : . .

A circumstance which crowns the defects of the Confederation remains yet to be mentioned,—the want of a judiciary power. Laws are a dead letter without courts to expound and define their true meaning and operation. The treaties of the United States, to have any force at all, must be considered as part of the law of the land. Their true import, as far as respects individuals, must, like all other laws, be ascertained by judicial determinations. To produce uniformity in these determinations, they ought to be submitted, in the last resort, to one SUPREME TRIBUNAL. And this tribunal ought to be instituted under the same authority which forms the treaties themselves. These ingredients are both indispensable. If there is in each State a court of final jurisdiction, there may be as many different final determinations on the same point as there are courts. There are endless diversities in the opinions of men. We often see not only different courts but the judges of the same court differing from each other. To avoid the confusion which would unavoidably result from the contradictory decisions of a number of independent judicatories, all nations have found it necessary to establish one court paramount to the rest, possessing a general superintendence, and authorized to settle and declare in the last resort a uniform rule of civil justice.

This is the more necessary where the frame of the government is so compounded that the laws of the whole are in danger of being contravened by the laws of the parts. In this case, if the particular tribunals are invested with a right of ultimate jurisdiction, besides the contradictions to be expected from differences of opinion there will be much to fear from the bias of local views and prejudices, and from the interference of local regulations. As often as such an interference was to happen, there would be reason to apprehend that the provisions of the particular laws might be preferred to those of the general laws; for nothing is more natural to men in office than to look with peculiar deference towards that authority to which they owe their official existence. The treaties of the United States, under the present Constitution, are liable to the infractions of thirteen different legislatures, and as many different courts of final jurisdiction, acting under the authority of those legislatures. The faith, the reputation, the peace of the whole Union, are thus continually at the mercy of the prejudices, the passions, and the interests of every member of which it is composed. Is it possible that foreign nations can either respect or confide in such a government? Is it possible that the people of America will longer consent to trust their honor, their happiness, their safety, on so precarious a foundation?

*   *   *   *

The organization of Congress is itself utterly improper for the exercise of those powers which are necessary to be deposited in the Union. A single assembly may be a proper receptacle of those slender, or rather fettered, authorities, which have been heretofore delegated to the federal head; but it would be inconsistent with all the principles of good government, to intrust it with those additional powers which, even the moderate and more rational adversaries of the proposed Constitution admit, ought to reside in the United States. If that plan should not be adopted, and if the necessity of the Union should be able to withstand the ambitious aims of those men who may indulge magnificent schemes of personal aggrandizement from its dissolution, the probability would be, that we should run into the project of conferring supplementary powers upon Congress, as they are now constituted; and either the machine, from the intrinsic feebleness of its structure, will moulder into pieces, in spite of our ill-judged efforts to prop it; or, by successive augmentations of its force and energy, as necessity might prompt, we shall finally accumulate, in a single body, all the most important prerogatives of sovereignty, and thus entail upon our posterity one of the most execrable forms of government that human infatuation ever contrived. Thus we should create in reality that very tyranny which the adversaries of the new Constitution either are, or affect to be, solicitous to avert.

It has not a little contributed to the infirmities of the existing federal system, that it never had a ratification by the PEOPLE. Resting on no better foundation than the consent of the several legislatures, it has been exposed to frequent and intricate questions concerning the validity of its powers, and has, in some instances, given birth to the enormous doctrine of a right of legislative repeal. Owing its ratification to the law of a State, it has been contended that the same authority might repeal the law by which it was ratified. However gross a heresy it may be to maintain that a *party* to a *compact* has a right to revoke that *compact*, the doctrine itself has had respectable advocates. The possibility of a question of this nature proves the necessity of laying the foundations of our national government deeper than in the mere sanction of delegated authority. The fabric of American empire ought to rest on the solid basis of THE CONSENT OF THE PEOPLE. The streams of national power ought to flow immediately from that pure, original foundation of all legitimate authority.

PUBLIUS

23 [ALEXANDER HAMILTON]

✰✰

The Necessity of an Energetic and Active National Government

✰✰

To the People of the State of New York:

The necessity of a Constitution, at least equally energetic with the one proposed, to the preservation of the Union, is the point at the examination of which we are now arrived.

This inquiry will naturally divide itself into three branches— the objects to be provided for by the federal government, the quantity of power necessary to the accomplishment of those objects, the persons upon whom that power ought to operate. Its distribution and organization will more properly claim our attention under the succeeding head.

The principal purposes to be answered by union are these— the common defence of the members; the preservation of the public peace, as well against internal convulsions as external attacks; the regulation of commerce with other nations and between the States; the superintendence of our intercourse, political and commercial, with foreign countries.

The authorities essential to the common defence are these: to raise armies; to build and equip fleets; to prescribe rules for the government of both; to direct their operations; to provide for their support. These powers ought to exist without limitation, *because it is impossible to foresee or define the extent and variety of national exigencies, or the correspondent extent and variety of the means which may be necessary to satisfy them.* The circumstances that endanger the safety of nations are infinite, and for this reason no constitutional shackles can wisely be imposed on the power to which the care of it is committed. This power ought to be co-extensive with all the possible combinations of such circumstances; and ought to be under the direction of the same councils which are appointed to preside over the common defence.

This is one of those truths which, to a correct and unprejudiced mind, carries its own evidence along with it; and may be obscured, but cannot be made plainer by argument or reasoning. It rests upon axioms as simple as they are universal; the *means* ought to be proportioned to the *end;* the persons, from whose agency the attainment of any *end* is expected, ought to possess the *means* by which it is to be attained.

Whether there ought to be a federal government intrusted with the care of the common defence, is a question in the first instance, open for discussion; but the moment it is decided in the affirmative, it will follow, that that government ought to be clothed with all the powers requisite to complete execution of its trust. And unless it can be shown that the circumstances which may affect the public safety are reducible within certain determinate limits; unless the contrary of this position can be fairly and rationally disputed, it must be admitted, as a necessary consequence, that there can be no limitation of that authority which is to provide for the defence and protection of community, in any matter essential to its efficacy—that is, in any matter essential to the *formation, direction,* or *support* of the NATIONAL FORCES.

Defective as the present Confederation has been proved to be, this principle appears to have been fully recognized by the framers of it; though they have not made proper or adequate provision for its exercise. Congress have an unlimited discretion to make requisitions of men and money; to govern the army and navy; to direct their operations. As their requisitions are made constitutionally binding upon the States, who are in fact under the most solemn obligations to furnish the supplies required of them, the intention evidently was, that the United States should command whatever resources were by them judged requisite to the "common defence and general welfare." It was presumed that a sense of their true interests, and a regard to the dictates of good faith, would be found sufficient pledges for the punctual performance of the duty of the members to the federal head.

The experiment has, however, demonstrated that this expectation was ill-founded and illusory; and the observations, made under the last head, will, I imagine, have sufficed to convince the impartial and discerning, that there is an absolute necessity for an entire change in the first principles of the system; that if we are in earnest about giving the Union energy and duration, we must abandon the vain project of legislating upon the States in their collective capacities; we must extend the laws of the federal government to the individual citizens of America; we must discard the fallacious scheme of quotas and requisitions, as equally impracticable and unjust. The result from all this is that the Union ought to be invested with full power to levy troops; to build and equip fleets; and to raise the revenues which will be required for the formation and support of an army and navy, in the customary and ordinary modes practised in other governments.

If the circumstances of our country are such as to demand a compound instead of a simple, a confederate instead of a sole, government, the essential point which will remain to be adjusted will be to discriminate the OBJECTS, as far as it can be done, which shall appertain to the different provinces or departments of power; allowing to each the most ample authority for fulfilling the objects committed to its charge. Shall the Union be constituted the guardian of the common safety? Are fleets and armies and revenues necessary to this purpose? The government of the Union must be empowered to pass all laws, and to make all regulations which have relation to them. The same must be the case in respect to commerce, and to every other matter to which its jurisdiction is permitted to extend. Is the administration of justice between the citizens of the same State the proper department of the local governments? These must possess all the authorities which are connected with this object, and with every other that may be allotted to their particular cognizance and direction. Not to confer in each case a degree of power commensurate to the end, would be to violate the most obvious rules of prudence and propriety, and improvidently to trust the great interests of the nation to hands which are disabled from managing them with vigor and success.

Who so likely to make suitable provisions for the public defence, as that body to which the guardianship of the public safety is confided; which, as the centre of information, will best understand the extent and urgency of the dangers that threaten; as the representative of the WHOLE, will feel itself most deeply interested in the preservation of every part; which, from the responsibility implied in the duty assigned to it, will be most sensibly impressed with the necessity of proper exertions; and which, by the extension of its authority throughout the States, can alone establish uniformity and concert in the plans and measures by which the common safety is to be secured? Is there not a manifest inconsistency in devolving upon the federal government the care of the general defence, and leaving in the State governments the *effective* powers by which it is to be provided for? Is not a want of co-operation the infallible consequence of such a system? And will not weakness, disorder, and undue distribution of the burdens and calamities of war, an unnecessary and intolerable increase of expense, be its natural and inevitable concomitants? Have we not had unequivocal experience of its effects in the course of the revolution which we have just accomplished?

. . . [It] is both unwise and dangerous to deny the federal government an unconfined authority, as to all those objects which are intrusted to its management. It will indeed deserve the most vigilant and careful attention of the people, to see that it be modelled in such a manner as to admit of its being safely vested with the requisite powers. If any plan which has been, or may be, offered to our consideration, should not, upon a dispassionate inspection, be found to answer this description, it ought to be rejected. A government, the constitution of which renders it unfit to be trusted with all the powers which a free people *ought to delegate to any government,* would be an unsafe and improper depositary of the NATIONAL INTERESTS. Whereever THESE can with propriety be confided, the coincident powers may safely accompany them. This is the true result of all just reasoning upon the subject. And the adversaries of the plan promulgated by the convention ought to have confined themselves to showing, that the internal structure of the proposed government was such as to render it unworthy of the confidence of the people. They ought not to have wandered into inflammatory declamations and unmeaning cavils about the extent of the powers. The POWERS are not too extensive for the OBJECTS of federal administration, or, in other words, for the management of our NATIONAL INTERESTS; nor can any satisfactory argument be framed to show that they are chargeable with such an excess. If it be true, as has been insinuated by some of the writers on the other side, that the difficulty arises from the nature of the thing, and that the extent of the country will not permit us to form a government in which such ample powers can safely be reposed, it would prove that we ought to contract our views, and resort to the expedient of separate confederacies, which will move within more practicable spheres. For the absurdity must continually stare us in the face of confiding to a government the direction of the most essential national interests, without daring to trust it to the authorities which are indispensable to their proper and efficient management. Let us not attempt to reconcile contradictions, but firmly embrace a rational alternative.

I trust, however, that the impracticability of one general system cannot be shown. . . . This, at all events, must be evident, that the very difficulty itself, drawn from the extent of the country, is the strongest argument in favor of an energetic government; for any other can certainly never preserve the Union of so large an empire. If we embrace the tenets of those who oppose the adoption of the proposed Constitution, as the standard of our political creed, we cannot fail to verify the gloomy doctrines which predict the impracticability of a national system pervading entire limits of the present Confederacy.

PUBLIUS

33 [ALEXANDER HAMILTON]

★★

The Constitutionality of National Tax Laws

★★

To the People of the State of New York:

The residue of the argument against the provisions of the Constitution in respect to taxation is ingrafted upon the following clauses;—the last clause of the eighth section of the first article of the plan under consideration authorizes the national legislature "to make all laws which shall be *necessary* and *proper* for carrying into execution *the powers* by that Constitution vested in the government of the United States, or in any department or officer thereof"; and the second clause of the sixth article declares, "that the Constitution and the laws of the United States made *in pursuance thereof,* and the treaties made by their authority shall be the *supreme law* of the land, any thing in the constitution or laws of any State to the contrary notwithstanding."

These two clauses have been the source of much virulent invective and petulant declamation against the proposed Constitution. They have been held up to the people in all the exaggerated colors of misrepresentation as the pernicious engines by which their local governments were to be destroyed and their liberties exterminated; as the hideous monster whose devouring jaws would spare neither sex nor age, nor high nor low, nor sacred nor profane; and yet, strange as it may appear, after all this clamor, to those who may not have happened to contemplate them in the same light, it may be affirmed with perfect confidence that the constitutional operation of the intended government

297

would be precisely the same, if these clauses were entirely obliterated, as if they were repeated in every article. They are only declaratory of a truth which would have resulted by necessary and unavoidable implication from the very act of constituting a federal government, and vesting it with certain specified powers. . . .

What is a power, but the ability or faculty of doing a thing? What is the ability to do a thing, but the power of employing the *means* necessary to its execution? What is a LEGISLATIVE power, but a power of making LAWS? What are the *means* to execute a LEGISLATIVE power, but LAWS? What is the power of laying and collecting taxes, but a *legislative power,* or a power of *making laws,* to lay and collect taxes? What are the proper means of executing such a power, but *necessary* and *proper* laws?

This simple train of inquiry furnishes us at once with a test by which to judge of the true nature of the clause complained of. It conducts us to this palpable truth, that a power to lay and collect taxes must be a power to pass all laws *necessary* and *proper* for the execution of that power; and what does the unfortunate and calumniated provision in question do more than declare the same truth, to wit, that the national legislature, to whom the power of laying and collecting taxes had been previously given, might, in the execution of that power, pass all laws *necessary* and *proper* to carry it into effect? I have applied these observations thus particularly to the power of taxation, because it is the immediate subject under consideration, and because it is the most important of the authorities proposed to be conferred upon the Union. But the same process will lead to the same result, in relation to all other powers declared in the Constitution. And it is *expressly* to execute these powers that the sweeping clause, as it has been affectedly called, authorizes the national legislature to pass all *necessary* and *proper* laws. If there is any thing exceptionable, it must be sought for in the specific powers upon which this general declaration is predicated. The declaration itself, though it may be chargeable with tautology or redundancy, is at least perfectly harmless.

* * * *

But it may be again asked, Who is to judge of the *necessity* and *propriety* of the laws to be passed for executing the powers of the Union? I answer, first that this question arises as well and as fully upon the simple grant of those powers as upon the declaratory clause; and I answer, in the second place, that the national government, like every other, must judge, in the first instance, of the proper exercise of its powers, and its constituents in the last. If the federal government should overpass the just bounds of its authority and make a tyrannical use of its powers, the people, whose creature it is, must appeal to the standard they have formed, and take such measures to redress the injury done to the Constitution as the exigency may suggest and prudence justify. The propriety of a law, in a constitutional light, must always be determined by the nature of the powers upon which it is founded. Suppose, by some forced constructions of its authority (which, indeed, cannot easily be imagined), the Federal legislature should attempt to vary the law of descent in any State, would it not be evident that, in making such an attempt, it had exceeded its jurisdiction, and infringed upon that of the State? Suppose, again, that upon the pretence of an interference with its revenues, it should undertake to abrogate a land-tax imposed by the authority of a State; would it not be equally evident that this was an invasion of that concurrent jurisdiction in respect to this species of tax, which its Constitution plainly supposes to exist in the State governments? . . .

But it is said that the laws of the Union are to be the *supreme law* of the land. But what inference can be drawn from this, or what would they amount to, if they were not to be supreme? It is evident they would amount to nothing. A LAW, by the very meaning of the term, includes supremacy. It is a rule which those to whom it is prescribed are bound to observe. This results from every political association. If individuals enter into a state of society, the laws of that society must be the supreme regulator of their conduct. If a number of political societies enter into a larger political society, the laws which the latter may enact, pursuant to the powers intrusted to it by its constitution, must necessarily be supreme over those societies, and the individuals of whom they are composed. It would otherwise be a mere treaty, dependent on the good faith of the parties, and not a government, which is only another word for POLITICAL POWER AND SUPREMACY. But it will not follow from this doctrine that acts of the larger society which are *not pursuant* to its constitutional powers, but which are invasions of the residuary authorities of the smaller societies, will become the supreme law of the land. These will be merely acts of usurpation, and will deserve to be treated as such. Hence we perceive that the clause which declares the supremacy of the laws of the Union, like the one we have just before considered, only declares a truth, which flows immediately and necessarily from the institution of a federal government. It will not, I presume, have escaped observation, that it *expressly* confines this supremacy to laws made *pursuant to the Constitution;* which I mention merely as an instance of caution in the convention; since that limitation would have been to be understood, though it had not been expressed.

Though a law, therefore, laying a tax for the use of the United States would be supreme in its nature, and could not legally be opposed or controlled, yet a law for abrogating or preventing the collection of a tax laid by the authority of the State (unless upon imports and exports), would not be the supreme law of the land, but a usurpation of power not granted by the Constitution. As far as an improper accumulation of taxes on the same object might tend to render the collection difficult or precarious, this would be a mutual inconvenience, not arising from a superiority or defect of power on either side, but from an injudicious exercise of power by one or the other, in a manner equally disadvantageous to both. It is to be hoped and presumed, however, that mutual interest would dictate a concert in this respect which would avoid any material inconvenience. The inference from the whole is, that the individual States would, under the proposed Constitution, retain an independent and uncontrollable authority to raise revenue to any extent of which they may stand in need, by every kind of taxation, except duties on imports and exports. It will be shown in the next paper that this CONCURRENT JURISDICTION in the article of taxation was the only admissible substitute for an entire subordination, in respect to this branch of power, of the State authority to that of the Union.

PUBLIUS

37 [JAMES MADISON]

Problems Confronting the Federal Convention

To the People of the State of New York:

In reviewing the defects of the existing Confederation, and showing that they cannot be supplied by a government of less energy than that before the public, several of the most important principles of the latter fell of course under consideration. But as the ultimate object of these papers is to determine clearly and fully the merits of this Constitution, and the expediency of adopting it, our plan cannot be complete without taking a more critical and thorough survey of the work of the convention, without examining it on all its sides, comparing it in all its parts, and calculating its probable effects.

❖   ❖   ❖   ❖

. . . [Many] allowances ought to be made for the difficulties inherent in the very nature of the undertaking referred to the convention.

The novelty of the undertaking immediately strikes us. It has been shown in the course of these papers, that the existing Confederation is founded on principles which are fallacious; that we must consequently change this first foundation, and with it the superstructure resting upon it. It has been shown, that the other confederacies which could be consulted as precedents have been vitiated by the same erroneous principles, and can therefore furnish no other light than that of beacons, which give

302

warning of the course to be shunned, without pointing out that which ought to be pursued. The most that the convention could do in such a situation, was to avoid the errors suggested by the past experience of other countries, as well as of our own; and to provide a convenient mode of rectifying their own errors, as future experience may unfold them.

Among the difficulties encountered by the convention, a very important one must have lain in combining the requisite stability and energy in government, with the inviolable attention due to liberty and to the republican form. Without substantially accomplishing this part of their undertaking, they would have very imperfectly fulfilled the object of their appointment, or the expectation of the public; yet that it could not be easily accomplished, will be denied by no one who is unwilling to betray his ignorance of the subject. Energy in government is essential to that security against external and internal danger, and to that prompt and salutary execution of the laws which enter into the very definition of good government. Stability in government is essential to national character and to the advantages annexed to it, as well as to that repose and confidence in the minds of the people, which are among the chief blessings of civil society. An irregular and mutable legislation is not more an evil in itself than it is odious to the people; and it may be pronounced with assurance that the people of this country, enlightened as they are with regard to the nature, and interested, as the great body of them are, in the effects of good government, will never be satisfied till some remedy be applied to the vicissitudes and uncertainties which characterize the State administrations. On comparing, however, these valuable ingredients with the vital principles of liberty, we must perceive at once the difficulty of mingling them together in their due proportions. The genius of republican liberty seems to demand on one side, not only that all power should be derived from the people, but that those intrusted with it should be kept in dependence on the people, by a short duration of their appointments; and that even during this short period the trust should be placed not in a few, but a number of hands. Stability, on the contrary, requires that the hands in which power is lodged should continue for a length of time the same. A frequent change of men will result from a frequent return of elections; and a frequent change of measures from a frequent change of men: whilst energy in government requires not only a certain duration of power, but the execution of it by a single hand.

How far the convention may have succeeded in this part of their work, will better appear on a more accurate view of it. From the cursory view here taken, it must clearly appear to have been an arduous part.

Not less arduous must have been the task of marking the proper line of partition between the authority of the general and that of the State governments. Every man will be sensible of this difficulty, in proportion as he has been accustomed to contemplate and discriminate objects extensive and complicated in their nature. . . .

* * * *

. . . Experience has instructed us that no skill in the science of government has yet been able to discriminate and define, with sufficient certainty, its three great provinces—the legislative, executive, and judiciary; or even the privileges and powers of the different legislative branches. Questions daily occur in the course of practice, which prove the obscurity which reigns in these subjects, and which puzzle the greatest adepts in political science.

The experience of ages, with the continued and combined labors of the most enlightened legislators and jurists, has been equally unsuccessful in delineating the several objects and limits of different codes of laws and different tribunals of justice. . . . Besides the obscurity arising from the complexity of objects, and the imperfection of the human faculties, the medium through which the conceptions of men are conveyed to each other adds a fresh embarrassment. The use of words is to express ideas.

Perspicuity, therefore, requires not only that the ideas should be distinctly formed, but that they should be expressed by words distinctly and exclusively appropriate to them. But no language is so copious as to supply words and phrases for every complex idea, or so correct as not to include many equivocally denoting different ideas. . . .

Here, then, are three sources of vague and incorrect definitions: indistinctness of the object, imperfection of the organ of conception, inadequateness of the vehicle of ideas. Any one of these must produce a certain degree of obscurity. The convention, in delineating the boundary between the federal and State jurisdictions, must have experienced the full effect of them all.

To the difficulties already mentioned may be added the interfering pretensions of the larger and smaller States. We cannot err in supposing that the former would contend for a participation in the government, fully proportioned to their superior wealth and importance; and that the latter would not be less tenacious of the equality at present enjoyed by them. We may well suppose that neither side would entirely yield to the other, and consequently that the struggle could be terminated only by compromise. It is extremely probable, also, that after the ratio of representation had been adjusted, this very compromise must have produced a fresh struggle between the same parties, to give such a turn to the organization of the government, and to the distribution of its powers, as would increase the importance of the branches, in forming which they had respectively obtained the greatest share of influence. There are features in the Constitution which warrant each of these suppositions; and as far as either of them is well founded, it shows that the convention must have been compelled to sacrifice theoretical propriety to the force of extraneous considerations.

Nor could it have been the large and small States only, which would marshal themselves in opposition to each other on various points. Other combinations, resulting from a difference of local position and policy, must have created additional difficulties. As every state may be divided into different districts, and its citizens into different classes, which give birth to contending interests and local jealousies, so the different parts of the United States are distinguished from each other by a variety of circumstances, which produce a like effect on a larger scale. And although this variety of interests, for reasons sufficiently explained in a former paper, may have a salutary influence on the administration of the government when formed, yet every one must be sensible of the contrary influence, which must have been experienced in the task of forming it.

Would it be wonderful if, under the pressure of all these difficulties, the convention should have been forced into some deviations from that artificial structure and regular symmetry which an abstract view of the subject might lead an ingenious theorist to bestow on a Constitution planned in his closet or in his imagination? The real wonder is that so many difficulties should have been surmounted, and surmounted with a unanimity almost as unprecedented as it must have been unexpected. It is impossible for any man of candor to reflect on this circumstance without partaking of the astonishment. It is impossible for the man of pious reflection not to perceive in it a finger of that Almighty hand which has been so frequently and signally extended to our relief in the critical stages of the revolution.

. . . The history of almost all the great councils and consultations held among mankind for reconciling their discordant opinions, assuaging their mutual jealousies, and adjusting their respective interests, is a history of factions, contentions, and disappointments, and may be classed among the most dark and degraded pictures which display the infirmities and depravities of the human character. If, in a few scattered instances, a brighter aspect is presented, they serve only as exceptions to admonish us of the general truth; and by their lustre to darken the gloom of the adverse prospect to which they are contrasted. In revolving the causes from which these exceptions result, and applying them to the particular instance before us, we are necessarily led to two important conclusions. The first is, that the convention must have enjoyed, in a very singular degree, an exemption from the pestilential influence of party animosities—the disease most incident to deliberative bodies, and most apt to contaminate their proceedings. The second conclusion is that all the deputations composing the convention were satisfactorily accommodated by the final act, or were induced to accede to it by a deep conviction of the necessity of sacrificing private opinions and partial interests to the public good, and by a despair of seeing this necessity diminished by delays or by new experiments.

PUBLIUS

39 [JAMES MADISON]

****

Republicanism, Nationalism, Federalism

****

To the People of the State of New York:

The last paper having concluded the observations which were meant to introduce a candid survey of the plan of government reported by the convention, we now proceed to the execution of that part of our undertaking.

The first question that offers itself is, whether the general form and aspect of the government be strictly republican? It is evident that no other form would be reconcilable with the genius of the people of America; with the fundamental principles of the Revolution; or with that honorable determination which animates every votary of freedom, to rest all our political experiments on the capacity of mankind for self-government. If the plan of the convention, therefore, be found to depart from the republican character, its advocates must abandon it as no longer defensible.

What, then, are the distinctive characters of the republican form? Were an answer to this question to be sought, not by recurring to principles, but in the application of the term by political writers, to the constitutions of different States, no satisfactory one would ever be found. Holland, in which no particle of the supreme authority is derived from the people, has passed almost universally under the denomination of a republic. The same title has been bestowed on Venice, where absolute power over the great body of the people is exercised, in the most absolute manner, by a small body of hereditary nobles. Poland, which is a mixture of aristocracy and of monarchy in their worst forms, has been dignified with the same appellation. The government of England, which has one republican branch only, combined with an hereditary aristocracy and monarchy, has, with equal impropriety, been frequently placed on the list of republics. These examples, which are nearly as dissimilar to each other as to a genuine republic, show the extreme inaccuracy with which the term has been used in political disquisitions.

If we resort for a criterion to the different principles on which different forms of government are established, we may define a republic to be, or at least may bestow that name on, a government which derives all its powers directly or indirectly from the great body of the people, and is administered by persons holding their offices during pleasure, for a limited period, or during good behavior. It is *essential* to such a government that it be derived from the great body of the society, not from an inconsiderable proportion, or a favored class of it; otherwise a handful of tyrannical nobles, exercising their oppressions by a delegation of their powers, might aspire to the rank of republicans, and claim for their government the honorable title of republic. It is *sufficient* for such a government that the persons administering it be appointed, either directly or indirectly, by the people; and that they hold their appointments by either of the tenures just specified; otherwise every government in the United States, as well as every other popular government that has been or can be well organized or well executed, would be degraded from the republican character. According to the constitution of every State in the Union, some or other of the offices of government are appointed indirectly only by the people. According to most of them, the chief magistrate himself is so appointed. And according to one, this mode of appointment is extended to one of the coördinate branches of the legislature. According to all the constitutions, also, the tenure of the highest offices is extended to a definite period, and in many instances, both within the legislative and executive departments, to a period of years. According to the provisions of most of the constitutions, again, as well as according to the most respectable and received opinions on the subject, the members of the judiciary department are to retain their offices by the firm tenure of good behavior.

On comparing the Constitution planned by the convention with the standard here fixed, we perceive at once that it is, in the most rigid sense, conformable to it. The House of Representatives, like that of one branch at least of all the State legislatures, is elected immediately by the great body of the people. The Senate, like the present Congress, and the Senate of Maryland, derives its appointment indirectly from the people. The President is indirectly derived from the choice of the people, according to the example in most of the States. Even the judges with all other officers of the Union, will, as in the several States, be the choice, though a remote choice, of the people themselves. The duration of the appointments is equally conformable to the republican standard, and to the model of State constitutions. The House of Representatives is periodically elective, as in all the States; and for the period of two years, as in the State of South Carolina. The Senate is elective, for the period of six years; which is but one year more than the period of the Senate of Maryland, and but two more than that of the Senates of New York and Virginia. The President is to continue in office for the period of four years; as in New York and Delaware the chief magistrate is elected for three years, and in South Carolina for two years. In the other States the election is annual. In several of the States, however, no constitutional provision is made for the impeachment of the chief magistrate. And in Delaware and Virginia he is not impeachable till out of office. The President of the United States is impeachable at any time during his continuance in office. The tenure by which the judges are to hold their places, is, as it unquestionably ought to be, that of good behavior. The tenure of the ministerial offices generally, will be a subject of legal regulation, conformably to the reason of the case and the example of the State constitutions.

Could any further proof be required of the republican complexion of this system, the most decisive one might be found in its absolute prohibition of titles of nobility, both under the federal and the State governments; and in its express guaranty of the republican form to each of the latter.

"But it was not sufficient," say the adversaries of the proposed Constitution, "for the convention to adhere to the republican form. They ought, with equal care, to have preserved the *federal* form, which regards the Union as a *Confederacy* of sovereign states; instead of which, they have framed a *national* government, which regards the Union as a *consolidation* of the States." And it is asked by what authority this bold and radical innovation was undertaken? The handle which has been made of this objection requires that it should be examined with some precision.

Without inquiring into the accuracy of the distinction on which the objection is founded, it will be necessary to a just estimate of its force, first, to ascertain the real character of the government in question; secondly, to inquire how far the convention were authorized to propose such a government; and thirdly, how far the duty they owed to their country could supply any defect of regular authority.

First.—In order to ascertain the real character of the government, it may be considered in relation to the foundation on which it is to be established; to the sources from which its ordinary powers are to be drawn; to the operation of those powers; to the extent of them; and to the authority by which future changes in the government are to be introduced.

On examining the first relation, it appears, on one hand, that the Constitution is to be founded on the assent and ratification of the people of America, given by deputies elected for the special purpose; but, on the other, that this assent and ratification is to be given by the people, not as individuals composing one entire nation, but as composing the distinct and independent States to which they respectively belong. It is to be the assent and ratification of the several States, derived from the supreme authority in each State,—the authority of the people themselves. The act, therefore, establishing the Constitution, will not be a *national,* but a *federal* act.

That it will be a federal and not a national act, as these terms are understood by the objectors; the act of the people, as forming so many independent States, not as forming one aggregate nation, is obvious from this single consideration, that it is to result neither from the decision of a *majority* of the people of the Union, nor from that of a *majority* of the States. It must result from the *unanimous* assent of the several States that are parties to it, differing no otherwise from their ordinary assent than in its being expressed, not by the legislative authority, but by that of the people themselves. Were the people regarded in this transaction as forming one nation, the will of the majority of the whole people of the United States would bind the minority, in the same manner as the majority in each State must bind the minority; and the will of the majority must be determined either by a comparison of the individual votes, or by considering the will of the majority of the States as evidence of the will of a majority of the people of the United States. Neither of these rules has been adopted. Each State, in ratifying the Constitution, is considered as a sovereign body, independent of all others, and only to be bound by its own voluntary act. In this relation, then, the new Constitution will, if established, be a *federal,* and not a *national* constitution.

The next relation is, to the sources from which the ordinary powers of government are to be derived. The House of Representatives will derive its powers from the people of America; and the people will be represented in the same proportion, and on the same principle, as they are in the legislature of a particular State. So far the government is *national,* not *federal.* The Senate, on the other hand, will derive its powers from the States, as political and coequal societies; and these will be represented on the principle of equality in the Senate, as they now are in the existing Congress. So far the government is *federal,* not *national.*

The executive power will be derived from a very compound source. The immediate election of the President is to be made by the States in their political characters. The votes allotted to them are in a compound ratio, which considers them partly as distinct and coequal societies, partly as unequal members of the same society. The eventual election, again, is to be made by that branch of the legislature which consists of the national representatives; but in this particular act they are to be thrown into the form of individual delegations, from so many distinct and coequal bodies politic. From this aspect of the government, it appears to be of a mixed character, presenting at least as many *federal* as *national* features.

The difference between a federal and national government, as it relates to the *operation of the government,* is supposed to consist in this, that in the former the powers operate on the political bodies composing the Confederacy, in their political capacities; in the latter, on the individual citizens composing the nation, in their individual capacities. On trying the Constitution by this criterion, it falls under the *national,* not the *federal* character; though perhaps not so completely as has been understood. In several cases, and particularly in the trial of controversies to which States may be parties, they must be viewed and proceeded against in their collective and political capacities only. So far the national countenance of the government on this side seems to be disfigured by a few federal features. But this blemish is perhaps unavoidable in any plan; and the operation of the government on the people, in their individual capacities, in its ordinary and most essential proceedings, may, on the whole, designate it, in this relation, a *national* government.

But if the government be national with regard to the *operation* of its powers, it changes its aspect again when we contemplate it in relation to the extent of its powers. The idea of a national government involves in it, not only an authority over the individual citizens, but an indefinite supremacy over all persons and things, so far as they are objects of lawful government. Among a people consolidated into one nation, this supremacy is completely vested in the national legislature. Among communities united for particular purposes, it is vested partly in the general and partly in the municipal legislatures. In the former case, all local authorities are subordinate to the supreme; and may be controlled, directed, or abolished by it at pleasure. In the latter, the local or municipal authorities form distinct and independent portions of the supremacy, no more subject, within their respective spheres, to the general authority, than the general authority is subject to them, within its own sphere. In this relation, then, the proposed government cannot be deemed a *national* one; since its jurisdiction extends to certain enumerated objects only, and leaves to the several States a residuary and inviolable sovereignty over all other objects. It is true that in controversies relating to the boundary between the two jurisdictions, the tribunal which is ultimately to decide, is to be established under the general government. But this does not change the principle of the case. The decision is to be impartially made, according to the rules of the Constitution; and all the usual and most effectual precautions are taken to secure this impartiality. Some such tribunal is clearly essential to prevent an appeal to the sword and a dissolution of the compact; and that it ought to be established under the general rather than under the local governments, or, to speak more properly, that it could be safely established under the first alone, is a position not likely to be combated.

If we try the Constitution by its last relation to the authority by which amendments are to be made, we find it neither wholly *national* nor wholly *federal*. Were it wholly national, the supreme and ultimate authority would reside in the *majority* of the people of the Union; and this authority would be competent at all times, like that of a majority of every national society, to alter or abolish its established government. Were it wholly federal, on the other hand, the concurrence of each State in the Union would be essential to every alteration that would be binding on all. The mode provided by the plan of the convention is not founded on either of these principles. In requiring more than a majority, and particularly in computing the proportion by *States*, not by *citizens*, it departs from the *national* and advances towards the *federal* character; in rendering the concurrence of less than the whole number of States sufficient, it loses again the *federal* and partakes of the *national* character.

The proposed Constitution, therefore, is, in strictness, neither a national nor a federal Constitution, but a composition of both. In its foundation it is federal, not national; in the sources from which the ordinary powers of the government are drawn, it is partly federal and partly national; in the operation of these powers, it is national, not federal; in the extent of them, again, it is federal, not national; and, finally, in the authoritative mode of introducing amendments, it is neither wholly federal nor wholly national.

PUBLIUS

45 [JAMES MADISON]

****

Powers and Continuing Advantages of the States

****

To the People of the State of New York:

Having shown that no one of the powers transferred to the federal government is unnecessary or improper, the next question to be considered is, whether the whole mass of them will be dangerous to the portion of authority left in the several States.

The adversaries to the plan of the convention, instead of considering in the first place what degree of power was absolutely necessary for the purposes of the federal government, have exhausted themselves in a secondary inquiry into the possible consequences of the proposed degree of power to the governments of the particular States. But if the Union, as has been shown, be essential to the security of the people of America against foreign danger; if it be essential to their security against contentions and wars among the different States; if it be essential to guard them against those violent and oppressive factions which embitter the blessings of liberty, and against those military establishments which must gradually poison its very fountain; if, in a word, the Union be essential to the happiness of the people of America, is it not preposterous, to urge as an objection to a government, without which the objects of the Union cannot be attained, that such a government may derogate from the importance of the governments of the individual States? Was, then, the American Revolution effected, was the American Confederacy formed, was the precious blood of thousands spilt, and the hard-earned substance of millions lavished, not that the people of America should enjoy peace, liberty, and safety, but that the government of the individual States, that particular municipal establishments, might enjoy a certain extent of power, and be arrayed with certain dignities and attributes of sovereignty? We have heard of the impious doctrine in the Old World, that the people were made for kings, not kings for the people. Is the same doctrine to be revived in the New, in another shape—that the solid happiness of the people is to be sacrificed to the views of political institutions of a different form? It is too early for politicians to presume on our forgetting that the public good, the real welfare of the great body of the people, is the supreme object to be pursued; and that no form of government whatever has any other value than as it may be fitted for the attainment of this object. Were the plan of the convention adverse to the public happiness, my voice would be, Reject the plan. Were the Union itself inconsistent with the public happiness, it would be, Abolish the Union. In like manner, as far as the sovereignty of the States cannot be reconciled to the happiness of the people, the voice of every good citizen must be, Let the former be sacrificed to the latter. How far the sacrifice is necessary, has been shown. How far the unsacrificed residue will be endangered, is the question before us.

Several important considerations have been touched in the course of these papers, which discountenance the supposition that the operation of the federal government will by degrees prove fatal to the State governments. The more I revolve the subject, the more fully I am persuaded that the balance is much more likely to be disturbed by the preponderancy of the last than of the first scale.

We have seen, in all the examples of ancient and modern confederacies, the strongest tendency continually betraying itself in the members, to despoil the general government of its authorities, with a very ineffectual capacity in the latter to defend itself against the encroachments. Although, in most of these examples, the system has been so dissimilar from that under consideration as greatly to weaken any inference concerning the latter from the fate of the former, yet, as the States will retain, under the proposed Constitution, a very extensive portion of active sovereignty, the inference ought not to be wholly disregarded. . . .

＊　　＊　　＊　　＊

The State governments will have the advantage of the Federal government, whether we compare them in respect to the immediate dependence of the one on the other; to the weight of personal influence which each side will possess; to the powers respectively vested in them to the predilection and probable support of the people; to the disposition and faculty of resisting and frustrating the measures of each other.

The State governments may be regarded as constituent and essential parts of the federal government: whilst the latter is nowise essential to the operation or organization of the former. Without the intervention of the State legislatures, the President of the United States cannot be elected at all. They must in all cases have a great share in his appointment, and will, perhaps, in most cases, of themselves determine it. The Senate will be elected absolutely and exclusively by the State legislatures. Even the House of Representatives, though drawn immediately from the people, will be chosen very much under the influence of that class of men, whose influence over the people obtains for themselves an election into the State legislatures. Thus, each of the principal branches of the federal government will owe its existence more or less to the favor of the State governments, and must consequently feel a dependence, which is much more likely to beget a disposition too obsequious than too overbearing towards them. On the other side, the component parts of the State governments will in no instance be indebted for their appointment to the direct agency of the federal government, and very little, if at all, to the local influence of its members.

The number of individuals employed under the Constitution of the United States will be much smaller than the number employed under the particular States. There will consequently be less of personal influence on the side of the former than of the latter. The members of the legislative, executive, and judiciary departments of thirteen and more States, the justices of peace, officers of militia, ministerial officers of justice, with all the county, corporation, and town officers, for three millions and more of people, intermixed, and having particular acquaintance with every class and circle of people, must exceed, beyond all proportion, both in number and influence, those of every description who will be employed in the administration of the federal system. Compare the members of the three great departments of the thirteen States, excluding from the judiciary department the justices of peace, with the members of the corresponding departments of the single government of the Union; compare the militia officers of three millions of people with the military and marine officers of any establishment which is within the compass of probability, or, I may add, of possibility, and in this view alone, we may pronounce the advantage of the States to be decisive. . . .

The powers delegated by the proposed Constitution to the federal government are few and defined. Those which are to remain in the State governments are numerous and indefinite. The former will be exercised principally on external objects, as war, peace, negotiation, and foreign commerce; with which last the power of taxation will, for the most part, be connected. The powers reserved to the several States will extend to all the objects which, in the ordinary course of affairs, concern the lives, liberties, and properties of the people; and the internal order, improvement, and prosperity of the State.

The operations of the federal government will be most extensive and important in times of war and danger; those of the State governments in times of peace and security. As the former periods will probably bear a small proportion to the latter, the State governments will here enjoy another advantage over the federal government. The more adequate, indeed, the federal powers may be rendered to the national defence, the less frequent will be those scenes of danger which might favor their ascendancy over the governments of the particular States.

If the new Constitution be examined with accuracy and candor, it will be found that the change which it proposes consists much less in the addition of NEW POWERS to the Union, than in the invigoration of its ORIGINAL POWERS. The regulation of commerce, it is true, is a new power; but that seems to be an addition which few oppose, and from which no apprehensions are entertained. The powers relating to war and peace, armies and fleets, treaties and finance, with the other more considerable powers, are all vested in the existing Congress by the articles of Confederation. The proposed change does not enlarge these powers; it only substitutes a more effectual mode of administering them. The change relating to taxation may be regarded as the most important; and yet the present Congress have as complete authority to REQUIRE of the States indefinite supplies of money for the common defence and general welfare, as the future Congress will have to require them of individual citizens; and the latter will be no more bound than the States themselves have been, to pay the quotas respectively taxed on them. Had the States complied punctually with the articles of Confederation, or could their compliance have been enforced by as peaceable means as may be used with success towards single persons, our past experience is very far from countenancing an opinion, that the State governments would have lost their constitutional powers, and have gradually undergone an entire consolidation. To maintain that such an event would have ensued, would be to say at once, that the existence of the State governments is incompatible with any system whatever that accomplishes the essential purposes of the Union.

PUBLIUS

State and Federal Powers Compared

To the People of the State of New York:

Resuming the subject of the last paper, I proceed to inquire whether the federal government or the State governments will have the advantage with regard to the predilection and support of the people. Notwithstanding the different modes in which they are appointed, we must consider both of them as substantially dependent on the great body of the citizens of the United States. I assume this position here as it respects the first, reserving the proofs for another place. The federal and State governments are in fact but different agents and trustees of the people, constituted with different powers, and designed for different purposes. The adversaries of the Constitution seem to have lost sight of the people altogether in their reasonings on this subject; and to have viewed these different establishments, not only as mutual rivals and enemies, but as uncontrolled by any common superior in their efforts to usurp the authorities of each other. These gentlemen must here be reminded of their error. They must be told that the ultimate authority, wherever the derivative may be found, resides in the people alone, and that it will not depend merely on the comparative ambition or address of the different governments, whether either, or which of them, will be able to enlarge its sphere of jurisdiction at the expense of the other. Truth, no less than decency, requires that the event in every case should be supposed to depend on the sentiments and sanction of their common constituents.

Many considerations, besides those suggested on a former occasion, seem to place it beyond doubt that the first and most natural attachment of the people will be to the governments of their respective States. Into the administration of these a greater number of individuals will expect to rise. From the gift of these a greater number of offices and emoluments will flow. By the superintending care of these, all the more domestic and personal interests of the people will be regulated and provided for. With the affairs of these, the people will be more familiarly and minutely conversant. And with the members of these, will a greater proportion of the people have the ties of personal acquaintance and friendship, and of family and party attachments; on the side of these, therefore, the popular bias may well be expected most strongly to incline.

Experience speaks the same language in this case. The federal administration, though hitherto very defective in comparison with what may be hoped under a better system, had, during the war, and particularly whilst the independent fund of paper emissions was in credit, an activity and importance as great as it can well have in any future circumstances whatever. It was engaged, too, in a course of measures which had for their object the protection of every thing that was dear, and the acquisition of every thing that could be desirable to the people at large. It was, nevertheless, invariably found, after the transient enthusiasm for the early Congresses was over, that the attention and attachment of the people were turned anew to their own particular governments; that the federal council was at no time the idol of popular favor; and that opposition to proposed enlargements of its powers and importance was the side usually taken by the men who wished to build their political consequence on the prepossessions of their fellow-citizens.

If, therefore, as has been elsewhere remarked, the people should in future become more partial to the federal than to the State governments, the change can only result from such manifest and irresistible proofs of a better administration, as will overcome all their antecedent propensities. And in that case, the people ought not surely to be precluded from giving most of their confidence where they may discover it to be most due; but even in that case the State governments could have little to apprehend, because it is only within a certain sphere that the federal power can, in the nature of things, be advantageously administered.

The remaining points on which I propose to compare the federal and State governments, are the disposition and the faculty they may respectively possess, to resist and frustrate the measures of each other.

It has been already proved that the members of the federal will be more dependent on the members of the State governments, than the latter will be on the former. It has appeared also, that the prepossessions of the people, on whom both will depend, will be more on the side of the State governments, than of the federal government. So far as the disposition of each towards the other may be influenced by these causes, the State governments must clearly have the advantage. But in a distinct and very important point of view, the advantage will lie on the same side. The prepossessions, which the members themselves will carry into the federal government, will generally be favorable to the States; whilst it will rarely happen, that the members of the State governments will carry into the public councils a bias in favor of the general government. A local spirit will infallibly prevail much more in the members of Congress, than a national spirit will prevail in the legislatures of the particular States. Every one knows that a great proportion of the errors committed by the State legislatures proceeds from the disposition of the members to sacrifice the comprehensive and permanent interest of the State, to the particular and separate views of the counties or districts in which they reside. And if they do not sufficiently enlarge their policy to embrace the collective welfare of their particular State, how can it be imagined that they will make the aggregate prosperity of the Union, and the dignity and respectability of its government, the objects of their affections and consultations? For the same reason that the members of the

State legislatures will be unlikely to attach themselves sufficiently to national objects, the members of the federal legislature will be likely to attach themselves too much to local objects. The States will be to the latter what counties and towns are to the former. Measures will too often be decided according to their probable effect, not on the national prosperity and happiness, but on the prejudices, interests, and pursuits of the governments and people of the individual States. What is the spirit that has in general characterized the proceedings of Congress? A perusal of their journals, as well as the candid acknowledgments of such as have had a seat in that assembly, will inform us, that the members have but too frequently displayed the character, rather of partisans of their respective States, than of impartial guardians of a common interest; that where on one occasion improper sacrifices have been made of local considerations, to the aggrandizement of the federal government, the great interests of the nation have suffered on an hundred, from an undue attention to the local prejudices, interests and views of the particular States. I mean not by these reflections to insinuate, that the new federal government will not embrace a more enlarged plan of policy than the existing government may have pursued; much less, that its views will be as confined as those of the State legislatures; but only that it will partake sufficiently of the spirit of both, to be disinclined to invade the rights of the individual States, or the prerogatives of their governments. The motives on the part of the State governments, to augment their prerogatives by defalcations from the federal government, will be overruled by no reciprocal predispositions in the members.

Were it admitted, however, that the Federal government may feel an equal disposition with the State governments to extend its power beyond the due limits, the latter would still have the advantage in the means of defeating such encroachments. If an act of a particular State, though unfriendly to the national government, be generally popular in that State, and should not too grossly violate the oaths of the State officers, it is executed immediately and, of course, by means on the spot and depending on the State alone. The opposition of the federal government, or the interposition of federal officers, would but inflame the zeal of all parties on the side of the State, and the evil could not be prevented or repaired, if at all, without the employment of means which must always be resorted to with reluctance and difficulty. On the other hand, should an unwarrantable measure of the federal government be unpopular in particular States, which would seldom fail to be the case, or even a warrantable measure be so, which may sometimes be the case, the means of opposition to it are powerful and at hand. The disquietude of the people; their repugnance and, perhaps, refusal to coöperate with the officers of the Union; the frowns of the executive magistracy of the State; the embarrassments created by legislative devices, which would often be added on such occasions, would oppose, in any State, difficulties not to be despised; would form, in a large State, very serious impediments; and where the sentiments of several adjoining States happened to be in unison, would present obstructions which the federal government would hardly be willing to encounter.

But ambitious encroachments of the federal government, on the authority of the State governments, would not excite the opposition of a single State, or of a few States only. They would be signals of general alarm. Every government would espouse the common cause. A correspondence would be opened. Plans of resistance would be concerted. One spirit would animate and conduct the whole. The same combinations, in short, would result from an apprehension of the federal, as was produced by the dread of a foreign, yoke; and unless the projected innovations should be voluntarily renounced, the same appeal to a trial of force would be made in the one case as was made in the other. But what degree of madness could ever drive the federal government to such an extremity. In the contest with Great Britain, one part of the empire was employed against the other. The more numerous part invaded the rights of the less numerous part. The attempt was unjust and unwise; but it was not in speculation absolutely chimerical. But what would be the contest in the case we are supposing? Who would be the parties? A few representatives of the people would be opposed to the people themselves; or rather one set of representatives would be contending against thirteen sets of representatives, with the whole body of their common constituents on the side of the latter.

* * * *

The argument under the present head may be put into a very concise form, which appears altogether conclusive. Either the mode in which the federal government is to be constructed will render it sufficiently dependent on the people, or it will not. On the first supposition, it will be restrained by that dependence from forming schemes obnoxious to their constituents. On the other supposition, it will not possess the confidence of the people, and its schemes of usurpation will be easily defeated by the State governments, who will be supported by the people.

On summing up the considerations stated in this and the last paper, they seem to amount to the most convincing evidence, that the powers proposed to be lodged in the federal government are as little formidable to those reserved to the individual States, as they are indispensably necessary to accomplish the purposes of the Union; and that all those alarms which have been sounded, of a meditated and consequential annihilation of the State governments must, on the most favorable interpretation, be ascribed to the chimerical fears of the authors of them.

PUBLIUS

The Separation of Powers: I

To the People of the State of New York:

Having reviewed the general form of the proposed government and the general mass of power allotted to it, I proceed to examine the particular structure of this government, and the distribution of this mass of power among its constituent parts.

One of the principal objections inculcated by the more respectable adversaries to the Constitution, is its supposed violation of the political maxim, that the legislative, executive, and judiciary departments ought to be separate and distinct. In the structure of the federal government, no regard, it is said, seems to have been paid to this essential precaution in favor of liberty. The several departments of power are distributed and blended in such a manner as at once to destroy all symmetry and beauty of form, and to expose some of the essential parts of the edifice to the danger of being crushed by the disproportionate weight of other parts.

No political truth is certainly of greater intrinsic value, or is stamped with the authority of more enlightened patrons of liberty, than that on which the objection is founded. The accumulation of all powers, legislative, executive, and judiciary, in the same hands, whether of one, a few, or many, and whether hereditary, self-appointed, or elective, may justly be pronounced the very definition of tyranny. Were the federal Constitution, therefore, really chargeable with the accumulation of power, or with a mixture of powers, having a dangerous tendency to such an accumulation, no further arguments would be necessary to inspire a universal reprobation of the system. I persuade myself, however, that it will be made apparent to every one, that the charge cannot be supported, and that the maxim on which it relies has been totally misconceived and misapplied. In order to form correct ideas on this important subject, it will be proper to investigate the sense in which the preservation of liberty requires that the three great departments of power should be separate and distinct.

The oracle who is always consulted and cited on this subject is the celebrated Montesquieu. If he be not the author of this invaluable precept in the science of politics, he has the merit at least of displaying and recommending it most effectually to the attention of mankind. Let us endeavor, in the first place, to ascertain his meaning on this point.

The British Constitution was to Montesquieu what Homer has been to the didactic writers on epic poetry. As the latter have considered the work of the immortal bard as the perfect model from which the principles and rules of the epic art were to be drawn, and by which all similar works were to be judged, so this great political critic appears to have viewed the Constitution of England as the standard, or to use his own expression, as the mirror of political liberty; and to have delivered, in the form of elementary truths, the several characteristic principles of that particular system. That we may be sure, then, not to mistake his meaning in this case, let us recur to the source from which the maxim was drawn.

On the slightest view of the British Constitution, we must perceive that the legislative, executive, and judiciary departments are by no means totally separate and distinct from each other. The executive magistrate forms an integral part of the legislative authority. He alone has the prerogative of making treaties with foreign sovereigns, which, when made, have, under certain limitations, the force of legislative acts. All the members of the judiciary department are appointed by him, can be removed by him on the address of the two Houses of Parliament, and form, when he pleases to consult them, one of his constitutional councils. One branch of the legislative department forms also a great constitutional council to the executive chief, as, on another hand, it is the sole depositary of judicial power in cases of impeachment, and is invested with the supreme appellate jurisdiction in all other cases. The judges, again, are so far connected with the legislative department as often to attend and participate in its deliberations, though not admitted to a legislative vote.

From these facts, by which Montesquieu was guided, it may clearly be inferred that, in saying "There can be no liberty where the legislative and executive powers are united in the same person, or body of magistrates," or, "if the power of judging be not separated from the legislative and executive powers," he did not mean that these departments ought to have no *partial agency* in, or no *control* over, the acts of each other. His meaning, as his own words import, and still more conclusively as illustrated by the example in his eye, can amount to no more than this, that where the *whole* power of one department is exercised by the same hands which possess the *whole* power of another department, the fundamental principles of a free constitution are subverted. This would have been the case in the constitution examined by him, if the king, who is the sole executive magistrate, had possessed also the complete legislative power, or the supreme administration of justice; or if the entire legislative body had possessed the supreme judiciary, or the supreme executive authority. This, however is not among the vices of that constitution. The magistrate in whom the whole executive power resides cannot of himself make a law, though he can put a negative on every law; nor administer justice in person, though he has the appointment of those who do administer it. The judges can exercise no executive prerogative, though they are shoots from the executive stock; nor any legislative function, though they may be advised with by the legislative councils. The entire legislature can perform no judiciary act, though by the joint act of two of its branches the judges may be removed from their offices, and though one of its branches is possessed of the judicial power in the last resort. The entire legislature, again, can exercise no executive prerogative, though one of its branches constitutes the supreme executive magistracy, and another, on the impeachment of a third, can try and condemn all the subordinate officers in the executive department.

The reasons on which Montesquieu grounds his maxim are a further demonstration of his meaning. "When the legislative and executive powers are united in the same person or body," says he, "there can be no liberty, because apprehensions may arise lest *the same* monarch or senate should *enact* tyrannical laws to *execute* them in a tyrannical manner." Again: "Were the power of judging joined with the legislative, the life and liberty of the subject would be exposed to arbitrary control, for *the judge* would then be *the legislator*. Were it joined to the executive power, *the judge* might behave with all the violence of *an oppressor*." Some of these reasons are more fully explained in other passages; but briefly stated as they are here, they sufficiently establish the meaning which we have put on this celebrated maxim of this celebrated author.

If we look into the constitutions of the several States, we find that, notwithstanding the emphatical and, in some instances, the unqualified terms in which this axiom has been laid down, there is not a single instance in which the several departments of power have been kept absolutely separate and distinct. New Hampshire, whose constitution was the last formed, seems to have been fully aware of the impossibility and inexpediency of avoiding any mixture whatever of these departments, and has qualified the doctrine by declaring "that the legislative, executive, and judiciary powers ought to be kept as separate from, and independent of, each other *as the nature of a free government will admit; or as is consistent with that chain of connection that binds the whole fabric of the constitution in one indissoluble bond of unity and amity."* Her constitution accordingly mixes these departments in several respects. The Senate, which is a branch of the legislative department, is also a judicial tribunal for the trial of impeachments. The President, who is the head of the executive department, is the presiding member also of the Senate; and, besides an equal vote in all cases, has a casting vote in case of a tie. The executive head is himself eventually elective every year by the legislative department, and his council is every year chosen by and from the members of the same department. Several of the officers of state are also appointed by the legislature. And the members of the judiciary department are appointed by the executive department.

The constitution of Massachusetts has observed a sufficient though less pointed caution, in expressing this fundamental article of liberty. It declares "that the legislative departments shall never exercise the executive and judicial powers, or either of them; the executive shall never exercise the legislative and judicial powers, or either of them; the judicial shall never exercise the legislative and executive powers, or either of them." This declaration corresponds precisely with the doctrine of Montesquieu, as it has been explained, and is not in a single point violated by the plan of the convention. It goes no farther than to prohibit any one of the entire departments from exercising the powers of another department. In the very Constitution to which it is prefixed, a partial mixture of powers has been admitted. The executive magistrate has a qualified negative on the legislative body, and the Senate, which is a part of the legislature, is a court of impeachment for members both of the executive and judiciary departments. The members of the judiciary department, again, are appointable by the executive department, and removable by the same authority on the address of the two legislative branches. Lastly, a number of the officers of government are annually appointed by the legislative department. As the appointment to offices, particularly executive offices, is in its nature an executive function, the compilers of the Constitution have, in this last point at least, violated the rule established by themselves.

I pass over the constitutions of Rhode Island and Connecticut, because they were formed prior to the Revolution, and even before the principle under examination had become an object of political attention.

The constitution of New York contains no declaration on this subject; but appears very clearly to have been framed with an eye to the danger of improperly blending the different departments. It gives, nevertheless, to the executive magistrate, a partial control over the legislative department; and, what is more, gives a like control to the judiciary department; and even blends the executive and judiciary departments in the exercise of this control. In its council of appointment members of the legislative are associated with the executive authority, in the appointment of officers, both executive and judiciary. And its court for the trial of impeachments and correction of errors is to consist of one branch of the legislature and the principal members of the judiciary department.

The constitution of New Jersey has blended the different powers of government more than any of the preceding. The governor, who is the executive magistrate, is appointed by the legislature; is chancellor and ordinary, or surrogate of the State; is a member of the Supreme Court of Appeals, and president, with a casting vote, of one of the legislative branches. The same legislative branch acts again as executive council of the governor, and with him constitutes the Court of Appeals. The members of the judiciary department are appointed by the legislative department, and removable by one branch of it, on the impeachment of the other.

According to the constitution of Pennsylvania, the president, who is the head of the executive department, is annually elected by a vote in which the legislative department predominates. In conjunction with an executive council, he appoints the members of the judiciary department, and forms a court of impeachment for trial of all officers, judiciary as well as executive. The judges of the Supreme Court and justices of the peace seem also to be removable by the legislature; and the executive power of pardoning in certain cases, to be referred to the same department. The members of the executive council are made EX-OFFICIO justices of peace throughout the State.

In Delaware, the chief executive magistrate is annually elected by the legislative department. The speakers of the two legislative branches are vice-presidents in the executive department. The executive chief, with six others, appointed, three by each of the legislative branches, constitutes the Supreme Court of Appeals; he is joined with the legislative department in the appointment of the other judges. Throughout the States, it appears that the members of the legislature may at the same time be justices of the peace; in this State, the members of one branch of it are EX-OFFICIO justices of the peace; as are also the members of the executive council. The principal officers of the executive department are appointed by the legislative; and one branch of the latter forms a court of impeachments. All officers may be removed on address of the legislature.

Maryland has adopted the maxim in the most unqualified terms; declaring that the legislative, executive, and judicial powers of government ought to be forever separate and distinct from each other. Her constitution, notwithstanding, makes the executive magistrate appointable by the legislative department; and the members of the judiciary by the executive department.

The language of Virginia is still more pointed on this subject. Her constitution declares, "that the legislative, executive, and judiciary departments shall be separate and distinct; so that neither exercise the powers properly belonging to the other; nor shall any person exercise the powers of more than one of them at the same time, except that the justices of county courts shall be eligible to either House of Assembly." Yet we find not only this express exception, with respect to the members of the inferior courts, but that the chief magistrate, with his executive council, are appointable by the legislature; that two members of the latter are triennially displaced at the pleasure of the legislature; and that all the principal offices, both executive and judiciary, are filled by the same department. The executive prerogative of pardon, also, is in one case vested in the legislative department.

The constitution of North Carolina, which declares "that the legislative, executive, and supreme judicial powers of government ought to be forever separate and distinct from each other," refers, at the same time, to the legislative department, the appointment not only of the executive chief, but all the principal officers within both that and the judiciary department.

In South Carolina, the constitution makes the executive magistracy eligible by the legislative department. It gives to the latter, also, the appointment of the members of the judiciary department, including even justices of the peace and sheriffs; and the appointment of officers in the executive department, down to captains in the army and navy of the State.

In the constitution of Georgia, where it is declared "that the legislative, executive, and judiciary departments shall be separate and distinct, so that neither exercise the powers properly belonging to the other," we find that the executive department is to be filled by appointments of the legislature; and the executive prerogative of pardon to be finally exercised by the same authority. Even justices of the peace are to be appointed by the legislature.

In citing these cases, in which the legislative, executive, and judiciary departments have not been kept totally separate and distinct, I wish not to be regarded as an advocate for the particular organizations of the several State governments. I am fully aware that among the many excellent principles which they exemplify, they carry strong marks of the haste, and still stronger of the inexperience, under which they were framed. It is but too obvious that in some instances the fundamental principle under consideration has been violated by too great a mixture, and even an actual consolidation, of the different powers; and that in no instance has a competent provision been made for maintaining in practice the separation delineated on paper. What I have wished to evince is, that the charge brought against the proposed Constitution, of violating the sacred maxim of free government, is warranted neither by the real meaning annexed to that maxim by its author, nor by the sense in which it has hitherto been understood in America. This interesting subject will be resumed in the ensuing paper.

PUBLIUS

The Separation of Powers: II

To the People of the State of New York:

It was shown in the last paper that the political apothegm there examined does not require that the legislative, executive, and judiciary departments should be wholly unconnected with each other. I shall undertake, in the next place, to show that unless these departments be so far connected and blended as to give to each a constitutional control over the others, the degree of separation which the maxim requires, as essential to a free government, can never in practice be duly maintained.

It is agreed on all sides, that the powers properly belonging to one of the departments ought not to be directly and completely administered by either of the other departments. It is equally evident, that none of them ought to possess, directly or indirectly, an overruling influence over the others, in the administration of their respective powers. It will not be denied, that power is of an encroaching nature, and that it ought to be effectually restrained from passing the limits assigned to it. After discriminating, therefore, in theory, the several classes of power, as they may in their nature be legislative, executive, or judiciary, the next and most difficult task is to provide some practical security for each, against the invasion of the others. What this security ought to be, is the great problem to be solved.

Will it be sufficient to mark, with precision, the boundaries of these departments, in the constitution of the government, and to trust to these parchment barriers against the encroaching spirit of power? This is the security which appears to have been principally relied on by the compilers of most of the American constitutions. But experience assures us, that the efficacy of the provision has been greatly overrated; and that some more adequate defence is indispensably necessary for the more feeble, against the more powerful, members of the government. The legislative department is everywhere extending the sphere of its activity, and drawing all power into its impetuous vortex.

The founders of our republics have so much merit for the wisdom which they have displayed, that no task can be less pleasing than that of pointing out the errors into which they have fallen. A respect for truth, however, obliges us to remark, that they seem never for a moment to have turned their eyes from the danger to liberty from the overgrown and all-grasping prerogative of an hereditary magistrate, supported and fortified by an hereditary branch of the legislative authority. They seem never to have recollected the danger from legislative usurpations, which, by assembling all power in the same hands, must lead to the same tyranny as is threatened by executive usurpations.

In a government where numerous and extensive prerogatives are placed in the hands of an hereditary monarch, the executive department is very justly regarded as the source of danger, and watched with all the jealousy which a zeal for liberty ought to inspire. In a democracy, where a multitude of people exercise in person the legislative functions, and are continually exposed, by their incapacity for regular deliberation and concerted measures, to the ambitious intrigues of their executive magistrates, tyranny may well be apprehended, on some favorable emergency, to start up in the same quarter. But in a representative republic, where the executive magistracy is carefully limited, both in the extent and the duration of its power; and where the legislative power is exercised by an assembly, which is inspired, by a supposed influence over the people, with an intrepid confidence in its own strength; which is sufficiently numerous to feel all the passions which actuate a multitude, yet not so numerous as to be incapable of pursuing the objects of its passions, by means which reason prescribes; it is against the enterprising ambition of this department that the people ought to indulge all their jealousy and exhaust all their precautions.

The legislative department derives a superiority in our governments from other circumstances. Its constitutional powers being at once more extensive, and less susceptible of precise limits, it can, with the greater facility, mask, under complicated and indirect measures, the encroachments which it makes on the coördinate departments. It is not unfrequently a question of real nicety in legislative bodies, whether the operation of a particular measure will, or will not, extend beyond the legislative sphere. On the other side, the executive power being restrained within a narrower compass, and being more simple in its nature, and the judiciary being described by landmarks still less uncertain, projects of usurpation by either of these departments would immediately betray and defeat themselves. Nor is this all: the legislative department alone has access to the pockets of the people, and has in some constitutions full discretion, and in all a prevailing influence, over the pecuniary rewards of those who fill the other departments, a dependence is thus created in the latter, which gives still greater facility to encroachments of the former.

I have appealed to our own experience for the truth of what I advance on this subject. Were it necessary to verify this experience by particular proofs, they might be multiplied without end. I might find a witness in every citizen who has shared in, or been attentive to, the course of public administrations. I might collect vouchers in abundance from the records and archives of every State in the Union. But as a more concise, and at the same time equally satisfactory, evidence, I will refer to the example of two States, attested by two unexceptionable authorities.

The first example is that of Virginia, a State which, as we have seen, has expressly declared in its constitution, that the three great departments ought not to be intermixed. The authority in support of it is Mr. Jefferson, who, besides his other advantages for remarking the operation of the government, was himself the chief magistrate of it. In order to convey fully the ideas with which his experience had impressed him on this subject, it will be necessary to quote a passage of some length from his very interesting "Notes on the State of Virginia," p. 195. "All the powers of government, legislative, executive, and judiciary, result to the legislative body. The concentrating these in the same hands, is precisely the definition of despotic government. It will be no alleviation, that these powers will be exercised by a plurality of hands, and not by a single one. One hundred and seventy-three despots would surely be as oppressive as one. Let those who doubt it, turn their eyes on the republic of Venice. As little will it avail us, that they are chosen by ourselves. An *elective despotism* was not the government we fought for; but one which should not only be founded on free principles, but in which the powers of government should be so divided and balanced among several bodies of magistracy, as that no one could transcend their legal limits, without being effectually checked and restrained by the others. For this reason, that convention which passed the ordinance of government, laid its foundation on this basis, that the legislative, executive, and judiciary departments should be separate and distinct, so that no person should exercise the powers of more than one of them at the same time. *But no barrier was provided between these several powers.* The judiciary and the executive members were left dependent on the legislative for their subsistence in office, and some of them for their continuance in it. If, therefore, the legislature assumes executive and judiciary powers, no opposition is likely to be made; nor, if made, can be effectual; because in that case they may put their proceedings into the form of acts of Assembly, which will render them obligatory on the other branches. They have accordingly, *in many* instances, *decided rights* which should have been left to *judiciary controversy,* and *the direction of the executive, dur-*

ing the whole time of their session, is becoming habitual and familiar."

The other State which I shall take for an example is Pennsylvania; and the other authority, the Council of Censors, which assembled in the years 1783 and 1784. A part of the duty of this body, as marked out by the constitution, was "to inquire whether the constitution had been preserved inviolate in every part; and whether the legislative and executive branches of government had performed their duty as guardians of the people, or assumed to themselves, or exercised, other or greater powers than they are entitled to by the constitution." In the execution of this trust, the council were necessarily led to a comparison of both the legislative and executive proceedings, with the constitutional powers of these departments; and from the facts enumerated, and to the truth of most of which both sides in the council subscribed, it appears that the constitution had been flagrantly violated by the legislature in a variety of important instances.

A great number of laws had been passed, violating, without any apparent necessity, the rule requiring that all bills of a public nature shall be previously printed for the consideration of the people; although this is one of the precautions chiefly relied on by the constitution against improper acts of the legislature.

The constitutional trial by jury had been violated, and powers assumed which had not been delegated by the constitution.

Executive powers had been usurped.

The salaries of the judges, which the constitution expressly requires to be fixed, had been occasionally varied; and cases belonging to the judiciary department frequently drawn within legislative cognizance and determination.

     ✲   ✲   ✲   ✲

It appears, also, that the executive department had not been innocent of frequent breaches of the constitution. There are three observations, however, which ought to be made on this head: *first,* a great proportion of the instances were either immediately produced by the necessities of the war, or recommended by Congress or the commander-in-chief; *secondly,* in most of the other instances, they conformed either to the declared or the known sentiments of the legislative department; *thirdly,* the executive department of Pennsylvania is distinguished from that of the other States by the number of members composing it. In this respect, it has as much affinity to a legislative assembly as to an executive council. And being at once exempt from the restraint of an individual responsibility for the acts of the body, and deriving confidence from mutual example and joint influence, unauthorized measures would, of course, be more freely hazarded, than where the executive department is administered by a single hand or by a few hands.

The conclusion which I am warranted in drawing from these observations is, that a mere demarcation on parchment of the constitutional limits of the several departments, is not a sufficient guard against those encroachments which lead to a tyrannical concentration of all the powers of government in the same hands.

PUBLIUS

49 [JAMES MADISON]

Appeal to the People in Cases of Disagreement

To the People of the State of New York:

The author of the "Notes on the State of Virginia," quoted in the last paper, has subjoined to that valuable work the draught of a constitution, which had been prepared in order to be laid before a convention expected to be called in 1783, by the legislature, for the establishment of a constitution for that commonwealth. The plan, like every thing from the same pen, marks a turn of thinking, original, comprehensive, and accurate; and is the more worthy of attention as it equally displays a fervent attachment to republican government and an enlightened view of the dangerous propensities against which it ought to be guarded. One of the precautions which he proposes, and on which he appears ultimately to rely as a palladium to the weaker departments of power against the invasions of the stronger, is perhaps altogether his own, and as it immediately relates to the subject of our present inquiry, ought not to be overlooked.

His proposition is, "that whenever any two of the three branches of government shall concur in opinion, each by the voices of two thirds of their whole number, that a convention is necessary for altering the constitution, or *correcting breaches of it,* a convention shall be called for the purpose."

As the people are the only legitimate fountain of power, and it is from them that the constitutional charter, under which the several branches of government hold their power, is derived, it seems strictly consonant to the republican theory, to recur to the same original authority, not only whenever it may be necessary to enlarge, diminish, or new-model the powers of the government, but also whenever any one of the departments may commit encroachments on the chartered authorities of the others. The several departments being perfectly coördinate by the terms of their common commission, none of them, it is evident, can pretend to an exclusive or superior right of settling the boundaries between their respective powers; and how are the encroachments of the stronger to be prevented, or the wrongs of the weaker to by redressed, without an appeal to the people themselves, who, as the grantors of the commission, can alone declare its true meaning, and enforce its observance?

There is certainly great force in this reasoning, and it must be allowed to prove that a constitutional road to the decision of the people ought to be marked out and kept open, for certain great and extraordinary occasions. But there appear to be insuperable objections against the proposed recurrence to the people, as a provision in all cases for keeping the several departments of power within their constitutional limits.

In the first place, the provision does not reach the case of a combination of two of the departments against the third. If the legislative authority, which possesses so many means of operating on the motives of the other departments, should be able to gain to its interest either of the others, or even one third of its members, the remaining department could derive no advantage from its remedial provision. I do not dwell, however, on this objection, because it may be thought to be rather against the modification of the principle, than against the principle itself.

In the next place, it may be considered as an objection inherent in the principle, that as every appeal to the people would carry an implication of some defect in the government, frequent appeals would, in a great measure, deprive the government of that veneration which time bestows on every thing, and without which perhaps the wisest and freest governments would not possess the requisite stability. If it be true that all governments rest on opinion, it is no less true that the strength of opinion in each individual, and its practical influence on his conduct, depend much on the number which he supposes to have entertained the same opinion. The reason of man, like man himself, is timid and cautious when left alone, and acquires firmness and confidence in proportion to the number with which it is associated. When the examples which fortify opinion are *ancient* as well as *numerous,* they are known to have a double effect. In a nation of philosophers, this consideration ought to be disregarded. A reverence for the laws would be sufficiently inculcated by the voice of an enlightened reason. But a nation of philosophers is as little to be expected as the philosophical race of kings wished for by Plato. And in every other nation, the most rational government will not find it a superfluous advantage to have the prejudices of the community on its side.

The danger of disturbing the public tranquillity by interesting too strongly the public passions, is a still more serious objection against a frequent reference of constitutional questions to the decision of the whole society. Notwithstanding the success which has attended the revisions of our established forms of government, and which does so much honor to the virtue and intelligence of the people of America, it must be confessed that the experiments are of too ticklish a nature to be unnecessarily multiplied. We are to recollect that all the existing constitutions were formed in the midst of a danger which repressed the passions most unfriendly to order and concord; of an enthusiastic confidence of the people in their patriotic leaders, which stifled the ordinary diversity of opinions on great national questions; of a universal ardor for new and opposite forms, produced by a universal resentment and indignation against the ancient government; and whilst no spirit of party connected with the changes to be made, or the abuses to be reformed, could mingle its leaven in the operation. The future situations in which we must expect to be usually placed, do not present any equivalent security against the danger which is apprehended.

But the greatest objection of all is, that the decisions which would probably result from such appeals would not answer the purpose of maintaining the constitutional equilibrium of the government. We have seen that the tendency of republican governments is to an aggrandizement of the legislative at the expense of the other departments. The appeals to the people, therefore, would usually be made by the executive and judiciary departments. But whether made by one side or the other, would each side enjoy equal advantages on the trial? . . . The members of the executive and judiciary departments are few in number, and can be personally known to a small part only of the people. . . . The members of the legislative department, on the other hand, are numerous. They are distributed and dwell among the people at large. Their connections of blood, of friendship, and of acquaintance embrace a great proportion of the most influential part of the society. The nature of their public trust implies a personal influence among the people, and that they are more immediately the confidential guardians of the rights and liberties of the people. With these advantages, it can hardly be supposed that the adverse party would have an equal chance for a favorable issue.

But the legislative party would not only be able to plead their cause most successfully with the people. They would probably be constituted themselves the judges. The same influence which had gained them an election into the legislature, would gain them a seat in the convention. If this should not be the case with all, it would probably be the case with many, and pretty certainly with those leading characters, on whom every thing depends in such bodies. The convention, in short, would be composed chiefly of men who had been, who actually were, or who expected to be, members of the department whose conduct was arraigned. They would consequently be parties to the very question to be decided by them.

It might, however, sometimes happen, that appeals would be made under circumstances less adverse to the executive and judiciary departments. The usurpations of the legislature might be so flagrant and so sudden, as to admit of no specious coloring. A strong party among themselves might take side with the other branches. The executive power might be in the hands of a peculiar favorite of the people. In such a posture of things, the public decision might be less swayed by prepossessions in favor of the legislative party. But still it could never be expected to turn on the true merits of the question. It would inevitably be connected with the spirit of preëxisting parties, or of parties springing out of the question itself. It would be connected with persons of distinguished character and extensive influence in the community. It would be pronounced by the very men who had been agents in, or opponents of, the measures to which the decision would relate. The *passions,* therefore, not the *reason,* of the public would sit in judgment. But it is the reason, alone, of the public, that ought to control and regulate the government. The passions ought to be controlled and regulated by the government.

We found in the last paper, that mere declarations in the written constitution are not sufficient to restrain the several departments within their legal rights. It appears in this, that occasional appeals to the people would be neither a proper nor an effectual provision for that purpose. . . .

PUBLIUS

51 [JAMES MADISON]

Checks and Balances

To the People of the State of New York:

To what expedient, then, shall we finally resort, for maintaining in practice the necessary partition of power among the several departments, as laid down in the Constitution? The only answer that can be given is, that as all these exterior provisions are found to be inadequate, the defect must be supplied, by so contriving the interior structure of the government as that its several constituent parts may, by their mutual relations, be the means of keeping each other in their proper places. . . .

In order to lay a due foundation for that separate and distinct exercise of the different powers of government, which to a certain extent is admitted on all hands to be essential to the preservation of liberty, it is evident that each department should have a will of its own; and consequently should be so constituted that the members of each should have as little agency as possible in the appointment of the members of the others. Were this principle rigorously adhered to, it would require that all the appointments for the supreme executive, legislative, and judiciary magistracies should be drawn from the same fountain of authority, the people, through channels having no communication whatever with one another. Perhaps such a plan of constructing the several departments would be less difficult in practice than it may in contemplation appear. Some difficulties, however, and some additional expense would attend the execution of it. Some deviations, therefore, from the principle must be admitted. In the constitution of the judiciary department in particular, it might be inexpedient to insist rigorously on the principle: first, because peculiar qualifications being essential in the members, the primary consideration ought to be to select that mode of choice which best secures these qualifications; secondly, because the permanent tenure by which the appointments are held in that department, must soon destroy all sense of dependence on the authority conferring them.

It is equally evident, that the members of each department should be as little dependent as possible on those of the others, for the emoluments annexed to their offices. Were the executive magistrate, or the judges, not independent of the legislature in this particular, their independence in every other would be merely nominal.

But the great security against a gradual concentration of the several powers in the same department, consists in giving to those who administer each department the necessary constitutional means and personal motives to resist encroachments of the others. The provision for defence must in this, as in all other cases, be made commensurate to the danger of attack. Ambition must be made to counteract ambition. The interest of the man must be connected with the constitutional rights of the place. It may be a reflection on human nature, that such devices should be necessary to control the abuses of government. But what is government itself, but the greatest of all reflections on human nature? If men were angels, no government would be necessary. If angels were to govern men, neither external nor internal controls on government would be necessary. In framing a government which is to be administered by men over men, the great difficulty lies in this: you must first enable the government to control the governed; and in the next place oblige it to control itself. A dependence on the people is, no doubt, the primary control on the government; but experience has taught mankind the necessity of auxiliary precautions.

This policy of supplying, by opposite and rival interests, the defect of better motives, might be traced through the whole system of human affairs, private as well as public. We see it particularly displayed in all the subordinate distributions of power, where the constant aim is to divide and arrange the several offices in such a manner as that each may be a check on the other—that the private interest of every individual may be a sentinel over the public rights. These inventions of prudence cannot be less requisite in the distribution of the supreme powers of the State.

But it is not possible to give to each department an equal power of self-defence. In republican government, the legislative authority necessarily predominates. The remedy for this inconveniency is to divide the legislature into different branches; and to render them, by different modes of election and different principles of action, as little connected with each other as the nature of their common functions and their common dependence on the society will admit. It may even be necessary to guard against dangerous encroachments by still further precautions. As the weight of the legislative authority requires that it should be thus divided, the weakness of the executive may require, on the other hand, that it should be fortified. An absolute negative on the legislature appears, at first view, to be the natural defence with which the executive magistrate should be armed. But perhaps it would be neither altogether safe nor alone sufficient. On ordinary occasions it might not be exerted with the requisite firmness, and on extraordinary occasions it might be perfidiously abused. May not this defect of an absolute negative be supplied by some qualified connection between this weaker department and the weaker branch of the stronger department, by which the latter may be led to support the constitutional rights of the former, without being too much detached from the rights of its own department?

If the principles on which these observations are founded be just, as I persuade myself they are, and they be applied as a criterion to the several State constitutions, and to the federal Constitution, it will be found that if the latter does not perfectly correspond with them, the former are infinitely less able to bear such a test.

There are, moreover, two considerations particularly applicable to the federal system of America, which place that system in a very interesting point of view.

First. In a single republic, all the power surrendered by the people is submitted to the administration of a single government; and the usurpations are guarded against by a division of the government into distinct and separate departments. In the compound republic of America, the power surrendered by the people is first divided between two distinct governments, and then the portion allotted to each subdivided among distinct and separate departments. Hence a double security arises to the rights of the people. The different governments will control each other, at the same time that each will be controlled by itself.

Second. It is of great importance in a republic not only to guard the society against the oppression of its rulers, but to guard one part of the society against the injustice of the other part. Different interests necessarily exist in different classes of citizens. If a majority be united by a common interest, the rights of the minority will be insecure. There are but two methods of providing against this evil: the one by creating a will in the community independent of the majority—that is, of the society itself; the other, by comprehending in the society so many separate descriptions of citizens as will render an unjust combination of a majority of the whole very improbable, if not impracticable. The first method prevails in all governments possessing an hereditary or self-appointed authority. This, at best, is but a precarious security; because a power independent of the society may as well espouse the unjust views of the major, as the rightful interests of the minor party, and may possibly be turned against both parties. The second method will be exemplified in the federal republic of the United States. Whilst all authority in it will be derived from and dependent on the society, the society itself will be broken into so many parts, interests and classes of citizens, that the rights of individuals, or of the minority, will be in little danger from interested combinations of the majority. In a free government the security for civil rights must be the same as that for religious rights. It consists in the one case in the multiplicity of interests, and in the other in the multiplicity of sects. The degree of security in both cases will depend on the number of interests and sects; and this may be presumed to depend on the extent of country and number of people comprehended under the same government. This view of the subject must particularly recommend a proper federal system to all the sincere and considerate friends of republican government, since it shows that in exact proportion as the territory of the Union may be formed into more circumscribed Confederacies, or States, oppressive combinations of a majority will be facilitated; the best security, under the republican forms, for the rights of every class of citizens will be diminished; and consequently the stability and independence of some member of the government, the only other security, must be proportionally increased. Justice is the end of government. It is the end of civil society. It ever has been and ever will be pursued until it be obtained, or until liberty be lost in the pursuit. In a society under the forms of which the stronger faction can readily unite and oppress the weaker, anarchy may as truly be said to reign as in a state of nature, where the weaker individual is not secured against the violence of the stronger; and as, in the latter state, even the stronger individuals are prompted, by the uncertainty of their condition, to submit to a government which may protect the weak as well as themselves; so, in the former state, will the more powerful factions or parties be gradually induced, by a like motive, to wish for a government which will protect all parties, the weaker as well as the more powerful. It can be little doubted that if the State of Rhode Island was separated from the Confederacy and left to itself, the insecurity of rights under the popular form of government within such narrow limits would be displayed by such reiterated oppressions of factious majorities that some power altogether independent of the people would soon be called for by the voice of the very factions whose misrule had proved the necessity of it. In the extended republic of the United States, and among the great variety of interests, parties, and sects which it embraces, a coalition of a majority of the whole society could seldom take place on any other principles than those of justice and the general good; whilst there being thus less danger to a minor from the will of a major party, there must be less pretext, also, to provide for the security of the former, by introducing into the government a will not dependent on the latter, or, in other words, a will independent of the society itself. It is no less certain than it is important, notwithstanding the contrary opinions which have been entertained, that the larger the society, provided it lie within a practical sphere, the more duly capable it will be of self-government. And happily for the *republican cause,* the practicable sphere may be carried to a very great extent, by a judicious modification and mixture of the *federal principle.*

PUBLIUS

55 [JAMES MADISON]

The House and Knowledge of Local Circumstances

To the People of the State of New York:

The number of which the House of Representatives is to consist, forms another and a very interesting point of view, under which this branch of the federal legislature may be contemplated. Scarce any article, indeed, in the whole Constitution seems to be rendered more worthy of attention, by the weight of character and the apparent force of argument with which it has been assailed. The charges exhibited against it are, first, that so small a number of representatives will be an unsafe depositary of the public interests; secondly, that they will not possess a proper knowledge of the local circumstances of their numerous constituents; thirdly, that they will be taken from that class of citizens which will sympathize least with the feelings of the mass of the people, and be most likely to aim at a permanent elevation of the few on the depression of the many; fourthly, that defective as the number will be in the first instance, it will be more and more disproportionate, by the increase of the people, and the obstacles which will prevent a correspondent increase of the representatives.

In general it may be remarked on this subject, that no political problem is less susceptible of a precise solution than that which relates to the number most convenient for a representative legislature; nor is there any point on which the policy of the several States is more at variance, whether we compare their legislative assemblies directly with each other, or consider the proportions which they respectively bear to the number of their constituents. Passing over the difference between the smallest and largest States, as Delaware, whose most numerous branch consists of twenty-one representatives, and Massachusetts, where it amounts to between three and four hundred, a very considerable difference is observable among States nearly equal in population. . . .

Another general remark to be made is, that the ratio between the representatives and the people ought not to be the same where the latter are very numerous as where they are very few. Were the representatives in Virginia to be regulated by the standard in Rhode Island, they would, at this time, amount to between four and five hundred; and twenty or thirty years hence, to a thousand. On the other hand, the ratio of Pennsylvania, if applied to the State of Delaware, would reduce the representative assembly of the latter to seven or eight members. Nothing can be more fallacious than to found our political calculations on arithmetical principles. Sixty or seventy men may be more properly trusted with a given degree of power than six or seven. But it does not follow that six or seven hundred would be proportionately a better depositary. And if we carry on the supposition to six or seven thousand, the whole reasoning ought to be reversed. The truth is, that in all cases a certain number at least seems to be necessary to secure the benefits of free consultation and discussion, and to guard against too easy a combination for improper purposes; as on the other hand, the number ought at most to be kept within a certain limit, in order to avoid the confusion and intemperance of a multitude. In all very numerous assemblies, of whatever character composed, passion never fails to wrest the sceptre from reason. Had every Athenian citizen been a Socrates, every Athenian assembly would still have been a mob.

It is necessary also to recollect here the observations which were applied to the case of biennial elections. For the same reason that the limited powers of the Congress, and the control of the State legislatures, justify less frequent election than the public safety might otherwise require, the members of Congress need be less numerous than if they possessed the whole power of legislation, and were under no other than the ordinary restraints of other legislative bodies.

❋   ❋   ❋   ❋

PUBLIUS

57 [JAMES MADISON]

The Popular Basis of the House

To the People of the State of New York:

The *THIRD* charge against the House of Representatives is, that it will be taken from the class of citizens which will have least sympathy with the mass of the people, and be most likely to aim at an ambitious sacrifice of the many to the aggrandizement of the few.

Of all the objections which have been framed against the federal Constitution, this is perhaps the most extraordinary. Whilst the objection itself is levelled against a pretended oligarchy, the principle of it strikes at the very root of republican government.

The aim of every political constitution is, or ought to be, first to obtain for rulers men who possess most wisdom to discern, and most virtue to pursue, the common good of the society; and in the next place, to take the most effectual precautions for keeping them virtuous whilst they continue to hold their public trust. The elective mode of obtaining rulers is the characteristic policy of republican government. The means relied on in this form of government for preventing their degeneracy are numerous and various. The most effectual one, is such a limitation of the term of appointments as will maintain a proper responsibility to the people.

Let me now ask what circumstance there is in the constitution of the House of Representatives that violates the principles of republican government, or favors the elevation of the few on the ruins of the many? Let me ask whether every circumstance is not, on the contrary, strictly conformable to these principles, and scrupulously impartial to the rights and pretensions of every class and description of citizens?

Who are to be the electors of the federal representatives? Not the rich, more than the poor; not the learned, more than the ignorant; not the haughty heirs of distinguished names, more than the humble sons of obscurity and unpropitious fortune. The electors are to be the great body of the people of the United States. They are to be the same who exercise the right in every State of electing the corresponding branch of the legislature of the State.

Who are to be the objects of popular choice? Every citizen whose merit may recommend him to the esteem and confidence of his country. No qualification of wealth, of birth, of religious faith, or of civil profession is permitted to fetter the judgment or disappoint the inclination of the people.

If we consider the situation of the men on whom the free suffrages of their fellow-citizens may confer the representative trust, we shall find it involving every security which can be devised or desired for their fidelity to their constituents.

In the first place, as they will have been distinguished by the preference of their fellow-citizens, we are to presume that in general they will be somewhat distinguished also by those qualities which entitle them to it, and which promise a sincere and scrupulous regard to the nature of their engagements.

In the second place, they will enter into the public service under circumstances which cannot fail to produce a temporary affection at least to their constituents. There is in every breast a sensibility to marks of honor, of favor, of esteem, and of confidence, which, apart from all considerations of interest, is some pledge for grateful and benevolent returns. Ingratitude is a common topic of declamation against human nature; and it must be confessed that instances of it are but too frequent and flagrant, both in public and in private life. But the universal and extreme indignation which it inspires is itself a proof of the energy and prevalence of the contrary sentiment.

In the third place, those ties which bind the representative to his constituents are strengthened by motives of a more selfish nature. His pride and vanity attach him to a form of government which favors his pretensions and gives him a share in its honors and distinctions. Whatever hopes or projects might be entertained by a few aspiring characters, it must generally happen that a great proportion of the men deriving their advancement from their influence with the people, would have more to hope from a preservation of the favor, than from innovations in the government subversive of the authority of the people.

All these securities, however, would be found very insufficient without the restraint of frequent elections. Hence, in the fourth place, the House of Representatives is so constituted as to support in the members an habitual recollection of their dependence on the people. Before the sentiments impressed on their minds by the mode of their elevation can be effaced by the exercise of power, they will be compelled to anticipate the moment when their power is to cease, when their exercise of it is to be reviewed, and when they must descend to the level from which they were raised; there forever to remain unless a faithful discharge of their trust shall have established their title to a renewal of it.

I will add, as a fifth circumstance in the situation of the House of Representatives, restraining them from oppressive measures, that they can make no law which will not have its full operation on themselves and their friends, as well as on the great mass of the society. This has always been deemed one of the strongest bonds by which human policy can connect the rulers and the people together. It creates between them that communion of interests and sympathy of sentiments, of which few governments have furnished examples; but without which every government degenerates into tyranny. If it be asked, what is to restrain the House of Representatives from making legal discriminations in favor of themselves and a particular class of the society? I answer: the genius of the whole system; the nature of just and constitutional laws; and above all, the vigilant and manly spirit which actuates the people of America—a spirit which nourishes freedom, and in return is nourished by it.

If this spirit shall ever be so far debased as to tolerate a law not obligatory on the legislature, as well as on the people, the people will be prepared to tolerate any thing but liberty.

Such will be the relation between the House of Representatives and their constituents. Duty, gratitude, interest, ambition itself, are the chords by which they will be bound to fidelity and sympathy with the great mass of the people. It is possible that these may all be insufficient to control the caprice and wickedness of man. But are they not all that government will admit, and that human prudence can devise? Are they not the genuine and the characteristic means by which republican government provides for the liberty and happiness of the people? Are they not the identical means on which every State government in the Union relies for the attainment of these important ends? What then are we to understand by the objection which this paper has combated? What are we to say to the men who profess the most flaming zeal for republican government, yet boldly impeach the fundamental principle of it; who pretend to be champions for the right and the capacity of the people to choose their own rulers, yet maintain that they will prefer those only who will immediately and infallibly betray the trust committed to them?

Were the objection to be read by one who had not seen the mode prescribed by the Constitution for the choice of representatives, he could suppose nothing less than that some unreasonable qualification of property was annexed to the right of suffrage; or that the right of eligibility was limited to persons of particular families or fortunes; or at least that the mode prescribed by the State constitutions was, in some respect or other, very grossly departed from. We have seen how far such a supposition would err, as to the two first points. Nor would it, in fact, be less erroneous as to the last. The only difference discoverable between the two cases is, that each representative of the United States will be elected by five or six thousand citizens; whilst in the individual States, the election of a representative is left to about as many hundreds. . . .

          ❋   ❋   ❋   ❋

PUBLIUS

62 [JAMES MADISON (?)]

The Nature and the Stabilizing Influence of the Senate

To the People of the State of New York:

Having examined the constitution of the House of Representatives, and answered such of the objections against it as seemed to merit notice, I enter next on the examination of the Senate.

The heads into which this member of the government may be considered are: I. The qualifications of senators; II. The appointment of them by the State legislatures; III. The equality of representation in the Senate; IV. The number of senators, and the term for which they are to be elected; V. The powers vested in the Senate.

I. The qualifications proposed for senators, as distinguished from those of representatives, consist in a more advanced age and a longer period of citizenship. A senator must be thirty years of age at least; as a representative must be twenty-five. And the former must have been a citizen nine years; as seven years are required for the latter. The propriety of these distinctions is explained by the nature of the senatorial trust, which, requiring greater extent of information and stability of character, requires at the same time that the senator should have reached a period of life most likely to supply these advantages; and which, participating immediately in transactions with foreign nations, ought to be exercised by none who are not thoroughly weaned from the

362

prepossessions and habits incident to foreign birth and education. The term of nine years appears to be a prudent mediocrity between a total exclusion of adopted citizens, whose merits and talents may claim a share in the public confidence, and an indiscriminate and hasty admission of them, which might create a channel for foreign influence on the national councils.

II. It is equally unnecessary to dilate on the appointment of senators by the State legislatures. Among the various modes which might have been devised for constituting this branch of the government, that which has been proposed by the convention is probably the most congenial with the public opinion. It is recommended by the double advantage of favoring a select appointment, and of giving to the State governments such an agency in the formation of the federal government as must secure the authority of the former, and may form a convenient link between the two systems.

III. The equality of representation in the Senate is another point, which, being evidently the result of compromise between the opposite pretensions of the large and the small States, does not call for much discussion. If indeed it be right, that among a people thoroughly incorporated into one nation, every district ought to have a *proportional* share in the government, and that among independent and sovereign States, bound together by a simple league, the parties, however unequal in size, ought to have an *equal* share in the common councils, it does not appear to be without some reason that in a compound republic, partaking both of the national and federal character, the government ought to be founded on a mixture of the principles of proportional and equal representation. But it is superfluous to try, by the standard of theory, a part of the Constitution which is allowed on all hands to be the result, not of theory, but "of a spirit of amity, and that mutual deference and concession which the peculiarity of our political situation rendered indispensable." A common government, with powers equal to its objects, is called for by the voice, and still more loudly by the political situation, of America. A government founded on principles more consonant to the wishes of the larger States, is not likely to be obtained from the smaller States. The only option, then, for the former, lies between the proposed government and a government still more objectionable. Under this alternative, the advice of prudence must be to embrace the lesser evil; and, instead of indulging a fruitless anticipation of the possible mischiefs which may ensue, to contemplate rather the advantageous consequences which may qualify the sacrifice.

In this spirit it may be remarked, that the equal vote allowed to each State is at once a constitutional recognition of the portion of sovereignty remaining in the individual States, and an instrument for preserving that residuary sovereignty. So far the equality ought to be no less acceptable to the large than to the small States; since they are not less solicitous to guard, by every possible expedient, against an improper consolidation of the States into one simple republic.

Another advantage accruing from this ingredient in the constitution of the Senate is, the additional impediment it must prove against improper acts of legislation. No law or resolution can now be passed without the concurrence, first, of a majority of the people, and then, of a majority of the States. It must be acknowledged that this complicated check on legislation may in some instances be injurious as well as beneficial; and that the peculiar defence which it involves in favor of the smaller States, would be more rational, if any interests common to them, and distinct from those of the other States, would otherwise be exposed to peculiar danger. But as the larger States will always be able, by their power over the supplies, to defeat unreasonable exertions of this prerogative of the lesser States, and as the facility and excess of law-making seem to be the diseases to which our governments are most liable, it is not impossible that this part of the Constitution may be more convenient in practice than it appears to many in contemplation.

IV. The number of senators, and the duration of their appointment, come next to be considered. In order to form an accurate judgment on both these points, it will be proper to inquire into the purposes which are to be answered by a senate; and in order to ascertain these, it will be necessary to review the inconveniences which a republic must suffer from the want of such an institution.

First. It is a misfortune incident to republican government, though in a less degree than to other governments, that those who administer it may forget their obligations to their constituents, and prove unfaithful to their important trust. In this point of view, a senate, as a second branch of the legislative assembly, distinct from, and dividing the power with, a first, must be in all cases a salutary check on the government. It doubles the security to the people, by requiring the concurrence of two distinct bodies in schemes of usurpation or perfidy, where the ambition or corruption of one would otherwise be sufficient. . . . I will barely remark, that as the improbability of sinister combinations will be in proportion to the dissimilarity in the genius of the two bodies, it must be politic to distinguish them from each other by every circumstance which will consist with a due harmony in all proper measures, and with the genuine principles of republican government.

Second. The necessity of a senate is not less indicated by the propensity of all single and numerous assemblies to yield to the impulse of sudden and violent passions, and to be seduced by factious leaders into intemperate and pernicious resolutions. Examples on this subject might be cited without number; and from proceedings within the United States, as well as from the history of other nations. But a position that will not be contradicted, need not be proved. All that need be remarked is, that a body which is to correct this infirmity ought itself to be free from it, and consequently ought to be less numerous. It ought, moreover, to possess great firmness, and consequently ought to hold its authority by a tenure of considerable duration.

Third. Another defect to be supplied by a senate lies in a want of due acquaintance with the objects and principles of legislation. It is not possible that an assembly of men called for the most part from pursuits of a private nature, continued in appointment for a short time, and led by no permanent motive to devote the intervals of public occupation to a study of the laws, the affairs, and the comprehensive interests of their country, should, if left wholly to themselves, escape a variety of important errors in the exercise of their legislative trust. It may be affirmed, on the best grounds, that no small share of the present embarrassments of America is to be charged on the blunders of our governments; and that these have proceeded from the heads rather than the hearts of most of the authors of them. What indeed are all the repealing, explaining, and amending laws, which fill and disgrace our voluminous codes, but so many monuments of deficient wisdom; so many impeachments exhibited by each succeeding against each preceding session; so many admonitions to the people, of the value of those aids which may be expected from a well-constituted senate?

A good government implies two things: first, fidelity to the object of government, which is the happiness of the people; secondly, a knowledge of the means by which that object can be best attained. Some governments are deficient in both these qualities; most governments are deficient in the first. I scruple not to assert, that in American governments too little attention has been paid to the last. The federal Constitution avoids this error; and what merits particular notice, it provides for the last in a mode which increases the security for the first.

Fourth. The mutability in the public councils arising from a rapid succession of new members, however qualified they may be, points out, in the strongest manner, the necessity of some stable institution in the government. Every new election in the States is found to change one half of the representatives. From this change of men must proceed a change of opinions; and from a change of opinions, a change of measures. But a continual change even of good measures is inconsistent with every rule of prudence and every prospect of success. The remark is verified in private life, and becomes more just, as well as more important, in national transactions.

To trace the mischievous effects of a mutable government, would fill a volume. I will hint a few only, each of which will be perceived to be a source of innumerable others.

In the first place, it forfeits the respect and confidence of other nations, and all the advantages connected with national character. . . . One nation is to another what one individual is to another; with this melancholy distinction perhaps, that the former, with fewer of the benevolent emotions than the latter, are under fewer restraints also from taking undue advantage from the indiscretion of each other. Every nation, consequently, whose affairs betray a want of wisdom and stability, may calculate on every loss which can be sustained from the more systematic policy of their wiser neighbors. But the best instruction on this subject is unhappily conveyed to America by the example of her own situation. She finds that she is held in no respect by her friends; that she is the derision of her enemies; and that she is a prey to every nation which has an interest in speculating on her fluctuating councils and embarrassed affairs.

The internal effects of a mutable policy are still more calamitous. It poisons the blessing of liberty itself. It will be of little avail to the people, that the laws are made by men of their own choice, if the laws be so voluminous that they cannot be read, or so incoherent that they cannot be understood; if they be repealed or revised before they are promulgated, or undergo such incessant changes that no man, who knows what the law is to-day, can guess what it will be to-morrow. Law is defined to be a rule of action; but how can that be a rule, which is little known, and less fixed?

Another effect of public instability is the unreasonable advantage it gives to the sagacious, the enterprising, and the moneyed few over the industrious and uninformed mass of the people. Every new regulation concerning commerce or revenue, or in any manner affecting the value of the different species of property, presents a new harvest to those who watch the change, and can trace its consequences; a harvest, reared not by themselves, but by the toils and cares of the great body of their fellow-citizens. This is a state of things in which it may be said with some truth that laws are made for the *few*, not for the *many*.

In another point of view, great injury results from an unstable government. The want of confidence in the public councils damps every useful undertaking, the success and profit of which may depend on a continuance of existing arrangements. What prudent merchant will hazard his fortunes in any new branch of commerce when he knows not but that his plans may be rendered unlawful before they can be executed? What farmer or manufacturer will lay himself out for the encouragement given to any particular cultivation or establishment, when he can have no assurance that his preparatory labors and advances will not render him a victim to an inconstant government? In a word, no great improvement or laudable enterprise can go forward which requires the auspices of a steady system of national policy.

But the most deplorable effect of all is that diminution of attachment and reverence which steals into the hearts of the people, towards a political system which betrays so many marks of infirmity, and disappoints so many of their flattering hopes. No government, any more than an individual, will long be respected without being truly respectable; nor be truly respectable, without possessing a certain portion of order and stability.

PUBLIUS

63 [JAMES MADISON (?)]

The Necessity of a Senate

To the People of the State of New York:

A *FIFTH* desideratum, illustrating the utility of a senate, is the want of a due sense of national character. Without a select and stable member of the government, the esteem of foreign powers will not only be forfeited by an unenlightened and variable policy, preceeding from the causes already mentioned, but the national councils will not possess that sensibility to the opinion of the world, which is perhaps not less necessary in order to merit, than it is to obtain, its respect and confidence.

An attention to the judgment of other nations is important to every government for two reasons: the one is, that, independently of the merits of any particular plan or measure, it is desirable, on various accounts, that it should appear to other nations as the offspring of a wise and honorable policy; the second is, that in doubtful cases, particularly where the national councils may be warped by some strong passion or momentary interest, the presumed or known opinion of the impartial world may be the best guide that can be followed. What has not America lost by her want of character with foreign nations; and how many errors and follies would she not have avoided, if the justice and propriety of her measures had, in every instance, been previously tried by the light in which they would probably appear to the unbiased part of mankind?

Yet however requisite a sense of national character may be,

it is evident that it can never be sufficiently possessed by a numerous and changeable body. It can only be found in a number so small that a sensible degree of the praise and blame of public measures may be the portion of each individual; or in an assembly so durably invested with public trust, that the pride and consequence of its members may be sensibly incorporated with the reputation and prosperity of the community. The half-yearly representatives of Rhode Island would probably have been little affected in their deliberations on the iniquitous measures of that State, by arguments drawn from the light in which such measures would be viewed by foreign nations, or even by the sister States; whilst it can scarcely be doubted that if the concurrence of a select and stable body had been necessary, a regard to national character alone would have prevented the calamities under which that misguided people is now laboring.

I add, as a *sixth* defect, the want, in some important cases, of a due responsibility in the government to the people, arising from that frequency of elections which in other cases produces this responsibility. This remark will, perhaps, appear not only new, but paradoxical. It must nevertheless be acknowledged, when explained, to be as undeniable as it is important.

Responsibility, in order to be reasonable, must be limited to objects within the power of the responsible party, and in order to be effectual, must relate to operations of that power, of which a ready and proper judgment can be formed by the constituents. The objects of government may be divided into two general classes: the one depending on measures which have singly an immediate and sensible operation; the other depending on a succession of well-chosen and well-connected measures, which have a gradual and perhaps unobserved operation. The importance of the latter description to the collective and permanent welfare of every country, needs no explanation. And yet it is evident that an assembly elected for so short a term as to be unable to provide more than one or two links in a chain of measures, on which the general welfare may essentially depend, ought not to be answerable for the final result, any more than a steward or tenant, engaged for one year, could be justly made to answer for plans or improvements which could not be accomplished in less than half a dozen years. Nor is it possible for the people to estimate the *share* of influence which their annual assemblies may respectively have on events resulting from the mixed transactions of several years. It is sufficiently difficult to preserve a personal responsibility in the members of a *numerous* body, for such acts of the body as have an immediate, detached, and palpable operation on its constituents.

The proper remedy for this defect must be an additional body in the legislative department, which, having sufficient permanency to provide for such objects as require a continued attention, and a train of measures, may be justly and effectually answerable for the attainment of those objects.

Thus far I have considered the circumstances which point out the necessity of a well-constructed Senate only as they relate to the representatives of the people. To a people as little blinded by prejudice or corrupted by flattery as those whom I address, I shall not scruple to add, that such an institution may be sometimes necessary as a defence to the people against their own temporary errors and delusions. As the cool and deliberate sense of the community ought, in all governments, and actually will, in all free governments, ultimately prevail over the views of its rulers; so there are particular moments in public affairs when the people, stimulated by some irregular passion, or some illicit advantage, or misled by the artful misrepresentations of interested men, may call for measures which they themselves will afterwards be the most ready to lament and condemn. In these critical moments, how salutary will be the interference of some temperate and respectable body of citizens, in order to check the misguided career, and to suspend the blow meditated by the people against themselves, until reason, justice, and truth can regain their authority over the public mind? What bitter anguish would not the people of Athens have often escaped if their government had contained so provident a safeguard against the tyranny of their own passions? Popular liberty might then have escaped the indelible reproach of decreeing to the same citizens the hemlock on one day and statues on the next.

It may be suggested, that a people spread over an extensive region cannot, like the crowded inhabitants of a small district, be subject to the infection of violent passions, or to the danger of combining in pursuit of unjust measures. I am far from denying that this is a distinction of peculiar importance. I have, on the contrary, endeavored in a former paper to show, that it is one of the principal recommendations of a confederated republic. At the same time, this advantage ought not to be considered as superseding the use of auxiliary precautions. It may even be remarked, that the same extended situation, which will exempt the people of America from some of the dangers incident to lesser republics, will expose them to the inconveniency of remaining for a longer time under the influence of those misrepresentations which the combined industry of interested men may succeed in distributing among them.

It adds no small weight to all these considerations, to recollect that history informs us of no long-lived republic which had not a senate. Sparta, Rome, and Carthage are, in fact, the only states to whom that character can be applied. In each of the two first there was a senate for life. The constitution of the senate in the last is less known. Circumstantial evidence makes it probable that it was not different in this particular from the two others. . . . These examples, though as unfit for the imitation, as they are repugnant to the genius, of America, are, notwithstanding, when compared with the fugitive and turbulent existence of other ancient republics, very instructive proofs of the necessity of some institution that will blend stability with liberty. I am not unaware of the circumstances which distinguish the American from other popular governments, as well ancient as modern; and which render extreme circumspection necessary, in reasoning from one case to the other. But after allowing due weight to this consideration, it may still be maintained, that there are many points of similitude which render these examples not unworthy of our attention. Many of the defects, as we have seen, which can only be supplied by a senatorial institution, are common to a numerous assembly frequently elected by the people, and to the people themselves. There are others peculiar to the former, which require the control of such an institution. The people can never wilfully betray their own interests; but they may possibly be betrayed by the representatives of the people; and the danger will be evidently greater where the whole legislative trust is lodged in the hands of one body of men, than where the concurrence of separate and dissimilar bodies is required in every public act.

The difference most relied on, between the American and other republics, consists in the principle of representation; which is the pivot on which the former move, and which is supposed to have been unknown to the latter, or at least to the ancient part of them. The use which has been made of this difference, in reasonings contained in former papers, will have shown that I am disposed neither to deny its existence nor to undervalue its importance. I feel the less restraint, therefore, in observing, that the position concerning the ignorance of the ancient governments on the subject of representation, is by no means precisely true in the latitude commonly given to it. . . .

In the most pure democracies of Greece, many of the executive functions were performed, not by the people themselves, but by officers elected by the people, and *representing* the people in their *executive* capacity.

* * * *

. . . [It] is clear that the principle of representation was neither unknown to the ancients nor wholly overlooked in their political constitutions. The true distinction between these and the American governments, lies *in the total exclusion of the people, in their collective capacity,* from any share in the *latter,* and not in the *total exclusion of the representatives of the people* from the administration of the *former*. The distinction, however, thus qualified, must be admitted to leave a most advantageous superiority in favor of the United States. But to insure to this advantage its full effect, we must be careful not to separate it from the other advantage, of an extensive territory. For it cannot be believed, that any form of representative government could have succeeded within the narrow limits occupied by the democracies of Greece.

In answer to all these arguments, suggested by reason, illustrated by examples, and enforced by our own experience, the jealous adversary of the Constitution will probably content himself with repeating, that a senate appointed not immediately by the people, and for the term of six years, must gradually acquire a dangerous preëminence in the government, and finally transform it into a tyrannical aristocracy.

To this general answer, the general reply ought to be sufficient, that liberty may be endangered by the abuses of liberty as well as by the abuses of power; that there are numerous instances of the former as well as of the latter; and that the former, rather than the latter, are apparently most to be apprehended by the United States. But a more particular reply may be given.

Before such a revolution can be effected, the Senate, it is to be observed, must in the first place corrupt itself; must next corrupt the State legislatures; must then corrupt the House of Representatives; and must finally corrupt the people at large. It is evident that the Senate must be first corrupted before it can attempt an establishment of tyranny. Without corrupting the State legislatures, it cannot prosecute the attempt, because the periodical change of members would otherwise regenerate the whole body. Without exerting the means of corruption with equal success on the House of Representatives, the opposition of that co-equal branch of the government would inevitably defeat the attempt; and without corrupting the people themselves, a succession of new representatives would speedily restore all things to their pristine order. Is there any man who can seriously persuade himself that the proposed Senate can, by any possible means within the compass of human address, arrive at the object of a lawless ambition, through all these obstructions?

❋   ❋   ❋   ❋

PUBLIUS

Advantages of a Single Executive

To the People of the State of New York:

There is an idea, which is not without its advocates, that a vigorous Executive is inconsistent with the genius of republican government. The enlightened well-wishers to this species of government must at least hope that the supposition is destitute of foundation; since they can never admit its truth, without at the same time admitting the condemnation of their own principles. Energy in the Executive is a leading character in the definition of good government. It is essential to the protection of the community against foreign attacks; it is not less essential to the steady administration of the laws; to the protection of property against those irregular and high-handed combinations which sometimes interrupt the ordinary course of justice; to the security of liberty against the enterprises and assaults of ambition, of faction, and of anarchy. Every man the least conversant in Roman story, knows how often that republic was obliged to take refuge in the absolute power of a single man, under the formidable title of Dictator, as well against the intrigues of ambitious individuals who aspired to the tyranny, and the seditions of whole classes of the community whose conduct threatened the existence of all government, as against the invasions of external enemies who menaced the conquest and destruction of Rome.

. . . A feeble Executive implies a feeble execution of the government. A feeble execution is but another phrase for a bad execution; and a government ill executed, whatever it may be in theory, must be, in practice, a bad government.

Taking it for granted, therefore, that all men of sense will agree in the necessity of an energetic Executive, it will only remain to inquire, what are the ingredients which constitute this energy? How far can they be combined with those other ingredients which constitute safety in the republican sense? And how far does this combination characterize the plan which has been reported by the convention?

The ingredients which constitute energy in the Executive are, unity; duration; an adequate provision for its support; competent powers.

The ingredients which constitute safety in the republican sense are, a due dependence on the people; a due responsibility.

Those politicans and statesmen who have been the most celebrated for the soundness of their principles and for the justice of their views, have declared in favor of a single Executive and a numerous legislature. They have, with great propriety, considered energy as the most necessary qualification of the former, and have regarded this as most applicable to power in a single hand; while they have, with equal propriety, considered the latter as best adapted to deliberation and wisdom, and best calculated to conciliate the confidence of the people and to secure their privileges and interests.

That unity is conducive to energy will not be disputed. Decision, activity, secrecy, and despatch will generally characterize the proceedings of one man in a much more eminent degree than the proceedings of any greater number; and in proportion as the number is increased, these qualities will be diminished.

This unity may be destroyed in two ways: either by vesting the power in two or more magistrates of equal dignity and authority; or by vesting it ostensibly in one man, subject, in whole or in part, to the control and cooperation of others, in the capacity of counsellors to him. Of the first, the two Consuls of Rome may serve as an example; of the last, we shall find examples in the constitutions of several of the States. New York and New Jersey, if I recollect right, are the only States which have intrusted the executive authority wholly to single men.[1] Both these methods of destroying the unity of the Executive have their partisans; but the votaries of an executive council are the most numerous. They are both liable, if not to equal, to similar objections, and may in most lights be examined in conjunction.

The experience of other nations will afford little instruction on this head. As far, however, as it teaches any thing, it teaches us not to be enamoured of plurality in the Executive. . . .

But quitting the dim light of historical research, attaching ourselves purely to the dictates of reason and good sense, we shall discover much greater cause to reject than to approve the idea of plurality in the Executive, under any modification whatever.

Wherever two or more persons are engaged in any common enterprise or pursuit, there is always danger of difference of opinion. If it be a public trust or office, in which they are clothed with equal dignity and authority, there is peculiar danger of personal emulation and even animosity. From either, and especially from all these causes, the most bitter dissensions are apt to spring. Whenever these happen, they lessen the respectability, weaken the authority, and distract the plans and operations of those whom they divide. If they should unfortunately assail the supreme executive magistracy of a country, consisting of a plurality of persons, they might impede or frustrate the most important measures of the government, in the most critical emergencies of the state. And what is still worse, they might split the community into the most violent and irreconcilable factions, adhering differently to the different individuals who composed the magistracy.

❖   ❖   ❖   ❖

[1] New York has no council except for the single purpose of appointing to offices; New Jersey has a council whom the governor may consult. But I think, from the terms of the constitution, their resolutions do not bind him. —PUBLIUS

. . . In the legislature, promptitude of decision is oftener an evil than a benefit. The differences of opinion, and the jarrings of parties in that department of the government, though they may sometimes obstruct salutary plans, yet often promote deliberation and circumspection, and serve to check excesses in the majority. When a resolution too is once taken, the opposition must be at an end. That resolution is a law, and resistance to it punishable. But no favorable circumstances palliate or atone for the disadvantages of dissension in the executive department. Here, they are pure and unmixed. There is no point at which they cease to operate. They serve to embarrass and weaken the execution of the plan or measure to which they relate, from the first step to the final conclusion of it. They constantly counteract those qualities in the Executive which are the most necessary ingredients in its composition,—vigor and expedition, and this without any counterbalancing good. In the conduct of war, in which the energy of the Executive is the bulwark of the national security, every thing would be to be apprehended from its plurality.

❋ ❋ ❋ ❋

But one of the weightiest objections to a plurality in the Executive . . . is, that it tends to conceal faults and destroy responsibility. Responsibility is of two kinds—to censure and to punishment. The first is the more important of the two, especially in an elective office. Man, in public trust, will much oftener act in such a manner as to render him unworthy of being any longer trusted, than in such a manner as to make him obnoxious to legal punishment. But the multiplication of the Executive adds to the difficulty of detection in either case. It often becomes impossible, amidst mutual accusations, to determine on whom the blame or the punishment of a pernicious measure, or series of pernicious measures, ought really to fall. It is shifted from one to another with so much dexterity, and under such plausible appearances, that the public opinion is left in suspense about the real author. The circumstances which may have led to any national miscarriage or misfortune are sometimes so complicated that, where there are a number of actors who may have had different degrees and kinds of agency, though we may clearly see upon the whole that there has been mismanagement, yet it may be impracticable to pronounce to whose account the evil which may have been incurred is truly chargeable.

*   *   *   *

In the single instance in which the governor of this State is coupled with a council—that is, in the appointment to offices, we have seen the mischiefs of it in the view now under consideration. Scandalous appointments to important offices have been made. Some cases, indeed, have been so flagrant that ALL PARTIES have agreed in the impropriety of the thing. When inquiry has been made, the blame has been laid by the governor on the members of the council, who, on their part, have charged it upon his nomination; while the people remain altogether at a loss to determine, by whose influence their interests have been committed to hands so unqualified and so manifestly improper. In tenderness to individuals, I forbear to descend to particulars.

It is evident from these considerations, that the plurality of the Executive tends to deprive the people of the two greatest securities they can have for the faithful exercise of any delegated power, *first*, the restraints of public opinion, which lose their efficacy, as well on account of the division of the censure attendant on bad measures among a number, as on account of the uncertainty on whom it ought to fall; and, *secondly*, the opportunity of discovering with facility and clearness the misconduct of the persons they trust, in order either to their removal from office, or to their actual punishment in cases which admit of it.

In England, the king is a perpetual magistrate; and it is a maxim which has obtained for the sake of the public peace, that he is unaccountable for his administration, and his person sacred. Nothing, therefore, can be wiser in that kingdom, than to annex to the king a constitutional council, who may be responsible to the nation for the advice they give. . . .

But in a republic, where every magistrate ought to be personally responsible for his behavior in office, the reason which in the British Constitution dictates the propriety of a council, not only ceases to apply, but turns against the institution. In the monarchy of Great Britain, it furnishes a substitute for the prohibited responsibility of the chief magistrate, which serves in some degree as a hostage to the national justice for his good behavior. In the American republic, it would serve to destroy, or would greatly diminish, the intended and necessary responsibility of the Chief Magistrate himself.

The idea of a council to the Executive, which has so generally obtained in the State constitutions, has been derived from that maxim of republican jealousy which considers power as safer in the hands of a number of men than of a single man. If the maxim should be admitted to be applicable to the case, I should contend that the advantage on that side would not counterbalance the numerous disadvantages on the opposite side. But I do not think the rule at all applicable to the executive power. I clearly concur in opinion, in this particular, with a writer whom the celebrated Junius pronounces to be "deep, solid, and ingenious," that "the executive power is more easily confined when it is ONE";[2] that it is far more safe there should be a single object for the jealousy and watchfulness of the people; and, in a word, that all multiplication of the Executive is rather dangerous than friendly to liberty.

❖   ❖   ❖   ❖

PUBLIUS

---

[2] De Lolme.—PUBLIUS

****

The Presidential Term of Office

****

To the People of the State of New York:

Duration in office has been mentioned as the second requisite to the energy of the Executive authority. This has relation to two objects: to the personal firmness of the executive magistrate, in the employment of his constitutional powers; and to the stability of the system of administration which may have been adopted under his auspices. With regard to the first, it must be evident, that the longer the duration in office, the greater will be the probability of obtaining so important an advantage. It is a general principle of human nature, that a man will be interested in whatever he possesses, in proportion to the firmness or precariousness of the tenure by which he holds it; will be less attached to what he holds by a momentary or uncertain title, than to what he enjoys by a durable or certain title; and, of course, will be willing to risk more for the sake of the one, than for the sake of the other. This remark is not less applicable to a political privilege, or honor, or trust, than to any article of ordinary property. The inference from it is, that a man acting in the capacity of chief magistrate, under a consciousness that in a very short time he *must* lay down his office, will be apt to feel himself too little interested in it to hazard any material censure or perplexity, from the independent exertion of his powers, or from encountering the ill-humors, however transient, which may happen to prevail, either in a considerable part of the society itself, or even in a predominant faction in the legislative body. If the case should only be, that he *might* lay it down, unless continued by a new choice, and if he should be desirous of being continued, his wishes, conspiring with his fears, would tend still more powerfully to corrupt his integrity, or debase his fortitude. In either case, feebleness and irresolution must be the characteristics of the station.

There are some who would be inclined to regard the servile pliancy of the Executive to a prevailing current, either in the community or in the legislature, as its best recommendation. But such men entertain very crude notions, as well of the purposes for which government was instituted, as of the true means by which the public happiness may be promoted. The republican principle demands that the deliberate sense of the community should govern the conduct of those to whom they intrust the management of their affairs; but it does not require an unqualified complaisance to every sudden breeze of passion, or to every transient impulse which the people may receive from the arts of men, who flatter their prejudices to betray their interests. It is a just observation, that the people commonly *intend* the PUBLIC GOOD. This often applies to their very errors. But their good sense would despise the adulator who should pretend that they always *reason right* about the *means* of promoting it. They know from experience that they sometimes err; and the wonder is that they so seldom err as they do, beset, as they continually are, by the wiles of parasites and sycophants, by the snares of the ambitious, the avaricious, the desperate, by the artifices of men who possess their confidence more than they deserve it, and those who seek to possess rather than to deserve it. When occasions present themselves, in which the interests of the people are at variance with their inclinations, it is the duty of the persons whom they have appointed to be the guardians of those interests, to withstand the temporary delusion, in order to give them time and opportunity for more cool and sedate reflection. Instances might be cited in which a conduct of this kind has saved the people from very fatal consequences of their own mistakes, and has procured lasting monuments of their gratitude to the men who had courage and magnanimity enough to serve them at the peril of their displeasure.

But however inclined we might be to insist upon an unbounded complaisance in the Executive to the inclinations of the people, we can with no propriety contend for a like complaisance to the humors of the legislature. The latter may sometimes stand in opposition to the former, and at other times the people may be entirely neutral. In either supposition, it is certainly desirable that the Executive should be in a situation to dare to act his own opinion with vigor and decision.

The same rule which teaches the propriety of a partition between the various branches of power, teaches us likewise that this partition ought to be so contrived as to render the one independent of the other. To what purpose separate the executive or the judiciary from the legislative, if both the executive and the judiciary are so constituted as to be at the absolute devotion of the legislative? Such a separation must be merely nominal, and incapable of producing the ends for which it was established. It is one thing to be subordinate to the laws, and another to be dependent on the legislative body. The first comports with, the last violates, the fundamental principles of good government; and, whatever may be the forms of the Constitution, unites all power in the same hands. The tendency of the legislative authority to absorb every other, has been fully displayed and illustrated by examples in some preceding numbers. In governments purely republican, this tendency is almost irresistible. The representatives of the people, in a popular assembly, seem sometimes to fancy that they are the people themselves, and betray strong symptoms of impatience and disgust at the least sign of opposition from any other quarter; as if the exercise of its rights, by either the executive or judiciary, were a breach of their privilege and an outrage to their dignity. They often appear disposed to exert an imperious control over the other departments; and as they commonly have the people on their side, they always act with such momentum as to make it very difficult for the other members of the government to maintain the balance of the Constitution.

It may perhaps be asked, how the shortness of the duration in office can affect the independence of the Executive on the legislature, unless the one were possessed of the power of appointing or displacing the other. One answer to this inquiry may be drawn from the principle already remarked—that is, from the slender interest a man is apt to take in a short-lived advantage, and the little inducement it affords him to expose himself, on account of it, to any considerable inconvenience or hazard. Another answer, perhaps more obvious, though not more conclusive, will result from the consideration of the influence of the legislative body over the people; which might be employed to prevent the reëlection of a man who, by an upright resistance to any sinister project of that body, should have made himself obnoxious to its resentment.

It may be asked also, whether a duration of four years would answer the end proposed; and if it would not, whether a less period, which would at least be recommended by greater security against ambitious designs, would not, for that reason, be preferable to a longer period, which was, at the same time, too short for the purpose of inspiring the desired firmness and independence of the magistrate.

It cannot be affirmed, that a duration of four years, or any other limited duration, would completely answer the end proposed; but it would contribute towards it in a degree which would have a material influence upon the spirit and character of the government. Between the commencement and termination of such a period, there would always be a considerable interval, in which the prospect of annihilation would be sufficiently remote, not to have an improper effect upon the conduct of a man imbued with a tolerable portion of fortitude; and in which he might reasonably promise himself, that there would be time enough before it arrived, to make the community sensible of the propriety of the measures he might incline to pursue. Though it be probable that, as he approached the moment when the public were, by a new election, to signify their sense of his conduct, his confidence, and with it his firmness, would decline; yet both the one and the other would derive support from the opportunities which his previous continuance in the station had afforded him, of establishing himself in the esteem and good-will of his constituents. He might, then, hazard with safety, in proportion to the proofs he had given of his wisdom and integrity, and to the title he had acquired to the respect and attachment of his fellow-citizens. As, on the one hand, a duration of four years will contribute to the firmness of the Executive in a sufficient degree to render it a very valuable ingredient in the composition; so, on the other, it is not enough to justify any alarm for the public liberty. If a British House of Commons, from the most feeble beginnings, *from the mere power of assenting or disagreeing to the imposition of a new tax,* have, by rapid strides, reduced the prerogatives of the crown and the privileges of the nobility within the limits they conceived to be compatible with the principles of a free government, while they raised themselves to the rank and consequence of a co-equal branch of the legislature; if they have been able, in one instance, to abolish both the royalty and the aristocracy, and to overturn all the ancient establishments, as well in the Church as State; if they have been able, on a recent occasion, to make the monarch tremble at the prospect of an innovation [1] attempted by them, what would be to be feared from an elective magistrate of four years' duration, with the con-

---

[1] This was the case with respect to Mr. Fox's India bill, which was carried in the House of Commons, and rejected in the House of Lords, to the entire satisfaction, as it is said, of the people.—PUBLIUS

fined authorities of a President of the United States? What, but that he might be unequal to the task which the Constitution assigns him? I shall only add, that if his duration be such as to leave a doubt of his firmness, that doubt is inconsistent with a jealousy of his encroachments.

PUBLIUS

****

The Judges as Guardians of the Constitution

****

To the People of the State of New York:

❖   ❖   ❖   ❖

In unfolding the defects of the existing Confederation, the utility and necessity of a federal judicature have been clearly pointed out. It is the less necessary to recapitulate the considerations there urged, as the propriety of the institution in the abstract is not disputed; the only questions which have been raised being relative to the manner of constituting it, and to its extent. . . .

The manner of constituting it seems to embrace these several objects: 1st. The mode of appointing the judges. 2d. The tenure by which they are to hold their places. 3d. The partition of the judiciary authority between different courts, and their relations to each other.

First. As to the mode of appointing the judges; this is the same with that of appointing the officers of the Union in general, and has been so fully discussed in the two last numbers, that nothing can be said here which would not be useless repetition.

Second. As to the tenure by which the judges are to hold their places: this chiefly concerns their duration in office; the provisions for their support; the precautions for their responsibility.

According to the plan of the convention, all judges who may be appointed by the United States are to hold their offices *during good behavior;* which is conformable to the most approved of the State constitutions, and among the rest, to that of this State. Its propriety having been drawn into question by the adversaries of that plan, is no light symptom of the rage for objection, which disorders their imaginations and judgments. The standard of good behavior for the continuance in office of the judicial magistracy, is certainly one of the most valuable of the modern improvements in the practice of government. In a monarchy it is an excellent barrier to the despotism of the prince; in a republic it is a no less excellent barrier to the encroachments and oppressions of the representative body. And it is the best expedient which can be devised in any government, to secure a steady, upright, and impartial administration of the laws.

Whoever attentively considers the different departments of power must perceive, that, in a government in which they are separated from each other, the judiciary, from the nature of its functions, will always be the least dangerous to the political rights of the Constitution; because it will be least in a capacity to annoy or injure them. The Executive not only dispenses the honors, but holds the sword of the community. The legislature not only commands the purse, but prescribes the rules by which the duties and rights of every citizen are to be regulated. The judiciary, on the contrary, has no influence over either the sword or the purse; no direction either of the strength or of the wealth of the society; and can take no active resolution whatever. It may truly be said to have neither FORCE nor WILL, but merely judgment; and must ultimately depend upon the aid of the executive arm even for the efficacy of its judgments.

This simple view of the matter suggests several important consequences. It proves incontestably, that the judiciary is beyond comparison the weakest of the three departments of power [1]; that it can never attack with success either of the other two; and

---

[1] The celebrated Montesquieu, speaking of them, says: "Of the three powers above mentioned, the judiciary is next to nothing."—"Spirit of Laws," vol. i., page 186.—PUBLIUS

that all possible care is requisite to enable it to defend itself against their attacks. It equally proves, that though individual oppression may now and then proceed from the courts of justice, the general liberty of the people can never be endangered from that quarter; I mean so long as the judiciary remains truly distinct from both the legislature and the Executive. For I agree, that "there is no liberty, if the power of judging be not separated from the legislative and executive powers." [2] And it proves, in the last place, that as liberty can have nothing to fear from the judiciary alone, but would have every thing to fear from its union with either of the other departments; that as all the effects of such a union must ensue from a dependence of the former on the latter, notwithstanding a nominal and apparent separation; that as, from the natural feebleness of the judiciary, it is in continual jeopardy of being overpowered, awed, or influenced by its coördinate branches; and that as nothing can contribute so much to its firmness and independence as permanency in office, this quality may therefore be justly regarded as an indispensable ingredient in its constitution, and, in a great measure, as the citadel of the public justice and the public security.

The complete independence of the courts of justice is peculiarly essential in a limited Constitution. By a limited Constitution, I understand one which contains certain specified exceptions to the legislative authority; such, for instance, as that it shall pass no bills of attainder, no *ex-post-facto* laws, and the like. Limitations of this kind can be preserved in practice no other way than through the medium of courts of justice, whose duty it must be to declare all acts contrary to the manifest tenor of the Constitution void. Without this, all the reservations of particular rights or privileges would amount to nothing.

Some perplexity respecting the rights of the courts to pronounce legislative acts void, because contrary to the constitution,

---

[2] *Idem.* page 181.—PUBLIUS

has arisen from an imagination that the doctrine would imply a superiority of the judiciary to the legislative power. It is urged that the authority which can declare the acts of another void, must necessarily be superior to the one whose acts may be declared void. As this doctrine is of great importance in all the American constitutions, a brief discussion of the ground on which it rests cannot be unacceptable.

There is no position which depends on clearer principles, than that every act of a delegated authority, contrary to the tenor of the commission under which it is exercised, is void. No legislative act, therefore, contrary to the Constitution, can be valid. To deny this, would be to affirm, that the deputy is greater than his principal; that the servant is above his master; that the representatives of the people are superior to the people themselves; that men acting by virtue of powers, may do not only what their powers do not authorize, but what they forbid.

If it be said that the legislative body are themselves the constitutional judges of their own powers, and that the construction they put upon them is conclusive upon the other departments, it may be answered, that this cannot be the natural presumption, where it is not to be collected from any particular provisions in the Constitution. It is not otherwise to be supposed, that the Constitution could intend to enable the representatives of the people to substitute their *will* to that of their constituents. It is far more rational to suppose, that the courts were designed to be an intermediate body between the people and the legislature, in order, among other things, to keep the latter within the limits assigned to their authority. The interpretation of the laws is the proper and peculiar province of the courts. A constitution is, in fact, and must be regarded by the judges, as a fundamental law. It therefore belongs to them to ascertain its meaning, as well as the meaning of any particular act proceeding from the legislative body. If there should happen to be an irreconcilable variance between the two, that which has the superior obligation and validity ought, of course, to be preferred; or, in other words, the Constitution ought to be preferred to the statute, the intention of the people to the intention of their agents.

Nor does this conclusion by any means suppose a superiority of the judicial to the legislative power. It only supposes that the power of the people is superior to both; and that where the will of the legislature, declared in its statutes, stands in opposition to that of the people, declared in the Constitution, the judges ought to be governed by the latter rather than the former. They ought to regulate their decisions by the fundamental laws, rather than by those which are not fundamental.

This exercise of judicial discretion, in determining between two contradictory laws, is exemplified in a familiar instance. It not uncommonly happens, that there are two statutes existing at one time, clashing in whole or in part with each other, and neither of them containing any repealing clause or expression. In such a case, it is the province of the courts to liquidate and fix their meaning and operation. So far as they can, by any fair construction, be reconciled to each other, reason and law conspire to dictate that this should be done; where this is impracticable, it becomes a matter of necessity to give effect to one, in exclusion of the other. The rule which has obtained in the courts for determining their relative validity is, that the last in order of time shall be preferred to the first. But this is a mere rule of construction, not derived from any positive law, but from the nature and reason of the thing. It is a rule not enjoined upon the courts by legislative provision, but adopted by themselves, as consonant to truth and propriety, for the direction of their conduct as interpreters of the law. They thought it reasonable, that between the interfering acts of an *equal* authority, that which was the last indication of its will should have the preference.

But in regard to the interfering acts of a superior and subordinate authority, of an original and derivative power, the nature and reason of the thing indicate the converse of that rule as proper to be followed. They teach us that the prior act of a superior ought to be preferred to the subsequent act of an inferior and subordinate authority; and that accordingly, whenever a particular statute contravenes the Constitution, it will be the duty of the judicial tribunals to adhere to the latter and disregard the former.

It can be of no weight to say that the courts, on the pretence of a repugnancy, may substitute their own pleasure to the constitutional intentions of the legislature. This might as well happen in the case of two contradictory statutes; or it might as well happen in every adjudication upon any single statute. The courts must declare the sense of the law; and if they should be disposed to exercise WILL instead of JUDGMENT, the consequence would equally be the substitution of their pleasure to that of the legislative body. The observation, if it prove any thing, would prove that there ought to be no judges distinct from that body.

If, then, the courts of justice are to be considered as the bulwarks of a limited Constitution against legislative encroachments, this consideration will afford a strong argument for the permanent tenure of judicial offices, since nothing will contribute so much as this to that independent spirit in the judges which must be essential to the faithful performance of so arduous a duty.

This independence of the judges is equally requisite to guard the Constitution and the rights of individuals from the effects of those ill humors, which the arts of designing men, or the influence of particular conjunctures, sometimes disseminate among the people themselves, and which, though they speedily give place to better information, and more deliberate reflection, have a tendency, in the meantime, to occasion dangerous innovations in the government, and serious oppressions of the minor party in the community. Though I trust the friends of the proposed Constitution will never concur with its enemies,[3] in questioning that fundamental principle of republican government, which admits the right of the people to alter or abolish the established Con-

---

[3] *Vide* "Protest of the Minority of the Convention of Pennsylvania," Martin's Speech, etc.—PUBLIUS

stitution, whenever they find it inconsistent with their happiness, yet it is not to be inferred from this principle, that the representatives of the people, whenever a momentary inclination happens to lay hold of a majority of their constituents, incompatible with the provisions in the existing Constitution, would, on that account, be justifiable in a violation of those provisions; or that the courts would be under a greater obligation to connive at infractions in this shape, than when they had proceeded wholly from the cabals of the representative body. Until the people have, by some solemn and authoritative act, annulled or changed the established form, it is binding upon themselves collectively, as well as individually; and no presumption, or even knowledge, of their sentiments, can warrant their representatives in a departure from it, prior to such an act. But it is easy to see, that it would require an uncommon portion of fortitude in the judges to do their duty as faithful guardians of the Constitution, where legislative invasions of it had been instigated by the major voice of the community.

But it is not with a view to infractions of the Constitution only, that the independence of the judges may be an essential safeguard against the effects of occasional ill humors in the society. These sometimes extend no farther than to the injury of the private rights of particular classes of citizens, by unjust and partial laws. Here also the firmness of the judicial magistracy is of vast importance in mitigating the severity and confining the operation of such laws. It not only serves to moderate the immediate mischiefs of those which may have been passed but it operates as a check upon the legislative body in passing them; who, perceiving that obstacles to the success of iniquitous intention are to be expected from the scruples of the courts, are in a manner compelled, by the very motives of the injustice they meditate, to qualify their attempts. This is a circumstance calculated to have more influence upon the character of our governments, than but few may be aware of. The benefits of the integrity and moderation of the judiciary have already been felt in more States than one: and though they may have displeased those whose sinister expectations they may have disappointed, they must have commanded the esteem and applause of all the virtuous and disinterested. Considerate men, of every description, ought to prize whatever will tend to beget or fortify that temper in the courts; as no man can be sure that he may not be to-morrow the victim of a spirit of injustice, by which he may be a gainer to-day. And every man must now feel, that the inevitable tendency of such a spirit is to sap the foundations of public and private confidence, and to introduce in its stead universal distrust and distress.

That inflexible and uniform adherence to the rights of the Constitution, and of individuals, which we perceive to be indispensable in the courts of justice, can certainly not be expected from judges who hold their offices by a temporary commission. Periodical appointments, however regulated, or by whomsoever made, would, in some way or other, be fatal to their necessary independence. If the power of making them was committed either to the Executive or legislature, there would be danger of an improper complaisance to the branch which possessed it; if to both, there would be an unwillingness to hazard the displeasure of either; if to the people, or to persons chosen by them for the special purpose, there would be too great a disposition to consult popularity, to justify a reliance that nothing would be consulted but the Constitution and the laws.

There is yet a further and a weightier reason for the permanency of the judicial offices, which is deducible from the nature of the qualifications they require. It has been frequently remarked, with great propriety, that a voluminous code of laws is one of the inconveniences necessarily connected with the advantages of a free government. To avoid an arbitrary discretion in the courts, it is indispensable that they should be bound down by strict rules and precedents, which serve to define and point out their duty in every particular case that comes before them; and it will readily be conceived from the variety of controversies which grow out of the folly and wickedness of mankind, that the records of those precedents must unavoidably swell to a very considerable bulk, and must demand long and laborious study to acquire a competent knowledge of them. Hence it is, that there can be but few men in the society who will have sufficient skill in the laws to qualify them for the stations of judges. And making the proper deductions for the ordinary depravity of human nature, the number must be still smaller of those who unite the requisite integrity with the requisite knowledge. These considerations apprise us, that the government can have no great option between fit character; and that a temporary duration in office, which would naturally discourage such characters from quitting a lucrative line of practice to accept a seat on the bench, would have a tendency to throw the administration of justice into hands less able, and less well qualified, to conduct it with utility and dignity. In the present circumstances of this country, and in those in which it is likely to be for a long time to come, the disadvantages on this score would be greater than they may at first sight appear; but it must be confessed, that they are far inferior to those which present themselves under the other aspects of the subject.

Upon the whole, there can be no room to doubt that the convention acted wisely in copying from the models of those constitutions which have established *good behavior* as the tenure of their judicial offices, in point of duration; and that so far from being blamable on this account, their plan would have been inexcusably defective, if it had wanted this important feature of good government. The experience of Great Britain affords an illustrious comment on the excellence of the institution.

PUBLIUS

Jurisdiction of the Federal Courts

To the People of the State of New York:

To judge with accuracy of the proper extent of the federal judicature, it will be necessary to consider, in the first place, what are its proper objects.

It seems scarcely to admit of controversy, that the judiciary authority of the Union ought to extend to these several descriptions of cases: 1st, to all those which arise out of the laws of the United States, passed in pursuance of their just and constitutional powers of legislation; 2d, to all those which concern the execution of the provisions expressly contained in the articles of Union; 3d, to all those in which the United States are a party; 4th, to all those which involve the PEACE of the CONFEDERACY, whether they relate to the intercourse between the United States and foreign nations, or to that between the States themselves; 5th, to all those which originate on the high seas, and are of admiralty or maritime jurisdiction; and, lastly, to all those in which the State tribunals cannot be supposed to be impartial and unbiased.

The first point depends upon this obvious consideration, that there ought always to be a constitutional method of giving efficacy to constitutional provisions. What, for instance, would avail restrictions on the authority of the State legislatures, without some constitutional mode of enforcing the observance of them? The States, by the plan of the convention, are prohibited from doing a variety of things, some of which are incompatible with the interests of the Union, and others with the principles of good government. The imposition of duties on imported articles, and the emission of paper money, are specimens of each kind. No man of sense will believe, that such prohibitions would be scrupulously regarded, without some effectual power in the government to restrain or correct the infractions of them. This power must either be a direct negative on the State laws, or an authority in the federal courts to overrule such as might be in manifest contravention of the articles of Union. There is no third course that I can imagine. The latter appears to have been thought by the convention preferable to the former, and, I presume, will be most agreeable to the States.

As to the second point, it is impossible, by any argument or comment, to make it clearer than it is in itself. If there are such things as political axioms, the propriety of the judicial power of a government being coextensive with its legislative, may be ranked among the number. The mere necessity of uniformity in the interpretation of the national laws, decides the question. Thirteen independent courts of final jurisdiction over the same causes, arising upon the same laws, is a hydra in government from which nothing but contradiction and confusion can proceed.

Still less need be said in regard to the third point. Controversies between the nation and its members or citizens, can only be properly referred to the national tribunals. Any other plan would be contrary to reason, to precedent, and to decorum.

The fourth point rests on this plain proposition, that the peace of the WHOLE ought not to be left at the disposal of a PART. The Union will undoubtedly be answerable to foreign powers for the conduct of its members. And the responsibility for an injury ought ever to be accompanied with the faculty of preventing it. As the denial or perversion of justice by the sentences of courts, as well as in any other manner, is with reason classed among the just causes of war, it will follow that the federal judiciary ought to have cognizance of all causes in which the citizens of other countries are concerned. This is not less essential to the preservation of the public faith, than to the security of the public tranquillity. A distinction may perhaps be imagined between cases arising upon treaties and the laws of nations and those which may stand merely on the footing of the municipal law. The former kind may be supposed proper for the federal jurisdiction, the latter for that of the States. But it is at least problematical, whether an unjust sentence against a foreigner, where the subject of controversy was wholly relative to the *lex loci*, would not, if unredressed, be an aggression upon his sovereign, as well as one which violated the stipulations of a treaty or the general law of nations. And a still greater objection to the distinction would result from the immense difficulty, if not impossibility, of a practical discrimination between the cases of one complexion and those of the other. So great a proportion of the cases in which foreigners are parties, involve national questions, that it is by far most safe and most expedient to refer all those in which they are concerned to the national tribunals.

The power of determining causes between two States, between one State and the citizens of another, and between the citizens of different States, is perhaps not less essential to the peace of the Union than that which has been just examined. . . .

       ❖   ❖   ❖   ❖

It may be esteemed the basis of the Union, that "the citizens of each State shall be entitled to all the privileges and immunities of citizens of the several States." And if it be a just principle that every government *ought to possess the means of executing its own provisions by its own authority,* it will follow, that in order to the inviolable maintenance of that equality of privileges and immunities to which the citizens of the Union will be entitled, the national judiciary ought to preside in all cases in which one State or its citizens are opposed to another State or its citizens. To secure the full effect of so fundamental a provision against all evasion and subterfuge, it is necessary that its construction should be committed to that tribunal which, having no local attachments, will be likely to be impartial between the different States and their citizens, and which, owing its official existence to the Union, will never be likely to feel any bias inauspicious to the principles on which it is founded.

The fifth point will demand little animadversion. The most bigoted idolizers of State authority have not thus far shown a disposition to deny the national judiciary the cognizance of maritime causes. . . .

The reasonableness of the agency of the national courts in cases in which the State tribunals cannot be supposed to be impartial, speaks for itself. No man ought certainly to be a judge in his own cause, or in any cause in respect to which he has the least interest or bias. This principle has no inconsiderable weight in designating the federal courts as the proper tribunals for the determination of controversies between different States and their citizens. And it ought to have the same operation in regard to some cases between citizens of the same State. Claims to land under grants of different States, founded upon adverse pretensions of boundary, are of this description. The courts of neither of the granting States could be expected to be unbiased. The laws may have even prejudged the question, and tied the courts down to decisions in favor of the grants of the State to which they belonged. And even where this had not been done, it would be natural that the judges, as men, should feel a strong predilection to the claims of their own government.

❊   ❊   ❊   ❊

PUBLIUS

The Lack of a Bill of Rights

To the People of the State of New York:

* * * *

The most considerable of the remaining objections is that the plan of the convention contains no bill of rights. Among other answers given to this, it has been upon different occasions remarked that the constitutions of several of the States are in a similar predicament. I add that New York is of the number. And yet the opposers of the new system, in this State, who profess an unlimited admiration for its constitution, are among the most intemperate partisans of a bill of rights. To justify their zeal in this matter, they allege two things: one is that, though the constitution of New York has no bill of rights prefixed to it, yet it contains, in the body of it, various provisions in favor of particular privileges and rights, which, in substance, amount to the same thing; the other is, that the Constitution adopts, in their full extent, the common and statute law of Great Britain, by which many other rights, not expressed in it, are equally secured.

To the first I answer, that the Constitution proposed by the convention contains, as well as the constitution of this State, a number of such provisions.

Independent of those which relate to the structure of the government, we find the following: Article 1, section 3, clause 7— "Judgment in cases of impeachment shall not extend further than to removal from office, and disqualification to hold and enjoy any office of honor, trust, or profit under the United States; but the party convicted shall, nevertheless, be liable and subject to indictment, trial, judgment, and punishment according to law." Section 9, of the same article, clause 2—"The privilege of the writ of *habeas corpus* shall not be suspended, unless when in cases of rebellion or invasion the public safety may require it." Clause 3— "No bill of attainder or *ex-post-facto* law shall be passed." Clause 7—"No title of nobility shall be granted by the United States; and no person holding any office of profit or trust under them, shall, without the consent of the Congress, accept of any present, emolument, office, or title of any kind whatever, from any king, prince, or foreign state." Article 3, section 2, clause 3—"The trial of all crimes, except in cases of impeachment, shall be by jury; and such trial shall be held in the State where the said crimes shall have been committed; but when not committed within any State, the trial shall be at such place or places as the Congress may by law have directed." Section 3, of the same article— "Treason against the United States shall consist only in levying war against them, or in adhering to their enemies, giving them aid and comfort. No person shall be convicted of treason, unless on the testimony of two witnesses to the same overt act, or on confession in open court." And clause 3, of the same section— "The Congress shall have power to declare the punishment of treason; but no attainder of treason shall work corruption of blood, or forfeiture, except during the life of the person attainted."

It may well be a question, whether these are not, upon the whole, of equal importance with any which are to be found in the constitution of this State. The establishment of the writ of *habeas corpus,* the prohibition of *ex-post-facto* laws, and of TITLES OF NOBILITY, *to which we have no corresponding provision in our Constitution,* are perhaps greater securities to liberty and republicanism than any it contains. The creation of crimes after the commission of the fact, or, in other words, the subjecting of men to punishment for things which, when they were done, were breaches of no law, and the practice of arbitrary imprisonments, have been, in all ages, the favorite and most formidable instruments of tyranny. The observations of the judicious Blackstone,[1] in reference to the latter, are well worthy of recital: "To bereave a man of life, [says he,] or by violence to confiscate his estate, without accusation or trial, would be so gross and notorious an act of despotism, as must at once convey the alarm of tyranny throughout the whole nation; but confinement of the person, by secretly hurrying him to jail, where his sufferings are unknown or forgotten, is a less public, a less striking, and therefore *a more dangerous engine* of arbitrary government." And as a remedy for this fatal evil he is everywhere peculiarly emphatical in his encomiums on the *habeas-corpus* act, which in one place he calls "the BULWARK of the British Constitution."[2]

Nothing need be said to illustrate the importance of the prohibition of titles of nobility. This may truly be denominated the corner-stone of republican government; for so long as they are excluded, there can never be serious danger that the government will be any other than that of the people.

To the second—that is, to the pretended establishment of the common and statute law by the Constitution, I answer, that they are expressly made subject "to such alterations and provisions as the legislature shall from time to time make concerning the same." They are therefore at any moment liable to repeal by the ordinary legislative power, and of course have no constitutional sanction. The only use of the declaration was to recognize the ancient law, and to remove doubts which might have been occasioned by the Revolution. This consequently can be considered as no part of a declaration of rights, which under our constitutions must be intended as limitations of the power of the government itself.

It has been several times truly remarked that bills of rights are, in their origin, stipulations between kings and their subjects,

---

[1] *Vide* Blackstone's "Commentaries," vol. i., p. 136.—PUBLIUS

[2] *Vide* Blackstone's "Commentaries," vol. iv., p. 438.—PUBLIUS

abridgments of prerogative in favor of privilege, reservations of rights not surrendered to the prince. Such was MAGNA CHARTA, obtained by the barons, sword in hand, from King John. Such were the subsequent confirmations of that charter by succeeding princes. Such was the *Petition of Right* assented to by Charles I., in the beginning of his reign. Such, also, was the Declaration of Right presented by the Lords and Commons to the Prince of Orange in 1688, and afterwards thrown into the form of an act of parliament called the Bill of Rights. It is evident, therefore, that, according to their primitive signification, they have no application to constitutions, professedly founded upon the power of the people, and executed by their immediate representatives and servants. Here, in strictness, the people surrender nothing; and as they retain every thing they have no need of particular reservations. "WE, THE PEOPLE of the United States, to secure the blessings of liberty to ourselves and our posterity, do *ordain* and *establish* this Constitution for the United States of America." Here is a better recognition of popular rights, than volumes of those aphorisms which make the principal figure in several of our State bills of rights, and which would sound much better in a treatise of ethics than in a constitution of government.

But a minute detail of particular rights is certainly far less applicable to a Constitution like that under consideration, which is merely intended to regulate the general political interests of the nation, than to a constitution which has the regulation of every species of personal and private concerns. If, therefore, the loud clamors against the plan of the convention, on this score, are well founded, no epithets of reprobation will be too strong for the constitution of this State. But the truth is, that both of them contain all which, in relation to their objects, is reasonably to be desired.

I go further, and affirm that bills of rights, in the sense and to the extent in which they are contended for, are not only unnecessary in the proposed Constitution, but would even be dangerous. They would contain various exceptions to powers not granted; and, on this very account, would afford a colorable pretext to claim more than were granted. For why declare that things shall not be done which there is no power to do? Why, for instance, should it be said that the liberty of the press shall not be restrained, when no power is given by which restrictions may be imposed? I will not contend that such a provision would confer a regulating power; but it is evident that it would furnish, to men disposed to usurp, a plausible pretence for claiming that power. They might urge with a semblance of reason, that the Constitution ought not to be charged with the absurdity of providing against the abuse of an authority which was not given, and that the provision against restraining the liberty of the press afforded a clear implication, that a power to prescribe proper regulations concerning it was intended to be vested in the national government. This may serve as a specimen of the numerous handles which would be given to the doctrine of constructive powers, by the indulgence of an injudicious zeal for bills of rights.

On the subject of the liberty of the press, as much as has been said, I cannot forbear adding a remark or two: in the first place, I observe, that there is not a syllable concerning it in the constitution of this State; in the next, I contend, that whatever has been said about it in that of any other State, amounts to nothing. What signifies a declaration, that "the liberty of the press shall be inviolably preserved"? What is the liberty of the press? Who can give it any definition which would not leave the utmost latitude of evasion? I hold it to be impracticable; and from this I infer, that its security, whatever fine declarations may be inserted in any constitution respecting it, must altogether depend on public opinion, and on the general spirit of the people and of the government.[3] And here, after all, as is intimated upon another occasion, must we seek for the only solid basis of all our rights.

There remains but one other view of this matter to conclude

---

[3] To show that there is a power in the Constitution by which the liberty of the press may be affected, recourse has been had to the power of taxation. It is said that duties may be laid upon the publications so high as to amount to a prohibition. I know not by what logic it could be maintained, that the declarations in the State constitutions, in favor of the freedom of

the point. The truth is, after all the declamations we have heard, that the Constitution is itself, in every rational sense, and to every useful purpose, A BILL OF RIGHTS. The several bills of rights in Great Britain form its Constitution, and conversely the constitution of each State is its bill of rights. And the proposed Constitution, if adopted, will be the bill of rights of the Union. Is it one object of a bill of rights to declare and specify the political privileges of the citizens in the structure and administration of the government? This is done in the most ample and precise manner in the plan of the convention; comprehending various precautions for the public security, which are not to be found in any of the State constitutions. Is another object of a bill of rights to define certain immunities and modes of proceeding, which are relative to personal and private concerns? This we have seen has also been attended to, in a variety of cases, in the same plan. Adverting therefore to the substantial meaning of a bill of rights, it is absurd to allege that it is not to be found in the work of the convention. It may be said that it does not go far enough, though it will not be easy to make this appear; but it can with no propriety be contended that there is no such thing. It certainly must be immaterial what mode is observed as to the order of declaring the rights of the citizens, if they are to be

---

the press, would be a constitutional impediment to the imposition of duties upon publications by the State legislatures. It cannot certainly be pretended that any degree of duties, however low, would be an abridgment of the liberty of the press. We know that newspapers are taxed in Great Britain, and yet it is notorious that the press nowhere enjoys greater liberty than in that country. And if duties of any kind may be laid without a violation of that liberty, it is evident that the extent must depend on legislative discretion, regulated by public opinion; so that, after all, general declarations respecting the liberty of the press, will give it no greater security than it will have without them. The same invasions of it may be effected under the State constitutions which contain those declarations through the means of taxation, as under the proposed Constitution, which has nothing of the kind. It would be quite as significant to declare that government ought to be free, that taxes ought not to be excessive, etc., as that the liberty of the press ought not to be restrained.—PUBLIUS

found in any part of the instrument which establishes the government. And hence it must be apparent, that much of what has been said on this subject rests merely on verbal and nominal distinctions, entirely foreign from the substance of the thing.

Another objection which has been made, and which, from the frequency of its repetition, it is to be presumed is relied on, is of this nature: "It is improper [say the objectors] to confer such large powers, as are proposed, upon the national government, because the seat of that government must of necessity be too remote from many of the States to admit of a proper knowledge on the part of the constituent, of the conduct of the representative body." This argument, if it proves any thing, proves that there ought to be no general government whatever. For the powers which, it seems to be agreed on all hands, ought to be vested in the Union, cannot be safely intrusted to a body which is not under every requisite control. But there are satisfactory reasons to show that the objection is in reality not well founded. There is in most of the arguments which relate to distance a palpable illusion of the imagination. What are the sources of information by which the people in Montgomery County must regulate their judgment of the conduct of their representatives in the State legislature? Of personal observation they can have no benefit. This is confined to the citizens on the spot. They must therefore depend on the information of intelligent men, in whom they confide; and how must these men obtain their information? Evidently from the complexion of public measures, from the public prints, from correspondences with their representatives, and with other persons who reside at the place of their deliberations. This does not apply to Montgomery County only, but to all the counties at any considerable distance from the seat of government.

It is equally evident that the same sources of information would be open to the people in relation to the conduct of their representatives in the general government, and the impediments to a prompt communication which distance may be supposed to create, will be overbalanced by the effects of the vigilance of the State governments. The executive and legislative bodies of each State will be so many sentinels over the persons employed in every department of the national administration; and as it will be in their power to adopt and pursue a regular and effectual system of intelligence, they can never be at a loss to know the behavior of those who represent their constituents in the national councils, and can readily communicate the same knowledge to the people. Their disposition to apprise the community of whatever may prejudice its interests from another quarter, may be relied upon, if it were only from the rivalship of power. And we may conclude with the fullest assurance that the people, through that channel, will be better informed of the conduct of their national representatives, than they can be by any means they now possess of that of their State representatives.

It ought also to be remembered that the citizens who inhabit the country at and near the seat of government will, in all questions that affect the general liberty and prosperity, have the same interest with those who are at a distance, and that they will stand ready to sound the alarm when necessary, and to point out the actors in any pernicious project. The public papers will be expeditious messengers of intelligence to the most remote inhabitants of the Union.

Among the many curious objections which have appeared against the proposed Constitution, the most extraordinary and the least colorable is derived from the want of some provision respecting the debts due *to* the United States. This has been represented as a tacit relinquishment of those debts, and as a wicked contrivance to screen public defaulters. The newspapers have teemed with the most inflammatory railings on this head; yet there is nothing clearer than that the suggestion is entirely void of foundation, the offspring of extreme ignorance or extreme dishonesty. In addition to the remarks I have made upon the subject in another place, I shall only observe that as it is a plain dictate of common-sense, so it is also an established doctrine of political law, that *"states neither lose any of their rights, nor are discharged from any of their obligations, by a change in the form of their civil government."* [4]

＊　　＊　　＊　　＊

PUBLIUS

---

[4] *Vide* Rutherford's "Institutes," vol. ii., book 11, chap. x., sect. xiv. and xv. *Vide* also Grotius, book II, chap. ix., sects. viii. and ix.—PUBLIUS

A SELECTED
BIBLIOGRAPHY

************   ************

COLLECTIONS OF DOCUMENTS

Borden, Morton, ed. *The Antifederalist Papers*. East Lansing: Michigan State University Press, 1965.

Cushing, H. A., ed. *The Writings of Samuel Adams*. New York: G. P. Putnam's Sons, 1904–1908.

Documentary History of the Constitution of the United States of America, 1786–1870. Vols. I–IV; Washington, D.C.: Department of State, 1893–1905.

Elliot, Jonathan, ed. *The Debates in the Several State Conventions on the Adoption of the Federal Constitution*. 4 vols., 2nd ed.; Washington, D.C., 1854.

Farrand, Max, ed. *The Records of the Federal Convention of 1787*. 3 vols.; New Haven, Conn.: Yale University Press, 1911.

Ford, Paul Leicester, ed. *Essays on the Constitution of the United States, Published During Its Discussion by the People, 1787–1788*. Brooklyn, N.Y., 1892.

————. *Pamphlets on the Constitution of the United States, Published During Its Discussion by the People, 1787–1788*. Brooklyn, N.Y., 1888.

————. *The Writings of Thomas Jefferson*. New York: G. P. Putnam's Sons, 1892–1899.

Hamilton, Alexander, John Jay, and James Madison. *The Federalist*. Benjamin Wright, ed. Cambridge, Mass.: Harvard University Press, 1961.

Kenyon, Cecelia M., ed. *The Anti-Federalists.* Indianapolis: Bobbs-Merrill Company, 1966.

McMaster, John B., and F. D. Stone, eds. *Pennsylvania and the Federal Constitution, 1787–1788.* Lancaster, Pa., 1888.

SECONDARY WORKS

Adair, Douglass. "The Authorship of the Disputed Federalist Papers," *William and Mary Quarterly,* I (1944), 97–122, 235–264.

_____. "The Tenth Federalist Revisited," *William and Mary Quarterly,* VIII (1951), 48–67.

Beard, Charles A. *An Economic Interpretation of the Constitution of the United States.* New York: The Macmillan Company, 1913.

Brant, Irving. *James Madison: Father of the Constitution, 1787–1800.* New York: Bobbs-Merrill Company, 1950.

Brown, Robert E. *Charles Beard and the Constitution.* Princeton, N.J.: Princeton University Press, 1956.

Diamond, Martin. "Democracy and the Federalist: A Reconsideration of the Framers' Intent," *American Political Science Review,* LIII (1959), 52–68.

Farrand, Max. *The Framing of the Constitution of the United States.* New Haven, Conn.: Yale University Press, 1913.

Kenyon, Cecelia M. " 'An Economic Interpretation of the Constitution' after Fifty Years," *The Centennial Review,* VII (1963), 327–352.

_____. "Men of Little Faith: The Anti-Federalists on the Nature of Representative Government," *William and Mary Quarterly,* XII (1955), 3–43.

McDonald, Forrest. *We the People: The Economic Origins of the Constitution.* Chicago: University of Chicago Press, 1958.

Main, Jackson T. *The Antifederalists: Critics of the Constitution, 1781–1788.* Chapel Hill: University of North Carolina Press, 1961.

Malone, Dumas. *Jefferson and the Rights of Man.* Boston: Little, Brown and Company, 1951. Chap. 9.

Mason, Alpheus T. "*The Federalist*—A Split Personality," *American Historical Review,* LVII (1952), 625–643.

_____. *The States Rights Debate: Antifederalism and the Constitution.* Englewood Cliffs, N.J.: Prentice-Hall, Inc., 1964.

Roche, John P. "The Founding Fathers: A Reform Caucus in Action," *American Political Science Review*, LV (1961), 799–816.

Rossiter, Clinton. *Alexander Hamilton and the Constitution*. New York: Harcourt, Brace and World, Inc., 1964.

_____. *1787: The Grand Convention*. New York: The Macmillan Company, 1966.

Smith, David G. *The Convention and the Constitution: The Political Ideas of the Founding Fathers*. New York: St. Martin's Press, 1965.

Warren, Charles. *The Making of the Constitution*. Boston: Little, Brown and Company, 1929.

Wright, Benjamin F. *Consensus and Continuity, 1776–1787*. Boston: Boston University Press, 1958.

_____. "*The Federalist* on the Nature of Political Man," *Ethics*, LIX (1949), No. 2, Part 2, 1–31.

★★★★★★★★★★★★ INDEX ★★★★★★★★★★★★

415